# Library Science Research and Database Books

# Library Science Research and Database Books

**Aashish Warekar**

**CYBER TECH PUBLICATIONS**
4264/3, Ansari Road, Daryaganj, New Delhi-110002 (India)
Ph.: 011-23244078, 011-43559448 Fax: 011-23280028
E-Mail: cyberpublicationsdelhi@yahoo.com
Website: www.cybertechpublications.com

# LIBRARY SCIENCE RESEARCH AND DATABASE BOOKS

**Aashish Warekar**



First Edition 2010



Asian Offset Printer

*Published by :*

**G.S. Rawat** for **Cyber Tech Publications**
4264/3, Ansari Road, Daryaganj, New Delhi-110002 (India)
Ph.: 011-23244078, 011-43559448 Fax: 011-23280028
E-Mail: cyberpublicationsdelhi@yahoo.com
Website: www.cybertechpublications.com

# Preface

An introduction to basic sources of information in Information and Library Science. Most of the University Libraries' books and periodicals on information and library science are located in the Dewey Graduate Library on the downtown campus. Books and periodicals on related subjects such as computer science and telecommunications are primarily located in the Science Library on the Main Campus. This guide is necessarily highly selective and only cites material located in the Dewey Library. The student in information science will be using a wide range of sources during the course of graduate study, including many resources held only at the University Library.

The fields of library and information science are changing and growing rapidly. Forty years ago, libraries were about books, journals, magazines, and newspapers. Information science, computing, and telecommunications were in their infancies. Today, libraries bring together people and all forms of information. Libraries make information content from various sources available online as well as in print. Academic librarians are providing valuable instruction to students in information finding, evaluation, and use, as well as expert research to ensure the latest and most reliable information for research and public service programs.

Different types of libraries have evolved in response to different kinds of problems. The public library, the special library, and the research library, for example, all differ in this regard. Nevertheless, all libraries are concerned in one way or another with acquiring, organizing, and providing effective access to recorded information. It might seem obvious that, to understand how to improve libraries, one should study how people seek and use information. Indeed, much research is so directed.

*—Author*

# CONTENTS

# 1

# Introduction

If you search in bibliographic databases using the search term "International librarianship", you will find a fair number of monographs that include these words in their titles. In a review of Carroll and Harvey's *International librarianship: cooperation and collaboration* (Carroll and Harvey, 2001), W.V. Jackson (Jackson, 2003), not to be confused with Miles Jackson, made the following observation:Although the literature of comparative and international librarianship has not flourished in recent years, one type of work seems to recur periodically. This is the anthology of articles... by various authors: such compilations generally include pieces both geographical (that is, about a country or region) or topical (for example, about cooperation, buildings and so on) in nature (Jackson, 2003).

Most books on "international librarianship" are compilations of chapters by various authors, describing library conditions in particular foreign countries or regions, along the lines of the following (real) examples:

- The standardisation of Chinese bibliography
- University libraries in West Africa
- Public libraries in Nigeria
- Library and information services in Bermuda
- Indonesian university libraries and their reference services

In these volumes we also find chapters on international library cooperation, the work of international agencies in the field of librarianship, and relations between countries in the field of librarianship. More real examples:

- Colonialism and the development of libraries and archives in French Indochina
- IFLA and international librarianship
- Anglo-Nordic library relationships
- International cultural exchange through libraries
- International influences in Thailand

The second group of examples come closer to what I understand by international librarianship, as I shall discuss shortly, but what has generally been missing is attempts to systematise or develop a conceptual framework for international librarianship. In most cases the introduction or preface to the compilation is extremely brief and provides only the most cursory attempt at defining what is meant by "international librarianship". For example, Miles Jackson's impressive volume of well over 600 pages offers no attempt to provide a systematic introduction or conceptual framework. The 1985 Festschift for William J Welsh (Price and Price, 1985) is an example of a book with the words "international librarianship" in its title, but which does not say anything about international librarianship as such.

Presumably the title, *International librarianship today and tomorrow*, was chosen because Welsh, at that time Deputy Librarian of Congress, was well-known in international circles and participated actively in forums such as IFLA and the Conference of Directors of National Libraries.

There is a striking exception to the general trend in books on international librarianship, the book *World librarianship: a comparative study*, by Richard Krzys and Gaston Litton (1983). This is an ambitious attempt to create a "world librarianship", defined as "the abstraction referring to the status of the profession in all parts of the world during a specified period of time" and its scientific investigation, which they call "world study in librarianship". Under this they subsume "international library science" and "comparative library science" (Krzys & Litton, 1982:3). Their work does not appear to have attracted followers; certainly the terminology they attempted to introduce has not been adopted by later writers. Generally, the field remains dominated by anthologies.

If you're not American you must be international It has struck me that the way we understand "international librarianship" may be related to the different ways in which the word "international" is used in American and British English. In the USA the word "international" is commonly used to mean "from another country". Thus an "international student" or an "international visitor" in most cases is just a student or visitor from another country. In British English we would call them *foreign* students or *foreign* visitors. In British English the expression "international scholar" would be used only for a foreign scholar who enjoys international renown.

This analysis suggests that the multilateral or multinational (many to many) connotation of the word "international" is lost in American English and replaced by a one to many connotation (American to other). What is not American is "international". This is illustrated by Stephen K. Bailey's 1966 definition of "international education" as "...non-American substance of school and university curriculums in the United States", cited by Carroll (1970:175). It is debatable whether the semantic shift of "international" from British to American English can be explained by the parochialism or isolationism so often attributed to Americans. This is also unkind. It is more likely (and charitable) to assume that "international" is simply used in the USA as a euphemism to avoid labelling other people as "foreign". Be that as it may, it would be interesting to determine whether the meaning given to the word "international" in the USA has had any effect on the conceptualisation of international librarianship, and whether this is different from the way international librarianship has been conceptualised in Britain.

## International and Comparative Librarianship

Louis Shores (1966) defined comparative librarianship as follows:

> *...the study and comparison of library theory and practice in all of the different countries of the world for the purpose of broadening and deepening our understanding of professional problems and solutions. (Cited in Appendix I, Definitions) of (Carroll, 1970).*

Here comparative librarianship is clearly international. Comparisons within countries (between cities, states or library types, for example) are excluded.

In the preface to his 1981 book, referred to earlier, Miles Jackson distinguishes international librarianship from comparative librarianship:

> *...the terms "international" and "comparative librarianship" are regarded as having different meanings but both are of importance in understanding world librarianship. International librarianship is limited strictly to those activities that involve librarianship and all its aspects across national boundaries. It would thereby exclude comparative analysis, but include such activities as exchange of librarians, books, ideas, and the study of library systems in different countries. On the other hand, comparative librarianship should lean on the tradition of comparative studies found in other fields such as political, government and legal studies (Jackson, 1981).*

Relating international librarianship to "activities that involve librarianship and all its aspects across national boundaries" is a good beginning, but I find the exclusion of comparative analysis unsatisfactory. It would be much simpler to use the words "international" and "comparative" as overlapping and not mutually exclusive, as in the following Venn diagram:

> *This suggests that comparative librarianship may be conducted at both national and international levels. After all, we can compare library systems or conditions between countries or within countries. It also suggests that international librarianship may or may not have a comparative dimension.*

## From Exoticism to Understanding

If this seems like splitting hairs, bear with me for a little longer. Comparison is a step up from mere description. This implies that we consider the aims or teleology of this intellectual activity. I would like to look briefly at the motives or rationales of those who have written about international librarianship, and how these relate to the results achieved. I suggest that authors who have contributed to what is broadly known as international librarianship have been variously motivated by the following, or combinations thereof:

- Exoticism
- Philanthropy
- Influence
- Internationalism
- Cooperation
- Innovation
- Understanding

### Exoticism

The first cluster of motives can be placed under the label of exoticism. It includes curiosity about how things are done in foreign countries, a love of travel and adventure, and the prestige that comes from having been where others have not. Writings motivated by exoticism tend to be anecdotal and descriptive.

### Philanthropy

The second motive is philanthropy, love of our fellow humans. Here we have accounts by librarians and students who have travelled to other countries to assist in library development there. Accounts of their experiences also tend to be anecdotal and descriptive, with occasional analytical and evaluative elements.

### Influence

Often interwoven with the previous motive is, thirdly, cultural or economic influence through foreign aid for library development, the intention being to extend or strengthen the influence of the country providing the assistance. Accounts in this genre tend to be descriptive or promotional, but insufficiently evaluative.

In this context it is interesting to consider Frances Laverne Carroll's systematic attempt, in a doctoral dissertation submitted in 1970, to analyse the goals of international education and to apply them to international librarianship in US library schools (Carroll, 1970). Carroll constructed an instrument for the evaluation of "internationalism in education for librarianship in the United States" (p.34).

As part of her research, Carroll analysed the schools' calendars ("catalogues") to see whether they contained any references to "internationalism". The results were somewhat meagre. The most cogent statement of the goals of internationalism in library education was found in the calendar of the Graduate Library School of the Pratt Institute, Brooklyn: "The post-war expansion of American education has created a need for librarians with the special skills necessary to acquire and process overseas and foreign language materials to support the multiplying number of language and area study programmes.

As an aside, it would be interesting to determine to what extent interest in international librarianship in the USA correlates with the development of area studies and teaching of foreign languages. A further question that arises is whether the apparent decline in international librarianship (in terms of literature and the teaching thereof in LIS schools) could be a result of declining interest in area studies and foreign language teaching.

Given the lack of explicit goals in the library school calendars, Carroll used the goals of international education as her point of departure. She undertook a detailed analysis to determine whether the goals found in the literature were major or minor goals or activities. The goals were then related to the goals of internationalism in library education (p.42-43). Without going into the details, the goals found in the literature (as discussed on pp. 43-55) can be summarised as follows:

- International understanding. This has three dimensions:
  - o Attitude (an affective dimension concerned with feelings of friendliness and willingness to cooperate)
  - o Knowledge (a cognitive dimension concerned with understanding the behaviour of other people)
  - o Strategic knowledge (another cognitive dimension concerned with understanding the intentions of

others with a view to decision-making, *e.g.* in foreign policy)

- Advancement of knowledge. This can be divided into two dimensions:
  - o Diffusion or transmission of existing knowledge, *e.g.* through primary, secondary and undergraduate education
  - o Discovery or production of new knowledge, including synthesis through research and scholarship
- Technical assistance
- To advance the objectives of US foreign policy (including the combating of communism and the strengthening of relations with the allies of the USA)
- To promote international understanding and appreciation of the United States
- To gain perspective on one's own values and traditions

In view of her objective of developing a checklist, Carroll eliminated the last four as minor goals, leaving only the first two goals as appropriate goal statements for library science. Her analysis highlights some of the ambivalence in inherent in international studies, particularly at the height of the Cold War. Do we study librarianship in other countries with altruistic or self-centred motives? Some goals are clearly subordinated to national policy interests. Others too, may not be as altruistic or idealistic as they look.

## Internationalism

In the context of international librarianship, and especially in the context of international library cooperation, internationalism frequently features as a shared value. This appears to be an idealistic motive: librarians engaged in international cooperation are described by Harrison (1989:xv) as "citizens of the world with a strong faith that what they are supporting is really worthwhile and that both short-term and long-term good will come from it". In the USA internationalism has had a strong protagonist in Frances Laverne Carroll, who devoted much research to the internationalisation of library and information science education. Internationalisation is defined by Carroll and Harvey (1987) as "the process by which a nationalistic library school topic, an entire curriculum, or an entire school is changed into one with a significant and varied international thrust, the process whereby it is permeated with international policies, viewpoints, ideas and facts"(p.x).

**Cooperation**

Librarians have a long and honourable tradition of cooperation. Peter Havard-Williams goes so far as to make cooperation the central theme of international librarianship. He wrote: "I define international librarianship as cooperative activity in the field of librarianship done for the benefit of the individual librarian in the whole of the world, and done frequently by the likes of you and me" (Havard-Williams, 1972:170). International cooperation in respect of document supply, bibliographic standards, preservation and other technical areas will undoubtedly remain an important motivation. But rapid developments in information and communications technologies and the accompanying phenomena of globalization and disintermediation, efficient cooperation among librarians worldwide is needed for us to participate effectively in the global forums. These are forums such as the World Intellectual Property Organisation (WIPO), the World Trade Organisation (WTO) and the World Summit on the Information Society (WSIS), where far-reaching decisions are made that affect free and fair access to information resources in libraries serving the peoples of the world (cf. Schleihagen 2004).

**Innovation**

A fifth motive is innovation. As K. C. Harrison (1989:xii) has put it: "...librarians with weather-eyes on professional practices in other countries have been able to adopt, adapt and apply many of these to their own library situations." Such transplanting has occurred particularly in technical library processes. This has led to writings of a technical and evaluative nature.

**Understanding**

Finally, there is the quest for understanding. Earlier I cited Louis Shores's statement of the purpose of what he calls comparative librarianship: "broadening and deepening our understanding of professional problems and solutions" (Shores 1970).

In his Foreword (Asheim, 1989) to Harrison's International librarianship (Harrison, 1989), Lester Asheim points to the value of "learning-through-participation... not only through actual practice as a librarian in some other country, but also through the mutual exchange of ideas and viewpoints made possible through international associations... Both of these... provide the librarian with the opportunity to have direct contact with the practice and philosophy of library service in varying circumstances and at different levels of societal development, and from this insight, to identify and appreciate the many factors outside of librarianship itself that shape and define the nature of a library's services and its social role." (p.vii)

Asheim goes on to list a number of factors outside of librarianship that determine who uses libraries, how and why, and what barriers inhibit their use. Such factors operate everywhere, "...but somehow we can see and understand this much more clearly in a foreign setting than we can when we are looking at a phenomenon with which we feel comfortably "at home"(p.viii). What I find significant about this motive is that is concerned with self-understanding, which represents considerable progress from the starting point of exoticism. (It can be said that self-understanding, achieved by seeing the self in relation to others, is the ultimate goal of travel.) A more recent statement of this motive is found in the introduction to a new column, "International perspectives on academic libraries" in the *Journal of academic librarianship*. The editors of the column, Philip J Calvert and Rowena Cullen, wrote:

> *It is hoped that this column will help broaden the journal's perspective outside North America; raise issues faced by academic librarians in the developing as well as the developed world; and identify issues that are common to all academic libraries, but to which the solutions must sometimes be modified to suit particular countries, cultures or economic environments. It should also be remembered that, although North America*

*academic libraries are the driving force behind much innovation in the LIS field and are the source of much new thinking in the discipline, librarians in other countries have sometimes to deal with certain issues before they become critical in the United States or Canada; hence there will be times that the flow of information will travel in the other direction (Calvert & Cullen, 2001).*

This statement raises interesting questions about the notion of librarians in different countries learning from one another.

**Each one Teach One? Learning from one Another**

In Miles M. Jackson's *International handbook of contemporary developments in librarianship* (Jackson, 1981), he refers briefly to LIS development in developing countries and poses some questions for researchers in international and comparative librarianship.

One such question is what can a nonindustrialized nation offer to an industrialized nation in terms of contemporary developments in librarianship?

Can American librarianship learn from Nigerian librarianship? Can librarianship in Papua New Guinea learn from librarianship in Jamaica?

Jackson's rationale appears to be mainly concerned with learning: librarians in country A learning from the library situation in country B. He touches on the issue of learning taking place between developed and developing countries. Diplomatically, the examples he gives involve a developed ("industrialized") country learning from a developing ("nonindustrialized") country, and a developing country learning from another, distant, developing country. The wholesale export of library concepts, ideologies and technologies from rich to poor countries is not touched on, but one does not have to be a Derrida to see it lurking under the surface, with all its political baggage.

We need to unpack the idealistic notion of learning from one another. What can one learn? The most obvious answer is there are techniques, technologies and systems invented or developed in country A that may not be known in country B, and that may fruitfully be adopted there. A typical expression of this is the visiting librarian or expert from country A, who says to colleagues in country B, "Gosh, don't you do/have/use XYZ? You must get it. It will solve your problems." Of course, things are not always as simple as they seem. Apart from the fact that libraries in country B may not be able to afford XYZ, there may be various local factors that would make it difficult to implement system XYZ successfully.

This could apply when both countries A and B are developed countries, but it is particularly the case when country A is a developed country and country B a developing country. There may be such a large gap between the countries, politically, culturally, economically, etc., that the advice, however well-meant, is quite unrealistic. Techniques, technologies and systems are not ideologically neutral. An attempt to import XYZ without also importing the conceptual and ideological schema and value system that underlies it in country A, may be doomed to failure. And country B may not want to import country A's ideologies and values.

When one thinks of librarians in one country learning from their colleagues in another, technology transfer comes to mind first. Techniques, technology and systems could cover a wide range of know-how: the use of 3x5 inch cards, the dictionary catalogue, AACR2, the Library of Congress Subject Headings, an integrated computer library management system, or an electromagnetic book theft detection system. But it does not always have to be so tangible. Other imports could include library legislation, the system of legal deposit, the organisation of an interlibrary lending system, the organisation structure of the country's public library system, or the system of training librarians and information workers, with the hierarchy and names of qualifications awarded.

Sometimes it is as interesting to see what is *not* learned. In an article entitled "A distant mirror: the story of libraries in South Africa", published in *Daedalus* in 1996, I looked at US influence on South African librarianship (Lor 1996). During the apartheid years the South African library community continued to adopt American technical innovations, for on-line searching, example integrated library management systems, and electronic book detection systems, but significant elements in the white leadership of the profession filtered out professional values such as freedom of expression and equal rights for all library clients. What about two developing countries learning from one another? Jackson's example of librarianship in Papua New Guinea learning from librarianship in Jamaica is appropriate here. This is not so much a question of political correctness, but one of commonalities. Two developing countries might have a great deal in common. In the case of Papua New Guinea and Jamaica, both are islands, they have a tropical climate, they underwent a period of British or British-influenced colonial rule, are members of the (British) Commonwealth and use English as the official language.

But there are also significant differences, for example in their ethnic composition and heritage, number of languages spoken, duration of British colonial rule, per capita GDP, literacy rate, etc. Intuitively one feels that, to learn from one another, it might be wiser to pair Jamaica with Trinidad and Tobago and Papua New Guinea with Guiana. Underlying such a judgement are certain assumptions about what countries should have in common to make possible sensible comparisons, mutual learning or technology transfer. Therefore a major task of a systematic international librarianship would be to surface and test the assumptions. This would require identifying the factors that influence library development in different countries, evaluating their impact, and understanding why they impact on libraries the way they do. Finally I come to Jackson's example of what American librarianship can learn from Nigerian librarianship. A very obvious answer is: how very fortunate American librarians are. International librarians can impart a sense of perspective: "Go home Americans, " one might say, "and thank your lucky stars for your magnificent resources and your great free public library tradition, to mention just a few privileges."

One might be tempted to add: "And stop complaining that you don't have enough." But international librarianship should not form the basis for smugness or complacency. Rather, it may enable some of us to at least exercise our profession with a greater awareness and appreciation for what is so easily taken for granted. And American librarians should not thank their lucky stars, but the library pioneers, the farsighted philanthropists and educational leaders, democracy, and (possibly) free-market capitalism. This of course raises more questions and underlines the importance of understanding what one observes in other countries. There are other things American librarians can learn from Nigerian librarians. For example, some Nigerian experience in serving small rural communities, serving illiterate users, and dealing with oral history, oral traditions and indigenous knowledge may be of value.

Finally, a greater understanding of the situation in a developing country would help librarians and others in developed countries who want to do good through aid programmes, staff exchanges, book donations and the like, to do so more sensibly and with greater sensitivity to the needs of the beneficiaries.

In the foreword I referred to earlier, Lester Asheim (1989) also refers to the value of international librarianship in preventing errors in assisting developing countries: "...all-too-often the actual attempts of the more advanced countries to assist the developing ones in the establishment or development of library services are marked by incredible errors and miscalculations, arising out of the failure to take these outside influences into account" (p.viii). He cites the gift of a number of bookmobiles to a country with a shortage of fuel and poor road network. Such donations are made out of "...ignorance born of the belief that whatever works for us will work for everyone" (p.viii). Librarians from developing countries can tell many horror stories of well-intentioned but useless book donations. A better and more sensitive understanding of needs and circumstances in the recipient countries could go a long way in avoiding such errors.

## The Scope of International Librarianship

To conclude the lecture I would like to look briefly at the scope of the field and the major themes that should be addressed in contemporary studies in international librarianship. The following is an outline of the material that comes to mind:

- Terminology, definitions, scope, conceptual structures of international librarianship
- Sources: journals and other sources in the field
- Values and orientations: internationalism, social responsibility, third world solidarity; American, British, European and Soviet approaches
- Research method: international surveys, case studies, etc.; assumptions and validity of comparisons
- International comparative studies, regional studies, and country comparisons: national and regional non-library factors; explanatory theories (*e.g.* influence of Calvinism, climate, orality & literacy)
- International diffusion of library theories and techniques: technology transfer; adoption of innovations, adaptation, rejection
- International influences: Transatlantic, Anglo-American, Continental European, colonial, post-colonial
- Role of cultural and information agencies (USIS, British Council etc.) and philanthropic foundations (Carnegie Corporation, Andrew W. Mellon Foundation, Soros, etc.); Book donations (Ranfurly, Sabre, etc.)
- International non-governmental organisations in LIS: IFLA, FID, regional library associations, specialised international associations
- UNESCO and other intergovernmental organisations; international attempts to promote national library and information policies (UNISIST, NATIS, etc.); literacy, reading and book development policies Journals that regularly contain articles relevant to international librarianship include *COMLA newsletter*, *Focus on international and comparative librarianship*, *IFLA journal*, *Information development*, *International information and library review*, *Library times international*, and *Libri*. Mention should also be made of the *Unesco bulletin for libraries*, long deceased. *Library and information science abstracts (LISA)* and *Library literature* are indispensable tools for literature searching

in international librarianship. A significant proportion of the literature is not yet on the Web.

- International cooperation in library and information services: international interlending and UAP, bibliographic control and UBC, preservation, international advocacy, etc.
- Development aid to libraries in the emerging and developing countries; role of development agencies active in LIS-related projects (Danida, Sida, IDRC, etc.); development assumptions and concepts; evolution of development efforts
- International information relations: North-South, South-North and South-South power relations and information flows; digital divide; intellectual property issues, WIPO, WTO, GATS etc.; barriers to expression and access; WSIS Considering this list, it seems that the topics can be grouped under three broad themes within international librarianship: international relations and influences, international organisations, and international comparisons. A comprehensive treatment of international librarianship would require that all three be covered. For the discipline to develop, it is necessary us to move beyond the anecdotal and descriptive contributions to those that serve explanation and understanding. We need to develop a more coherent conceptual framework for our research and find appropriate methodologies. We should explore whether we can draw on comparative studies in disciplines such as education and political science, to help us in this endeavour.

## Conclusion

People get involved in international librarianship for different reasons. As in all international relations, the practice of international librarianship involves a mixture of good intentions, ignorance and self-interest. The task of the discipline or sub-discipline as it is researched and taught, should be to reinforce the good intentions, dispel the ignorance, and expose the self-interest.

## FIVE LAWS OF LIBRARY SCIENCE

S. R. Ranganathan, known as the "the father of library science in India, " and respected by librarians all over the world, proposed five laws of library science. Most librarians worldwide accept them as the foundations of their philosophy.

These laws are:

1. Books are for use.
2. Every reader his or her book.
3. Every book its reader.
4. Save the time of the reader.
5. The library is a growing organism.

The Five Laws of Library Science are some of the most influential concepts in that field. Since they were published in 1931, these five laws "have remained a centerpiece of professional values..." (Rubin 2004). These basic theories of Library Science continue to directly affect the development of this discipline and the service of all libraries. S. R. Ranganathan's early education was of a mathematic background. This systematic way of thinking, he later applied to his work in library science, most notably his work on library classification and administration. (Indian Statistical Institute Library, et al 2007) "From the middle of the nineteenth century, librarians in the west felt the need and started emphasizing the importance of enhanced services to library patrons. Formulation of the Five Laws of Library Science at long last, provided a solid and lasting foundation in this direction." (Kabir 2003)

***First Law:*** Books are for use. (Ranganathan 1931) This may seem obvious within the context of today's libraries, but books were not always accessible to patrons at their libraries. There was a time when books were literally chained to the stacks on which they were shelved. Later, it was not uncommon for libraries to have stacks that were completely closed to the public. There a still a few types of libraries that work this way today, but the libraries that most people are familiar with have stacks that are open to the public.

***Second Law:*** Books are for all. (Ranganathan 1931) Any patron from the library community should have access to the books in the library. Any person has a right to use the collections housed in the library. There are not certain books or collections that some audiences within the population can not access. Collections should be developed that every part of the population will be interested in.

***Third Law:*** Every book its reader. (Ranganathan 1931) This law is about items in the library's collection, and who uses them. Each book in the library has a member of the community that will find the book useful or interesting. One of the major developments that Ranganathan contributed through this law is the idea that if a book is not being used often it needs exposure to groups of readers who will find it useful.

***Fourth Law:*** Save the time of the Reader. (Ranganathan 1931) This law makes it clear that if readers find what they are looking for in a timely manner they will be more satisfied, and more likely to feel like their needs have been met. This not only makes library service more efficient, but also makes the reader feel like their search has been an effective one.

***Fifth Law:*** The library is a growing organism. (Ranganathan 1931) This law says that the library is dependent on life and change. Without the human and organizational changes that occur, the library would neither function properly, nor meet its purpose.

## Variants

In 1998, librarian Michael Gorman (past president of the American Library Association, 2005-2006), recommended the following laws in addition to Ranganathan's five in his small book, "Our Singular Strengths":

1. Libraries serve humanity.
2. Respect all forms by which knowledge is communicated.
3. Use technology intelligently to enhance service.
4. Protect free access to knowledge.
5. Honour the past and create the future.

In 2004, librarian Alireza Noruzi recommended applying Ranganathan's laws to the web in his paper, "Application of Ranganathan's Laws to the Web":

1. Web resources are for use.

2. Every user his or her web resource.
3. Every web resource its user.
4. Save the time of the user.
5. The Web is a growing organism.

## HISTORY

Academic libraries have a close relationship with learning and research and have influenced these things as well. Their history is one of evolution and change that parallels the history of their parent institutions. Leaders and innovators championed features of libraries that are now taken for granted. Responsiveness to student and faculty needs, quality of service, and resilience have been hallmarks of academic libraries in the US. A chronological review of the literature demonstrates these characteristics. This paper is divided into the major periods of the history of US academic libraries: the Colonial period, the Nineteenth Century, and the Twentieth Century.

Included in this review of the literature are journal articles, books, and dissertations published between 1980 and 2003 that discuss historical aspects of the library in four-year colleges and universities in the United States. Histories of individual libraries are usually omitted. Histories of libraries in two-year colleges, architectural history, conference proceedings, and editorials have not been included; nor have publications on specialized libraries in academic institutions such as medical, law, or music, or research collections that are not a part of an academic institution (Library of Congress, Centre for Research Libraries). Citations were identified by exhaustive searching of the *Library Literature, ERIC, America History and Life, Digital Dissertations*, and *WorldCat* databases. Bibliographies of those citations were reviewed to identify additional sources. Key authors were identified and author searches were then performed in the databases listed.

### Mirror of Higher Education

That the history of academic libraries mirrors the development of higher education implies a process of growth, assimilation, and diversification (Shiflett 1994). The role of the library has evolved as the priorities of the institutions have evolved. At the same time, academic librarianship has developed into a distinct profession with its own set of ideals, objectives, and commitments within the academic community (Wiegand 1983). Shiflett's work on the origins of academic librarianship is a classic and an excellent summary of the literature and research on this topic that was published before 1980. He states that it is necessary to understand the history of American higher education to truly comprehend American academic librarianship. The library "prospered or suffered in proportion to its value to the college" (Shiflett 1981). and the status of the librarian was directly related to the library's place in the college. He concludes that academic librarianship has failed to become fully defined because it lacks a body of theory and research (Shiflett 1981).

Libraries "can be viewed as information systems that both reflect and influence, and even help to create, paradigms and authority, for they set limits in various ways on the ideas and information available to users" (Dain 1990). Due to a process called *transparency*, in which an entity is taken for granted and not well understood, the contexts and institutional structures of libraries are for the most part explored only in the library literature by librarian-historians. It is a disturbing indicator of the relative invisibility of libraries in higher education that there are few articles or books about them in the literature of that discipline. Their role in acquiring and producing knowledge within intellectual, institutional, and social contexts needs to be developed with a research base and disseminated in the literature of disciplines that are related to and affected by them.

## Colonial Libraries

Until the American Revolution, most books were imported from England. Local presses produced materials such as pamphlets, school texts, newspapers and business or legal forms. From 1639 to 1776, they produced about 60 books per year. After 1776, there was an increase in publications produced in America. An 1804 catalogue listed 1, 338 American publications in print (Hanson 1989). When John Harvard donated approximately 300 of his books to Harvard University, he created the first academic library in the colonies. The colonial college libraries were characterized by small, eclectic collections of donated books. There was no funding from parent institutions to systematically purchase materials to supplement the colleges' programmes. Libraries were vulnerable to fire because the buildings were made of wood. They were open for only a few hours per week and were operated by a professor who was assigned to be caretaker of the library as part of his teaching responsibilities. In some colleges, he had to pay for books that disappeared from the inventory himself.

Since a classical curriculum was fixed, there was little need to read anything but textbooks (Shiflett 1994). Most books in libraries were theological works, as well as some classics and standard treatises in philosophy, logic, and history. There was no standard way to categorize books so they were arranged either by size, donor, subject, or author until the adoption of the Dewey Decimal classification scheme in 1876. The library usually consisted of one or two rooms of books located in the main building or in the chapel. Harvard constructed the first freestanding library building in 1841 (Hanson 1989). Before the late 19th century, "academic libraries, with the exceptions of Harvard and Yale and a few others, were as undistinguished and arid as the colleges themselves" (Dain 1990).

**Nineteenth Century**

Changes in scholarship and learning during the late nineteenth and early twentieth centuries greatly affected libraries. The emphasis on publishing results of research during this period led to a proliferation of journals and scholarly monographs and the need for primary source materials (Shiflett 1981). Serial publications gained in importance in the early 1800s. There were fewer than 100 periodicals other than newspapers published in 1825; by 1885, there were 9, 000. Due to the difficulties inherent in such business ventures, they had a life expectancy of about three years (Hanson 1989).

**First Endowments**

Harvard and Yale were the first libraries to establish endowments during this period. This created a more stable financial base for those libraries. John L. Sibley began working in Harvard's library in 1841 and "was indefatigable in building the collections, enormously resourceful in attracting gifts and had never a doubt as to the vital importance of amassing the published and written record of all events and discoveries, great or small" (Hamlin 1981). He increased the library hours from one hour per week for freshmen and sophomores and two hours per week for juniors and seniors to seven hours daily Monday through Friday.

## Literary Society Libraries

College libraries during this period were not adequate for the students due to their limited hours of operation and limited collections. From 1800 to 1880, literary society libraries flourished. Members paid dues that supported their libraries and selected the books that were bought for the collection. The books were in English and encompassed fiction, drama, history, political science, biography, and travel. They were scholarly and classical and included encyclopedias, dictionaries, and other reference works. The libraries were open to all students and faculty and sometimes to alumni and townspeople. These libraries could be considered the predecessors of present day undergraduate libraries (Dain 1990). The literary societies declined when the natural sciences became more prominent in the curriculum, graduate instruction increased, and the course elective system came into existence. As literary society libraries declined in importance, college libraries correspondingly increased.

When Johns Hopkins University was established, faculty used the German seminar method for instruction instead of the recitation method. This created new demands for library services and materials. The librarians responded by keeping the library open longer, building stronger collections with primary and secondary sources, providing bibliographic instruction and reference service, and erecting multipurpose buildings designed to accommodate people as well as services (Wiegand 1983). As a result, there was a tremendous growth in collections. College libraries assimilated the student literary society libraries and gifts increased. Departmental libraries, rather than one centralized college library, predominated. The metaphor of the library as the "heart of the university" is assumed to have been first stated by Charles Eliot, longtime President of Harvard, in 1873.

**Growth in Collections**

The number of volumes in the collection at Harvard increased by an average of 63% per year from 1856 to 1876; from 1776-1856, the number had only increased by 7.5% per year. This occurred concurrently with the course elective system, an expanded curriculum, the rise of graduate schools, and new instruction methods. "By the end of the nineteenth century the typical small college library could be characterized as containing 6, 000 to 20, 000 volumes comprised mainly of donations. Emphasis was primarily on supporting the curriculum rather than research" (Hanson 1989).

**Improved Use**

At the end of the nineteenth century and into the twentieth, there was a definite shift in emphasis from conservation and protection of books to making them accessible and encouraging students and faculty to use them. There was recognition of the need to provide effective and personalized service as well as instruction in the use of the library and reference materials. It became accepted that books should be classified according to subject and not according to fixed shelf locations. Each book was to be listed with an adequate bibliographic description and this information was to be made easily available to users by author and subject. Cooperation with other libraries was seen as advantageous for borrowing materials (Hamlin, 48-9). Hours were extended and facilities improved to provide a comfortable work environment for students from early morning to late evening on weekdays and for some hours on weekends. Financing the library became an accepted responsibility of the parent institution. Placing books on reserve for use by students in a particular course was a new practice. Book catalogues of materials held by individual institutions or by groups of libraries were published to facilitate the sharing of resources (Dain 1990).

## Gender Bias

Almost all research university library directors were male, as were most deputy and assistant directors. This demographic only began to change in the 1970s (Dain 1990); however, a noteworthy regional phenomenon occurred in the Midwest. Bailey discusses the great increase and influence of female academic librarians in the Midwest during the last quarter of the nineteenth century. Students from this period required better library resources to support the changes in curriculum and teaching methods. The Midwest accepted coeducational institutions before other parts of the country. "The availability of college-educated women in conjunction with the low status accorded academic librarianship enabled women to enter college and university library work in growing numbers" (Bailey 1986). Faculty wives sometimes served as librarians because they were seen as "cultured, conveniently available, and an inexpensive source of labour" (Bailey 1986). Some of the dedicated women who led these libraries founded state library associations or published articles and books. One-third left their jobs when they married; one-quarter remained in their jobs for 20 years or more. Although not formally trained in library practices, they learned by observing other libraries, attending conferences, and reading the professional literature (Bailey 1986).

## Beginnings of Research Libraries

Wiegand believes that "the role the research library assumed in the scholarly communication system fostered by the modern American university in the last quarter of the nineteenth century in large part determined the way the research library profession defined its responsibilities to the research community" (Wiegand 1990). He explains that the ideology of reading at the time was that it should be done for a purpose and it should be done systematically. There were many lists of recommended reading. "Because institutions and their instructors did not regard independent reading very highly, college librarians felt little pressure to build large collections. Instead, they merely guarded collections donated from estates of deceased faculty members or alumni" (Wiegand 1990). After the publication of Darwin's *Origin of the Species* and the establishment of land grant colleges, education adopted a philosophy of scientific inquiry. As universities became interested in finding and communicating new knowledge, libraries began to build supporting collections.

**Collection Building**

Competitive collection-building was characteristic of academic libraries of the late nineteenth and early twentieth centuries. Yale's library was the second largest and third oldest in the country. Yale was the first American college to award a Ph.D. in 1861. An 1871 faculty report emphatically states the importance of a comprehensive library and so the library participated in the transformation of the college into a university (O'Connor 1987). Since no library could have a "complete" collection of all published works, libraries began to specialize. Libraries in large cities could cooperate with each other in acquiring and sharing materials; however, Yale was an institution that was isolated from other research libraries and so tried to acquire as comprehensive a collection as possible. Rare books were acquired through alumni donations (O'Connor 1987). Libraries achieved distinction because of donations of unique or rare collections. They were evolving from storehouses to workshops for research (O'Connor 1987).

**Leaders in Librarianship**

Several highly influential and innovative figures in academic librarianship appeared during the nineteenth century. Justin Winsor was appointed head librarian at Harvard in 1877. He served in this capacity for twenty years and brought about evolutionary changes and a new role for the library. Winsor is said to have humanized the library. He was recognized as a scholar, innovator, national leader in professional concerns, and builder of the Harvard library (Hamlin, 50-56).

Archibald Cary Coolidge became director of the Harvard Library in 1910. He had been a chair of the history department and had travelled extensively, all the while formulating a vision of what the library should be. He identified his priorities as finding space for the collections and research, addressing a patchwork cataloguing and classification system, and building a quality collection. He provided vision and leadership and also encouraged teamwork and shared responsibility (Byrnes 1982). He aggressively built an outstanding collection of foreign research materials and donated much to the library himself. Because of his efforts, the Widener Library was constructed, which "remains the physical and spiritual centre of the university a base and a centre for research and instruction at Harvard." Coolidge "helped make the library an essential part of the university organization, an intellectual symbol of the university. The skill with which Coolidge anticipated future needs of the collection and the library as a whole created a magnet that has helped Harvard to attract and retain scholars and thereby to make it a great university" (Byrnes 1982).

In 1883, Melvil Dewey became head librarian at Columbia University. His approach there was described as "revolutionary" (Hamlin, 49). Some of the changes he implemented were: extending library hours from 10 per week to 84; permitting students to access the shelves; invention of the card catalogue system for locating materials; lecturing or the use of the library; organizing the first reference department to "counsel and direct readers;" making available writing paper and ice water for the students; setting aside an area of the library where readers could talk; instituting a suggestion box to obtain feedback; and hiring six female Wellesley graduates as library assistants (Hamlin 1981). During his tenure, the acquisitions budget doubled, the personnel budget quadrupled, and book circulation increased by 500%. "His initiatives were being copied by other academic (and public) libraries across the country and around the world" (Wiegand, 1996; 108).

In 1887, Melvil Dewey opened the first library school at Columbia University with seventeen female and three male students. Before this event, academic librarians learned their profession by trial and error or by learning from other librarians. He moved the school to the New York State Library in Albany in 1889 because Columbia objected to admitting female students (Wiegand 1996). By 1900, a library school degree or certificate was necessary to be a chief librarian of a university. Students who graduated from Dewey's school formed small enclaves in different parts of the country to share professional training. Some of these developed into library schools (McElderry 1976).

### Twentieth Century

By World War I, most academic libraries had reference departments. Their purpose was instruction and guidance of the library user. The goal of reference work was to foster the independence of the user in locating research information. There was a trend toward specialization in reference service by subject (*i.e.*, art librarian), type of material (*i.e.*, rare books librarian; government documents librarian); and function (*i.e.*, reference librarian or cataloguing librarian) (Wiegand 1996). Library services to undergraduates were a focus. In 1947, Harvard opened the first library building dedicated to undergraduate services. Shortage of seating and collection space combined with the difficulty in accessing and using large research collections accelerated this trend. In the 1970s, more than 40 institutions had separate undergraduate libraries. That number has decreased to 25 in 1987 primarily due the cost of duplicating collections and services (Person 1988).

### Evolving Criteria for Library Performance

From 1906 to 1941, the Carnegie Corporation of New York gave grant funding to 248 college libraries to develop book collections for undergraduate students and to 108 institutions for library buildings. The foundation decided to award funding only to those institutions that were willing to support their libraries adequately. Data gathering done by the foundation staff determined that teachers' college libraries were especially deficient and so they had priority for funding. Several significant publications resulted from the work of the Corporation. As a result of the influence of the Foundation's Advisory Group on College Libraries, a list of recommended books for undergraduate libraries was developed and became a measure of the quality of library collections. This authoritative guide to purchasing books became known as the "Shaw List" and was a "landmark of the greatest importance" (Radford 1984). The Advisory Group then tackled the issue of defining standards for college libraries.

## Library Innovators

Louis Shores was a significant figure in academic librarianship in the twentieth century. His comment to a colleague, "You're too worried about the what and the where of libraries when you should be thinking about why libraries matter" is an indication of his philosophical perspective (Shiflett 1996). He was a leader in the area of reference librarianship, in his advocacy and development of the concept of "bibliographic instruction, " and as a library educator. He became the director of the Fisk University Library in Nashville, Tennessee, in 1928 and attempted unsuccessfully to establish a library school for African American librarians there.

He was a supporter of racial integration. He became head of the library school at Peabody College for Teachers in 1933 and received a Ph.D. from Peabody College for Teachers in 1934. His dissertation on the history of the colonial college libraries became a "cornerstone in the historiography of American library history" when it was published as a book (Shiflett 1996). He was influential in the launching of the *Journal of Library History* in 1966.

He was the founder of the innovative Library College movement of the 1960s. This was an attempt to "mate librarianship and education to produce a hybrid that would be greater than either" (Shiflett 1996). He believed that library-centred education was necessary for a good undergraduate education. In this model, teachers would work with students in the library during time that would have been spent in the classroom.

## Evolution of Staffing

Orne reviewed the evolution of staffing in the academic library. He relayed a historic desire by librarians to be accepted equally by faculty, but concluded that "acceptance of librarians by the academic community has not improved very much" (Orne 1980). The first instance of union participation by library staff was in 1940 at the Library of Congress. Whether scholarship should be a required qualification for a library director is an unresolved issue (Hamlin 1981). Academic librarians have struggled with their professional role in colleges and universities.

There has been ongoing debate about whether librarians should have faculty status and whether they can claim the same academic freedom rights as teaching faculty (DeVinney 1986). College library work in the 1970s was described as simple, traditional, and changing little. In university libraries, complex organizational dynamics resulted in "a progressive reduction of the ability to obtain hard decisions on matters having to do with improved performance" (Orne 1980).

## Organizational Models

Kaplan's review of the history of participative management in academic libraries revealed a 40-year delay from the time that the concept originated in the business world to its adoption by libraries. "Pioneer" librarians during the latent period published articles that tried to convince colleagues of the benefits of participative management. But the idea did not gain the attention of the profession until the social upheavals caused by the egalitarianism of the New Deal and the rebellious sixties occurred. Even then, the hierarchical structure of libraries was so strongly entrenched that widespread change in management style occurred slowly (Kaplan 1988).

The twenty-five year history of a successful model of management at Dickinson College Library described collegiality and flexibility with a rotating chair. It is based on a group decision-making model with shared responsibility. In 1975, a holistic model of librarianship was implemented that eliminated artificial barriers between technical and public services. Librarians were expected to be highly competent in a number of areas. Although considered radical at the time that it was adopted, the new model is now described as a system that works very well in a small to moderate size academic library (McKinzie 2000).

## Growth in Research

After World War II, federal funding stimulated increased research. Libraries had to deal with a great increase in the volume of published materials. As a result, the government provided support for research libraries to build their collections. The Cooperative Acquisitions Project for Wartime Publications resulted in the purchase of almost two million European books (Dain 1990). The Farmington Plan was a programme of cooperative acquisition of foreign publications that was established by the Association of Research Libraries in 1948 and terminated in 1972. Its original goal was that at least one copy of every newly published book that had research value would be acquired by at least one American library. This was the result of the recognition of a need for information during World War II and the corresponding dearth of foreign publications in the U.S. Agents in each country acquired monographs and distributed them to the appropriate library. There was an underlying assumption that library collections were a resource of value to the country, not just the parent institution (Wagner 2002).

### Consortia

Library consortia have a long history of cooperation in sharing collections or technical processing. They experienced their greatest growth in the 1960s and 1970s. Their greatest advantage is economy of scale. Certain items did not need to be purchased by every library. Consortia have led to different relationships with vendors and publishers and have redefined library collections and services (Bostick 2001).

### Resilience and Creativity

Miller's review of issues related to electronic resources cited the serials pricing crisis of the early 1980s as the catalyst for a new model that favoured access to materials rather than ownership of them. She believed that librarians must continually reassess what they do and why they do it, creatively move forward, and set standards, not merely react. She said that the literature showed that librarianship is "impressively resilient" and is willing to question, to reorganize, to build on its past, and adapt to change (Miller 2000).

The library of the Dine College, a Navajo tribal college, is an example of this resilience and creativity. The library addressed an information need and the desire to make accessible a source of knowledge that is not in a standard written form. Hurley (2002) describes the issues in collecting and preserving knowledge of the Navajo Nation. Communication of history and tradition through oral stories is common to North American Native people. Providing access to those stories is a challenge because there may not be a written form of the language and because different people tell different versions of the same stories. Capturing the stories in a static document loses the dynamic, context-driven, and fluid aspects that are essential (Hurley 2002). The library is determining how to make this rich source of information available while respecting the concerns and communication preferences of the tribe.

### Libraries in Historically Black Colleges and Universities

The story of the libraries of nine historically black colleges in Texas concluded that black academic libraries never became the "heart" of the institution. They were not a priority for the college administration "and almost never catalyzed the intellectual life of their communities. As adjunct activities, library operations failed to figure prominently in institutional reports." The librarians did not have allies among the faculty who could influence improvements because of high turnover among the professors (Olbrich 1986). The first freestanding library was built in 1907; the others followed after World War II. The Southern Association of Colleges and Secondary Schools began requiring relatively stringent quantitative library standards. Owens stated that there have been no comprehensive in-depth analyses of the libraries of historically black colleges and universities or of the quality of the collections (Owens 2001).

### Computerization

The Ohio College Library Centre (OCLC) was founded in 1967 by the colleges and universities in the state of Ohio. Its purpose was to develop a computerized system that would allow the libraries of these academic institutions to share resources and reduce costs (OCLC website). In 1972, OCLC offered online cataloguing data to subscribing libraries. OCLC began as a shared cataloguing resource based on a central catalogue for the Ohio college libraries. It was also highly useful as a union catalogue for all member libraries

(Maciuszko 1984). The OCLC database now includes the holdings for almost every library in the country and also some international libraries. Interlibrary loan requests are sent electronically to libraries that are listed as owning the material, saving time and providing great efficiency. The database is called "WorldCat" and can be searched by anyone in subscribing institutions. It is an unparalleled resource for finding citations to published and much unpublished material including books, journal titles, newsletters, audiovisuals, theses, government reports, and conference proceedings.

### Future of Libraries

A review of articles that predicted the future of libraries from 1990-2000 included sections on the issues of envisioning and planning the future of libraries; visions of digital libraries and new theories for information management; access/ownership and the transformation of scholarly communication; the arrival of the information society in 2000; and the Internet and new meanings for library collections. There were many articles that speculated on the future of libraries during the period from 1975 to 2000. This was evidence of a changing and uncertain profession. The author finds that by 2000, there were few articles that predicted the demise of traditional libraries (Sapp 2003). A possible area for further analysis was postulated by Dain, who speculates that libraries tend to reflect rather than create intellectual trends. She states that it would be interesting to study the intellectual origins and impact of library collections and operations through time and across disciplines and institutions (Dain 1990).

### Summary

The literature on the history of academic libraries was explored for three important periods in the evolution of higher education in the United States. Libraries in the Colonial period were minimal and peripheral to the college function and mission. In the nineteenth and early twentieth centuries, academic libraries developed a formal structure and became more integral to the mission of the university, serving students and faculty in supporting more diversified curricula and research. These trends blossomed following World War II when increases in funding allowed libraries to acquire larger collections and become important resources in research and teaching Changes in technology beginning in the 1970s caused major changes in availability and use of electronic resources. Since the 1980s, increased economic pressures on university administers has caused some to question the role and function of the traditional library. Throughout U.S. history, libraries have changed in response to external influences. As they find ways to connect with the mission of their parent institutions, the academic library will continue to be considered the "heart" of the university.

## A COMPARATIVE STUDY OF NATIONAL PUBLIC LIBRARY

Through an analytical and comparative study, this paper examines the development and current status of the United States' and China's national library statistical systems, their natural functions and key system characteristics, usability of performance measures, and each system's strengths and shortcomings. A distinction is made between government centred and profession centred systems. Four f actors are identified influencing the systems' characteristics. By finding commonalities and discrepancies between the two countries' statistical systems, the article provides library professionals, governmental administrators, and educators with the opportunity to learn from each other's practices and experiences, to conduct further investigations into the purpose and characteristics of the statistical systems, and ultimately, to improve nationwide library planning and evaluation in their own country.

### Paper

National statistical measures of library operations have been used in both the United States and People's Republic of China for over half a century. These national systems of statistical measurement provide a variety of information concerning service effectiveness, operational management, staff administration, national planning, and professional competitiveness. However, compared with the efforts expended in collection and dissemination of the numerical information, analyses of the differing character of national systems or of the contributions of these systems have rarely received attention. A study that compares characteristics of these systems can increase understanding of the function of each and can suggest approaches to improving their effectiveness.

Objectives of this study therefore are fourfold. First, the national statistical system in both the U.S. and P.R. China are described. Second, key characteristics of these system are examined. These include system function, data manipulation, and standardization and implementation. Third, the relation of the data utilization and library performance measures is discussed. Initial comparison between two countries of the national systems is supplied, and is based on the latest information on each system that I can find. Finally, an attempt is made to provide some insight into possible future developments as well as a system assessment.

## Description of the National Systems Government Centred versus Profession Centred Systems

With long library histories and large populations of public libraries, both countries have a natural need to trace meaningful numbers about libraries. In the U.S., plans to collect library statistics on a national basis began approximately one hundred years ago. The first milestone in public library statistics occurred in the end of 19th century. In a matter of nine years, after the establishment of the U.S. Office of Education in 1867, "a massive report, Public libraries in the United States, containing descriptive and statistical data was issued" (Adams, 1990).

In P.R. China, public library statistics can be traced back to the beginning of this century. The first nationwide library survey authorized by Ministry of Culture of China was distributed in 1950 (Li, 1988). This was just one year earlier than the dispatch of a very simple questionnaire from the UNESCO Office of Statistics in 1951. The practice of collecting national public library statistics in both the U.S. and China preceded the UNESCO's request for international collaboration on library data collection (Thi, 1987).

After years of efforts to find a better way to report useful and up to date data on public libraries, librarians in both the countries have built up their own unique statistical systems on national public libraries. Such systems, this study's subjects, can be categorized as government centred systems or professional or non governmental systems. The distinction between the two kinds of systems is based on the clients served by each system and their missions. The systems of the U.S. and China, respectively, are described below.

**The Systems in the United States**

Formally started in 1988 (Lynch, 1989), the current U.S. government public library data system is funded by the National Centre for Education Statistics (NCES), U.S. Department of Education Office of Educational Research and Improvement, and conducted through the Federal State Cooperative System for Public Library Data (FSCS).

The support of the system includes the local public librarians who provide the data; the FSCS State Data Coordinators who collect and verify data at the state level; the Chief Officers of State Library Agencies; the American Library Association (ALA); and the National Commission on Libraries and Information Science (NCLIS) which collects data disks from Data Coordinators.

To run this system, NCES is the executive agency and funds the programme; FSCS is responsible for questionnaire design and definitions of standardization. Over ninety five percent of public libraries anywhere in the country respond to the system yearly. Its clients include governmental officers, legislators, and professionals. As of 1995, the system issues the U.S. public library data on paper, diskette and the Internet each year.

The Public Library Data Service (PLDS) is the major public library professional system of the United States. The system, in which data were collected starting in 1987 (Johnson, 1993), is supported by Public Library Association (PLA), a division of American Library Association (ALA). Its executive agencies have included School of Library and Information Studies at

University of Wisconsin Madison, and Library Research Centre at the University of Illinois at Urbana Champaign. As a voluntary data collection project this system annually collects data from public libraries of all sizes, almost covering libraries serving more than 100, 000 population (79.8% were included in 1995). Data collected in February/March are published in an annual report in June. Clients include public library directors and library educators. The system is designed by the public library profession for its own use. Running for eight years, this system has become an invaluable reference for librarians, trustees, governmental officials and the media.

### The Systems in People's Republic of China

As a part of the statistical system on national social cultural affairs, statistics on public libraries in China are officially reported by the Ministry of Culture. The Ministry gathers library data through local government agencies and reports the data to the Bureau of National Statistics, the national statistical office. Data obtained at the end of each year are reported early the next year, and are published in The Annual Report of Public Library Statistical Records (PLSR). This government funded system was established in early 1950s, and has been continuing for four decades, although information during Cultural Revolution is fragmentary.

Using the basic pattern of data design in PLSR, the National Library and Bureau of Library Administration (a unit of the Ministry of Culture) have conducted national public library survey and published Overall Conditions of China Public Libraries (OCCPL) irregularly every several years starting in 1959 (OCCPL, 1989).

Statistical information published includes not only numerical data of the libraries but also narrative descriptions of the history and physical facilities. The summerized accounts were only for provincial or city public libraries. The purpose of this system is to report the current development of public librarianship and to serve the public library profession. Its clients include library administrators and researchers. Responses rates varied from year to year, and usually lower than PLSR.

## System Characteristics, Commonalities and Discrepancies

Built on different social cultural backgrounds, the statistical systems contain their own unique features. In some aspects, such as central organization and relationship between central organization and local participation, variation of national systems may make comparison difficult. However, on the other hand, some characteristics, such as system functions, data manipulation, standardization, and publications, have international concerns and commonalities that can be analyzed for the comparison.

## System Functions

Both of these systems include functions that address the following needs or issues:

1. *Accountability:* By tracking movement over time and historical trends/accounts, the intention is that the development and evolution of libraries nationwide can be traced through a national system.
2. *Feasibility and Measurability:* Data elements can be established and measured to reflect library key conditions and services that were particularly considered when the US systems were founded (Zweizig, 1979). Data established should have generizability and also serve accountability.
3. *Comparability and Uniformity:* Data can be used within and between libraries for library quality control and service improvement, and commonly to exchange information. "As states achieve greater uniformity of data, there will be greater comparability of data" (Adams, 1990).
4. *Reliability and Validity:* Accuracy of data reported is emphasized.
5. *Accessibility:* Data are open to public. NCES data were available through Web and Gopher starting last year.

Although the aims of all these systems are to support administration and decision making, their individual objectives are not really quite the same. In China the government system tends to use statistical data for making budget guidelines or for library information exchange.

The U.S. professional system on other hand intends to use these data for library professionals to make observations on the effectiveness of library services, to demonstrate accountability, to identify staff development needs, and to improve service design. NCES conducts its surveys in fulfilment of its legislative mission "to collect, and analyze, and disseminate statistics and other data related to education in the United States and in other nations" (USCA, 1988). It intends to primarily serve federal government executive and legislative needs.

### Data Manipulation

The differences between the U.S. and Chinese systems on data manipulation illustrate the systems' intention and expertise, and are often seen within many aspects such as elements structure, survey instrument, data treatment and statistical techniques used. Basically, contrasted to Chinese systems, information selected in the U.S. systems includes not only a public library and its service, but also its communities served.

Data in the U.S. systems are treated analytically, not only as input. Relations between library resources and service (what a library has and what is used) are reported by percentage distributions, and relations between library output and communities served are calculated as per capita figures. Statistical analysis is these systems' important feature.

The data element as a crucial part of the statistical system embodies and condenses a system's platform and guidelines. NCES includes a total of 44 items collected from each library 33 basic data elements including population of legal services area, service outlets, staffing, collection, circulation, visits and facilities; and 11 identifying items including name, address, interlibrary relationship and administrative structure.

There are also an additional 12 items collected on each public library outlet and state library outlet. PLDS has more than 50 data elements that are arranged into five categories:

Library Identification, Financial Information, Library Resources and Community Measure, Annual Use Figures, and Output Measures and Role Selection.

Additionally, a sixth category changes from year to year (*e.g.*, 1995 was Technology in Public Libraries, and 1994 was Children's Services Survey). Each category is formed by three parts: instruction, data elements, and summary table and comparison charts. Formulas used to derive numbers, notations used in summary tables, and the questionnaire used to collect these data are listed as appendixes. Software used for data manipulation in both U.S. systems include DECPLUS (Data Entry, Conversion, Table, Output Programme), LOTUS, dBASE, and Fourth Dimensions.

Data elements used in the Chinese systems, as in the U.S. systems, cover basic resources (funding, building, and holdings) and key services of each public library, but unlike the U.S. systems, do not cover population of the community served. The 48 data elements grouped within 18 categories in PLSR, include library name, number of staff, annual circulation, number of seats, and great detail on collections and expenditures. With almost the same categories of data as PLSR, OCCPL has only 11 data elements in its 1989 publication.

Methods of statistical analysis and techniques for comparing detailed percentages have not been used as much as the U.S. systems. Some data elements such as size of library facilities are useful and valuable to show how resources are allocated. To communicate the nature of service provided in China, the number of seats and size of reading rooms can be major indicators for these closed stack libraries. Opposed to this, the U.S. systems don't report these items because their stacks are open and seats do not appropriately express the use of libraries.

### Standardization

A legitimate usability and comparison of data are based on quality of standards used for data collection. To keep data consistent and reduce error and confusion, U.S. systems use standardized definition to define each itemized element. During the preparation for developing a comprehensive national system, FSCS conducted a pilot project in 1985 to standardize the collection of public library data. The definitions used in this system are from the National Information Standards Organization (NISO) manual Z39.7 (NCES 1995 and 1991). PLDS was designed in conjunction with the Public Library Development Programme by the New Standards Task Force of PLA (PLDS, 1988). Terms used in its questionnaire were carefully defined. As a check list of the standardized definition, Entity Data Element Definitions are published with data in both systems' publications. Code systems accompanying each data element ensure data quantification.

### Use of Statistics for Measuring Performance

Library statistics generated are expected to describe and compare effectiveness and efficiency of libraries. Even though endeavours of library performance measures in both the U.S. and China can be traced back to 1960s (Zhu, 1994; Kaplan, 1964), the natural use of library statistics to support improvement and facilitation of management in public libraries was really recognized only in the past decade.

In particular, PLDS was initiated to play a role of measuring library output nationwide with uniform measurements. Five major measures adopted in PLDS include circulation per capita, registration as a percent of the population, library holdings per capita, collection turnover, and reference transactions per capita (Johnson, 1992). These had been identified as useful in promoting efficiency, cost effectiveness and increased comparability in public libraries by a number of contributors, such as DeProspo et al. (1973), Zweizig and Rodger (1982) and Van House et al. (1987). Systems designers who worked for both NCES and PLDS developed the national systems with the uniform measurements in order to make them a powerful tool for performance measures in public libraries nationwide.

The measurements reported in NCES also concentrate on uses and the services a library provides for its community. Its focus is "what a public library delivers to the community it serves" (Lynch, 1990). Example measures are percentages of registration of population and per registered borrower, in library use, rates of reference completion, and title filled.

Facilities or non service related information such as library funding and staff salaries is measured, but the emphasis is on effectiveness and efficiency of uses and the services a library provides to its community.

Instances of these measurements include per capita holdings, per capital operating expenditures, and per capital library operating income. Focuses of measures in Chinese systems are based on their management intention, which includes not only how well a library is used, but also how well a library is developed. PLSR was designed to determine investment of government resources in library development. Measurements are basically functioning the same as data elements.

The main measures, such as number of seats and volumes, size of library stacks and reading rooms, and annual book purchasing budget are examined and used to compare quantity and quality of library development. OCCPL was originated to play the role of measuring effective use of a library. But measuring each library's resource in order to study the use of library funds also plays an important role. The different focuses between the two countries' systems reflect social cultural backgrounds and level of library developments.

During 1992 to 1994, a national assessment of public library work was made in China. To give a series of national criteria to the appraisal, the Library Bureau of Ministry of Culture issued The Appraisal Indicator Series for Provincial Libraries (AISPL), and Appraisal Standards for City/County Libraries (ASCCL).

The purpose of the national evaluation is to promote level of professional work and quality of library service, and to accelerate development of public librarianship nationwide. AISPL comprises six categories and seventy two indicators 55 quantitative indicators and 17 qualitative indicators. These indicators comprise aspects from library service, to professional work, to library facilities, and are intended to be employed as standardized performance criteria used for public libraries with different roles, such as provincial, city, county and children's libraries.

A main feature of the assessment is the use of quantified measurements to promote library development by allowing comparability cross libraries on a number of dimensions. Over 2000 public libraries nationwide participated this activity. AS a result, 1144 libraries received awards and were designated as advanced units at onc of three levels. AISPL and ASCCL together with OCCPL comprise a complete professional system of performance measures for public libraries of all sizes and functions.

Because of the great differences between the data elements collected in the U.S. and in China, and between the services designs of each country, possibilities for comparing statistics indicating library operations between the countries' public libraries were extremely limited. Comparative totals or averages by per head between the two countries would be easy to see if the key source, community served, was originally included in China's public library statistics.

## Conclusion: Issues and Trends

Four factors appear to influence the system characteristics in these two countries:

1. *System's Background:* Genesis of a system affects its later development. The social and cultural environment influence the system's evolution;
2. *Funding Sources:* The organizing and executive agencies determine the system's properties;
3. *Programme Goals:* Government statistics serve government needs. Professional systems centre on the use of measures for library professionals;
4. *Data Manipulation:* Government systems have a higher response rate therefore a greater authority of statistics. Data are collected systematically moving from local to

central. Professional systems have to conduct their national surveys for data collection directly from each outlet. Great focus on questions of professional interest and emphasis on measures of performance are beneficial to public library colleagues.

As a trend, the parallel systems in both countries, reflecting modern needs for statistics support of library performance measures, will continue to serve the management needs.

Efforts made by both governmental officers and library professionals in library statistics have been rewarded with the development of comprehensive statistical systems in both countries, in which statistics can be readily used for management to examine and appraise library characteristics.

The system does not have the power to promote effectiveness and efficiency of library service on its own, b ut it does have the power to illuminate the policy of the service and to support the development of librarianship by means of statistics if they are appropriately used. The statistical systems used to examine library progress have evolved over time as a result of a variety of impulses and not as a result of a coherent strategy or plan.

Strengths of the US systems include sophisticated data manipulation, extensive standardization, and strong statistical analysis. Important library characteristics are represented well through statistical elements.

Data reported are made easy for public to access. A weakness in NCES is the delay of at least two years in reporting data after collection. On the other hand, higher response rate in P LDS is only from libraries that serve large communities. Both Chinese systems have a lack of statistical analysis and information about the community served. The information shown in these systems in both countries has not been effectively used in research on library performance.

Further investigation. Social economic background is different for the two countries, but the needs for statistical information appears to be the same. Most functions of these statistical systems and their problems and issues faced are also not different. Questions that a system administrator may ask, including what data should be included and relation between cost and effectiveness of data collection, still remain. Understanding these systems' development and function is hampered by their being considered "inevitable" and "natural" when in fact they have developed to serve unstated but definable purposes.

Study of two comparable systems from strongly contrasting cultures can reveal obscure characteristics and functions. Similarities and differences regarding the above categories can illuminate the inherent characteristics of the national systems, and will be worthwhile for understanding of the role and impact of nationwide library planning, evaluating, and service performance measures.

# 2

# Research in Library and Information Science

This chapter aims at reporting on an on-going investigation into research capacity in Library and Information Science in South Africa by using bibliometric analyses. The study objectives are to identify and represent research capacity in terms of: research themes but also with regard to individual research productivity, institutional productivity, size/quantity of publications, location, gender/race of researchers and size of registered research projects. For the purposes of this conference, the results of the first part of the study on the size and nature of graduate research are based on records of theses and dissertations indexed in the SABINET on-line database (as reported by gender, institutional affiliation, language of report, level of graduate research report, population group and research topic).

Our definition of library and information science will include: information content, theory, technology, users, processing, centres, systems, services and management.

## Literature Review

Society is becoming increasingly dependent on research for answers to a myriad of unresolved phenomenological and ontological issues and problems that affect life, sometimes on a daily basis. Both public and corporate organizations are spending enormous amounts of money, time and resources on research and development. Research capacity of an organization largely determines its development, influence, and wealth creation and distribution. When South Africa is positioned in

Africa according to number of articles in SCI and SSCI it is singled out to be the largest research producer in Africa (1996). The measurement of research capacity is based on several, often-debatable variables.

Three dominant variables, in my view, include the registered, on-going and completed research projects. The other one that is also widely favoured for research productivity analyses is based on publication output.

The most commonly used indicators in this case are: journal articles, corporate publications, editorship or research reports, books or chapters in books, published proceeding size of congresses, symposia or conferences, performances and exhibitions (quality control highly debated in scholarly circles), book reviews, and patents. The final category could be the size of industrial property or intellectual property ownership. Publication counts are widely used to measure research productivity by individuals, organizations and even countries.

Bibliometrics is a field that has attracted a great deal of attention among scholars of all disciplines. The existence of an International Society for Scientometrics and Informetrics Congress (organized to foster studies in this unique field for quantitative analysis and measurements of publications) is a manifestation of its popularity.

Widely viewed (Broadus 1987; Sengupta (1992), bibliometrics tends to focus on the study and analyses of information resources by country, authors, languages, words, type, research methodologies, articles, obsolescence and distribution of authors in literature. When Alan Prichard (1969) (some of us prefer Otlet) proposed a replacement of 'statistical bibliography' with 'bibliometrics, ' he perhaps foresaw that this quantitative method of study held potential for rapid growth.

By this time, evidently, 'statistical bibliography' had produced exceptional results, as witnessed by Lotka's law on 'Author Productivity' (1926), Zipf's law on 'The Distribution of Words in Text' in 1933 (Zipf 1935), Bradford's law on 'The Scatter of Literature', and "The Decline in the Use of Materials as They Age' or 'half-life' of literature proposed by Burton and

Kebler (1960). The quantity of research and publications based on the bibliometric method as well as its application, as reflected in standard bibliographic databases, suggest that the methods have been recognized and still enjoy significant support for scientific enquiry.

In Africa the bibliometric method has not been widely popularized as would be expected. There is evidence of its application by West African scholars, particularly in Nigeria (Aina 1997 & 1998) and Ghana (Alemna 1994 & 1996). There is not enough information available to suggest its use for library and information science research in South Africa during the covered period. However, we expect fresh publications from a recent doctoral work completed at the University of Natal (Jacobs 1999).

Boon and Zyl did a recognizable study on research capacity in library and information science in South Africa that covered the period 1979-1989 (1990) ten years ago. The authors focused on the quantity, relevance and quality of research in South Africa. They identified the disciplines researched frequently as well as those less researched and concurred with similar studies elsewhere that quality of research in "LIS tends to be mediocre rather than excellent or poor'.

There are significant commonalties between the current study and Boon's and Zyl's study in terms of the use of database records of completed masters and doctoral research as well as the South African Journal of Library and Information Science for determination of quantitative and qualitative indicators. However, differences in methodology, scope and focus are observed in both instances.

## METHODOLOGY

This database provides titles of research, authors, level of research work, affiliation and broad subject such as library science, information science, computer science and commerce. Information on narrow subjects such as those indexed in table are not provided. In addition, information on gender, language and population groups are omitted. A Boolean search by library and information science yielded 151 records while that done by information science not library science produced 81 records from 1993-2000. All information science dissertations and theses in question were for degrees/qualifications in fields other than library and information science and had a bearing on one of the following fields: computer science, commerce, business management, political science and information systems.

Although qualifications reflected the aforementioned fields, they dealt with familiar areas such as information systems, IT, IM, and information needs assessment that also featured in the degrees offered in library and information science.

After deleting duplications and irrelevant records, 218 records were analyzed by topic/theme, affiliation, and level of thesis or dissertation, language, gender and population group. A table consisting of relevant rows and columns representing the indicators was designed where the data was first recorded in frequencies using special symbols made for recording purposes.

The data items were then quantified and summed up in each case and the results represented systematically and ranked by frequencies, in subsequent tables using a word-processor and excel software programmes. The results have been verified by triangulation based on data obtained from the analysis of publications in the South African Journal of Library and Information Science covering 1990-1998. The results obtained from graduate research analysis are largely consistent with those in the journal. Unfortunately details from the journal analysis could not be made available for this paper due to technical constraints.

## Results

The results appearing in this section represent the research capacity based on 218 records in the Union Catalogue of Theses and Dissertations produced by SABINET on completed graduate masters and doctoral research in library and information science from 1993-2000 as at 20/5/2000.

The records have been analyzed by level of graduate work (*e.g.* masters and doctoral), by gender (male or female), by population group (emphasis falls on black involvement in research as opposed to other racial groups), by language, by affiliation and, finally, by subject orientation. Table eight collates tables for comparative data. A summary of the results appears on tables one to seven.

**Research Capacity by Levels of theses or Dissertation**

***Research Capacity by Levels of Graduate Work (N=218)***

| *Year* | *Masters* | *Doctoral* |
|---|---|---|
| 1999 | 12 | 6 |
| 1998 | 10 | 5 |
| 1997 | 25 | 8 |
| 1996 | 31 | 5 |
| 1995 | 43 | 7 |
| 1994 | 36 | 4 |
| 1993 | 25 | 1 |
| Total | 176 | 38 |

A large part of graduate research is dominated by masters' work (82%) as opposed to doctoral work (18%). Admission to masters in South Africa normally takes place during the sixth year of university education for LIS graduates and fifth year for non-professional degrees.

The duration for masters is a minimum of one year full-time or two years part-time. Doctoral degrees take a minimum of two years full-time and four years part-time after masters or equivalent qualification.

Masters work can be offered by both course work and mini-dissertation or by thesis/dissertation only. Doctoral work is still offered by thesis only. While high standards are achieved in both cases, the variations found in masters' work have an influence on the depth and breadth of the research report or dissertation and thesis.

There has been a decline in masters and doctoral research from 1998. The causes of the decline are worthy of investigation.

***Research Capacity by Gender:*** It is of interest to establish the ratio of male to female in regard to graduate research.

***Research Capacity by Gender (N=218)***

| *Year* | *Male* | *Female* |
|---|---|---|
| 1999 | 6 | 12 |
| 1998 | 6 | 9 |
| 1997 | 10 | 23 |
| 1996 | 13 | 23 |
| 1995 | 24 | 26 |
| 1994 | 17 | 23 |
| 1993 | 14 | 12 |
| Total | 90 | 128 |

Females (58.7%) dominate both masters and doctoral research output. Female research output in library and information science is higher than 80% while less than 5% in information science technology oriented subjects (computer science, business management and commerce). More males (over 80%) conduct work in information science technology oriented disciplines such as IT and information systems and tend to obtain most information oriented qualifications/degrees in computer science, business management, information systems, commerce, education and political science.

## Research Capacity by Population Group

Population group in this case refers to race. The nascent democracy in South Africa is yearning for black empowerment through redress. Affirmative action is one of the means employed to achieve empowerment. Analysis of research capacity by population group is therefore essential. Table three provides a summary in this category.

The major population groups in South Africa are categorized in terms of Black, White, Indian and Coloureds. Whereas I intended to provide a breakdown of research capacity by all four-population groups, their identification by names provided in the publication proved to be difficult. However, it was possible to identify African names and this made it possible for analysis of the records by black as opposed to other population groups. Indians and Coloureds sometimes use western names that confuse identity with the whites unless individuals are personally approached in order to establish the population group to which they belong.

***Research Capacity by Population Groups (N=218)***

| *Year* | *Black* | *White & Others* |
|---|---|---|
| 1999 | 6 | 12 |
| 1998 | 8 | 10 |
| 1997 | 9 | 24 |
| 1996 | 4 | 32 |
| 1995 | 6 | 44 |
| 1994 | 1 | 39 |
| 1993 | 1 | 25 |
| Total | 34 | 184 |

This may be regarded by some to be an unethical form of approach. The number of blacks involved in graduate research is insignificant, although numbers are slowly increasing (15.6%). There are several career opportunities in other challenging, prestigious, high-income earning fields that were not easily accessible for blacks in previous times. These include fields such as medicine and engineering.

Whether new opportunities in these fields have any influence on career options remains debatable. Attainment of final qualifications in these areas may continue to represent a "long walk" for blacks.

It is, however, clear that graduate research largely remains a field occupied by whites. A detailed breakdown by all population groups including non-South Africans may reveal a clearer picture for manpower planners.

## Research Capacity by Language

The South African constitution permits the usage of eleven official languages including Afrikaans, isindebele, siswati, Setswana, isizulu, English, Sesotho, Sepedi, Tshivenda, Xitsonga and isxhosa. It is interesting to establish whether the eleven languages are used in graduate research and, if not, which languages dominate graduate research and why. Table four provides a summary in this regard

***Research Capacity by Language Use (N=218)***

| *Year* | *English* | *Afrikaans* |
|---|---|---|
| 1999 | 17 | 1 |
| 1998 | 15 | 0 |
| 1997 | 29 | 4 |
| 1996 | 25 | 11 |
| 1995 | 44 | 6 |
| 1994 | 26 | 14 |
| 1993 | 19 | 7 |
| Total | 175 | 43 |

Presentation of dissertations and theses in English (80.28%) is increasing as opposed to Afrikaans (19.72%) which is in decline. There is no evidence that other nine remaining languages are used for graduate dissertations and theses.

The demise of the African languages in graduate research sets a social agenda to be tackled by those who are keen on the promotion of African languages and the African renaissance. More South Africans seem to write theses and dissertations in English, perhaps because of its popularity with regard to publication and scientific communication.

## Research Capacity by Affiliation

The breadth and depth of doctoral theses and dissertations are normally superior compared to masters studies. This may be indicative of the level and perhaps the quality of research undertaken. For purposes of identification with regard to research partnership and associates as well as affiliations for graduate studies, information appearing in table five on research capacity by affiliation may be extremely important.

A large part of graduate research in library and information science originates from the University of Natal in Pietermaritzburg 48 (22 %), the Rand Afrikaans University 41 (18.8%) and the University of the Witwatersrand 30 (13.76%) that largely offers information science oriented research in Business Management. Following those three closely are the University of Pretoria 29(13.3%), the University of Cape Town 23 (10.6%) and the University of South Africa 16 (7.4%).

Potchefstroom 13 (6. %), Stellenbosch 10 (4.6%) and the remaining universities make an insignificant contribution. In terms of advanced research leading to doctoral work, the leading universities, respectively, are Natal (Pietermaritzburg) (11), RAU (9), Pretoria (8), UNISA (4) and Cape Town (2). Most of the Rand Afrikaans University's doctoral are in information science based qualifications in computer science, commerce and information systems.

***Graduate Research Capacity by Institution Affiliation (N=218)***

| NAME OF INSTITUTION | 1999 | | 1998 | | 1997 | | 1996 | | 1995 | | 1994 | | 1993 | | TOTAL | |
|---|---|---|---|---|---|---|---|---|---|---|---|---|---|---|---|---|
| University of | U | M | U | M | U | M | U | M | U | M | U | M | U | M | U | M |
| Natal-Pietermaritzburg (UNP) | 5 | 5 | 1 | 6 | 1 | 7 | 1 | 3 | 2 | 13 | 1 | 3 | - | - | 11 | 37 |
| Rands Afrikaans University (RAU) | 2 | 1 | - | - | 3 | 5 | 2 | 5 | 2 | 5 | - | 12 | - | 4 | 9 | 32 |
| Pretoria (UO) | - | 3 | 3 | 1 | 1 | 3 | 1 | 3 | 1 | 3 | 1 | 4 | 1 | 4 | 9 | 20 |
| South Africa (UNISA) | - | - | 1 | 1 | 1 | 1 | - | 2 | 1 | 1 | 1 | 2 | - | 5 | 4 | 12 |
| Cape Town (UCT) | - | - | - | - | - | 3 | 1 | 11 | 1 | 2 | - | 3 | - | 2 | 2 | 21 |
| Potchestroom University (PUC) | - | 1 | - | - | 1 | 1 | - | 4 | - | 2 | - | 2 | - | 2 | 1 | 12 |
| Witwatersrand (WITTS) | - | 1 | - | 2 | 1 | - | - | - | - | 15 | - | 5 | - | 6 | 1 | 29 |
| Stellenbosch (Stell) | - | - | - | - | - | 2 | - | 2 | - | 1 | 1 | 3 | - | 1 | 1 | 9 |
| Zululand (UZ) | - | - | - | - | - | 2 | - | - | - | 1 | - | - | - | 1 | - | 4 |
| Orange Free State (UOFS) | - | - | - | - | - | 1 | - | - | - | - | - | 1 | - | - | - | 2 |
| Vista University (VU) | - | - | - | - | - | - | - | - | - | - | - | 1 | - | - | - | 1 |
| Western Cape (WCU) | - | - | - | - | - | - | - | 1 | - | - | - | - | - | - | - | 1 |
| Total | 7 | 11 | 5 | 10 | 8 | 25 | 5 | 31 | 7 | 43 | 4 | 36 | 1 | 25 | 38 | 180 |

It is believed that the success of most of the aforementioned universities is attributable to a strong graduate tradition and to the maintenance of a stable graduate supervisory capacity. Most senior academics are still found in the aforementioned universities, which carry on with the graduate tradition. Universities that specialize in graduate library and information science education such as the University of Natal (Pietermaritzburg) and the University of Cape Town are likely to lead in research and graduate work. Between 1993 and 1999 information science based masters and doctoral research in commerce, computer science, geography and environmental studies, political science, education and music were obtained at the following universities: Pretoria (7-D, 4-M), Rand Afrikaans (4-D, 9-M), Witwatersrand (I-D, 28-M), Cape Town (8-M), Natal (I-M), UNISA (M-4), Potchefstroom (M-2), and the Orange Free State (1-M). The University of Witwatersrand (it does not offer library and information science degrees) has a strong base for information oriented education in business management while the University of Natal (Pietermaritzburg) leads in both graduate masters and doctoral output in Library and Information Science. Research capacity by subject orientation and institutional affiliation. It is of particular interest to establish research subject orientation as a whole as well as by institutional affiliation in South Africa in order to determine the gap for manpower development as well as popular research topics for research partnership and graduate enrolment. Table six provides an indexed list of the research subjects and affiliations.

### *Research Capacity by Subject Orientation*

| SUBJECT | FREQUENCY | INSTITUTIONAL AFFILIATION |
|---|---|---|
| Information Technology | 47 | WITS,UCT, RAU,PUC, UP, UNISA, UNP |
| Management/information management | 42 | UP, UNP, PUC, UZ, RAU, UNISA, PUC, UCT, UOFS,STEL, UWC |
| Information systems (includes, EIS, GIS, etc) | 30 | WITS,RAU,UCT,UNISA,UP,UN |
| User studies/information needs assessment | 26 | UCT, PUC, UNISA, UNP, UOFS, RAU, VISTA, UZ, STELL |
| Information dissemination/services | 24 | UNISA,RAU,UNP,UOFS, VISTA,UCT,PUC |
| LIS -education and training | 19 | RAU,UNP,UNISA,PUC,UP |
| Library and Information theory | 13 | UNP,UCT,STELL,UP,RAU |
| Readership/information seeking | 13 | UNP,UCT,RAU,UCT,STEL,UZ |
| Information collection development/management | 12 | RAU,STELL,UNP,UNISA,UCT |
| Historical librarianship | 9 | UNISA,STELL,UNP,UCT |
| Children's literature | 8 | UCT,PUC,RAU,STEL |
| Information security management | 7 | UNISA,UZ,RAU |
| Community information services | 7 | UNISA,UNP,UZ,UP |
| Cataloguing/classification | 6 | UNP,RAU,UCT,PUC |
| Marketing information system/publicity & promotion of information services | 5 | UNP,RAU |
| Legal /ethical issues | 4 | UNP,UP,PUC,RAU |
| Records management/archiving | 4 | UNP,UZ,RAU,UNISA |
| Databases/CD -ROM/ bibliographical | 3 | UP |
| Searching and retrieval | 3 | UOFS, RAU |
| Information literacy | 3 | UP,RAU,UNP |
| Information sources | 3 | UNP,RAU,UP, |
| Interlending/resource sharing | 2 | UNP,RAU |
| Information mapping/information audit | 2 | RAU |
| Publishing | 2 | RAU |
| Health information systems and services | 2 | UP |
| Information brokerage/consultacy | 1 | UP |
| Legal information systems/services | 1 | UP |
| Economics information | 1 | RAU |
| Indexing | 1 | PUC |

The ranked list of subject orientation for graduate research shows fairly diversified distribution that may be divided into three zones with an interval of 20. Zone one constitutes those subjects that appear between 40 to 60 times. The highest distribution is concentrated in information technology and management.

The second zone ranges from 20 to 40 and includes information systems, user studies and information needs assessment and information dissemination. Information Technology and Information Systems largely emanate from non-library and information science degree/qualification programmes and departments such as computer science, commerce and business management.

However, there is evidence that collaborative research between LIS departments and the aforementioned programmes are ongoing. Zone three ranges from 1-20 as ranked on table six. Most of the 32 subjects ranked in this zone are offered for LIS degrees. Information security management, legal/ethical issues, databases; information mapping/audit and economic information are shared between degree qualifications.

***Graduate Research Capacity Indicators Compared (Masters and Doctoral Theses and Dissertation 1993-2000) N=218***

| YEAR | 1999 | 1998 | 1997 | 1996 | 1995 | 1994 | 1993 | Total |
|---|---|---|---|---|---|---|---|---|
| MASERS | 12 | 10 | 25 | 31 | 43 | 36 | 25 | 182 |
| DOCTORAL | 6 | 5 | 8 | 5 | 7 | 4 | 1 | 36 |
| FEMALE | 12 | 9 | 23 | 23 | 26 | 23 | 12 | 128 |
| MALE | 6 | 6 | 10 | 13 | 24 | 17 | 14 | 90 |
| BLACK | 8 | 5 | 9 | 4 | 6 | 1 | 1 | 34 |
| WHITE AND OTHERS | 10 | 10 | 24 | 32 | 44 | 39 | 25 | 184 |
| LANGUAGES | 17 | 15 | 29 | 25 | 44 | 26 | 19 | 175 |
| Eng | 1 | 0 | 4 | 11 | 6 | 14 | 7 | 43 |
| Afr | | | | | | | | |
| UNIVERSITY/INSTITUTIONAL AFFILIATION (by number of masters and doctoral research) | | | | | | | | |
| UNP | 10 | 7 | 8 | 4 | 15 | 4 | - | 48 |
| RAU | 3 | - | 8 | 7 | 7 | 12 | 4 | 41 |
| WITS | 1 | 2 | 1 | - | 15 | 5 | 6 | 30 |
| UP | 3 | 4 | 4 | 4 | 4 | 5 | 5 | 29 |
| UCT | - | - | 3 | 12 | 3 | 3 | 2 | 23 |
| UNISA | - | 2 | 2 | 2 | 2 | 3 | 5 | 16 |
| PUC | 1 | - | 2 | 4 | 2 | 2 | 2 | 13 |
| STEL | - | - | 2 | 2 | 1 | 4 | 1 | 10 |
| UZ | - | - | 2 | - | 1 | - | 1 | 4 |
| UOFS | - | - | 1 | - | - | 1 | - | 2 |
| VISTA | - | - | - | - | - | 1 | - | 1 |
| UWC | - | - | - | 1 | - | - | - | 1 |

It is observed that a large proportion of graduate research is produced in LIS departments located in previously advantaged universities and that white females dominate in numbers among those graduating with masters and doctoral degrees. The same gender group publishes the preponderance of articles. The masters and doctoral research output by African South Africans is alarmingly small. Whereas the University of Natal (Pietermaritzburg) leads in both masters and doctoral research output for graduate degree/qualifications in library and information science.

Other rankings appear in tables. The publications arising from the 218 analyzed completed research work are minimal and those publications are linked to tertiary institutions or to university education and training institutions. Where there is no pressure to publish for career growth graduates publish less or nothing. Arguably, research is complete only when it is published.

The tradition that requires research supervisors or promoters to produce joint publication with their students from the research project or encourage their students to publish should be encouraged. This would attract good research work, where the authors are reluctant to publish because they are not under any pressure or obliged to do so as opposed to university academics that is compelled to publish. Specialization and location of senior academics that determine graduate research levels, topics, output and other staff related variables, favour previously advantaged universities.

Information reflected in this ongoing study should, in my view, provide data for determining graduate research capacity in South Africa; for knowledge and comparison of graduate research potential; selection of graduate institutions by those aspiring for masters and doctoral research; for student exchange; for research partnership and for determination and developments in graduate research. The rapidly growing research capacity in the country offers promising opportunities for research and professional linkages as well as manpower training at graduate levels for the people of Africa. South African LIS institutions have the potential to play a leading role with regard to LIS research in Africa. The work done by SABINET with regard to the establishment of a database on graduate research in South Africa is commendable. A current data base on ongoing (registered) and completed LIS research for non-degree purposes is essential to supplement the SABINET. I believe that the forthcoming first biannual DISSA conference to be held in Pretoria during October will set a strong agenda in this regard.

## EXCELLENT PEOPLE-ORIENTED STRATEGIES FOR DIGITAL LIBRARIES

Libraries are information and knowledge service providers. Without service, libraries are indistinguishable from museums. Montanelli and Stenstrom (1999) stated that, "Although technology is a powerful tool, it is people—librarians and staff—who build user–centred libraries." It is the quality of the people who work inside the library that makes the difference between an excellent library (*e.g.* a five–star rated library) and a poor or an average library (*e.g.* a two–star rated library).

According to Sirkin (1993): "The bottom line is that all of the major causes of customer dissatisfaction are strongly linked to human performance. Therefore an organization's staff has the greatest impact on the satisfaction of its customers."

We need to set the focus on the quality and attributes of librarians. The issues that must be decided are what quality attributes are we looking for? How can we maximize the people aspect in this digital era? What are excellent customer service techniques to use for a digital library?

### Definition

Digital libraries marry the missions, techniques and cultures of physical libraries with the capabilities and cultures of computing and telecommunication, according to Marchionini. Chowdhury and Chowdhury reported that the Digital Library Federation (DLF) defines digital libraries as follows:

Digital libraries are organizations that provide the resources, including the *specialized staff* [emphasis added], to select, structure, offer intellectual access to, interpret, distribute, preserve the integrity of, and ensure the persistence over time of collections of digital works so that they are readily and economically available for use by a defined community or set of communities.

The word specialized staff was emphasized here. It shows that the success of digital library projects depends on the quality of the specialized staff (the people aspect). The difficulties of assessing the people aspect of digital libraries arise from the complexity of the process involved in building and maintaining a digital library.

Tan and Foo outlined three problems in assessing service quality. The first problem was the intangibility of service, which cannot be displayed, physically demonstrated or illustrated. The second problem was that service performance depends very much on the level of library users' demand. The third problem was the high degree of people involvement, both from librarians and users, in delivering a quality digital library service. Kebede identified shortage of staff, both in quantity and quality, to be one of the main problems for libraries in developing countries.

Gorman found the seven deadly sins of library service that can prevent a library from becoming user–centred to be apathy, brush–off, coldness, condescension, robotic, rulebook, and runaround library staffs. Apathy happens when the library staff lack the interest or enthusiasm or concern to serve customers. Brush–off happens when the library staff refuse to listen to the customers. Coldness happens when the library staff is neither friendly nor enthusiastic in serving their customers. Condescension happens when the library staff feel superior and look down on the customers. Robotic service happens when the library staff behave without thinking, and lack imagination and creativity. Rulebook service happens when the library staff is dependent on the library rules and less concerned with satisfying customer needs. Runaround happens when the library staff treats users badly by not giving them the help or information the user needs or by deceiving the users.

As Atkins and Stenstrom put it: "The success of the library in meeting user demand for collections rarely depends on organizational structure. The knowledge and skill of the selector rather than organizational structure is key to the development of high–quality user–oriented collections." Tan and Foo showed that reliability was ranked as the most important service dimension, followed by responsiveness, assurance, tangibles and empathy. Fifty percent of the respondents commented on the lack of prompt service, helpful and knowledgeable library staff.

Calvert (1994) analyzed the perceptions on New Zealand public library effectiveness. It was found that all librarians, local political councillors and users who participated in this survey agreed that one indicator, namely the helpfulness and courtesy of library staff, determines public library effectiveness. In the same way, sixty–one performance dimensions of public library effectiveness presented by Van House and Childers showed the importance of having educated, responsive, customer–oriented, adequate, helpful, quality and high–morale library staff.

Ahmad Bakeri identified 13 key IT competencies needed for information professionals in Malaysia: IT basics, word processing, electronic mail, Internet and intranet, graphics, presentation and publishing, spreadsheet, project management, design, development, and administration of databases, system maintenance, design and development of application in web, system analysis and programming. All were found to be important, except system maintenance. It is crucial for each librarian to possess strong technical expertise.

Poll used the percentage of staff devoted to IT services as one of the performance indicators for library's electronic services. Poll calculated the number of full time staff members involved in planning, maintaining, providing and developing IT and Web–based services. The calculation also included staff in reference and training. Shahar Banun and Norhayati projected that new criteria for librarians in Malaysian public libraries would be to be webmasters and Internet information managers who are capable of searching, scanning, analyzing and compiling selected information according to the library users' needs and capable of creating a special Web directory, hosting it, maintaining it and monitoring it in a way that benefits the library users. The authors further added that the librarians should have strong proficiency in English in order to assist library users in information searching on the Internet.

Fisher studied the impact of information technology on librarians' work tasks. The findings revealed that expertise in computer application ranked as the fifth most cited item in 298 job ads, followed by online searching skills. Knowledge and skills in Web technology were found to be the eighth most important job characteristic. Research by Robinson and Jacobson also supported this idea. The trends focused on a workforce skilled in information technology (IT). Information knowledge management; and database creation and management skills were ranked as most important, followed by Web development, intranet development, extranet development, information storage and information retrieval skills.

Jerabek outlined detailed job descriptions specifically for librarians handling interlibrary loan/document delivery. They were expected to have an operating knowledge of modern information management and technologies. They were expected to implement fully automated library system. They must have experience with computer hardware and software.

Librarians must meet or satisfy customer needs and provide extra services (*i.e.* value–added services) to customers. Hernon and Altman emphasized the following four aspects of service quality in a library: excellence, value, conformance to specifications, and meeting and exceeding the expectations of library users.

Meeting the needs of library users is the first step towards providing excellent library services. Devadason and Lingam introduced an information needs identifier (INI) for identifying the information needs of various types of library users. The major steps in the process of identifying information needs were: study of a subject of interest to the organization/client, study of the organization and its environment, study of the immediate environment of the clients, study of the clients, a formal interview, identification and recording of information needs, and analysis and refinement of the identified information needs. Devette showed how the Cetus Corporation in Emeryville, California was determined to satisfy seventy–five percent of its users' information requests within the subscription budget of $100, 000. This company spent three years collecting the first page of all photocopied materials. This extra copy was placed in a box next to the photocopier. Then the details were keyed into database software which kept track of the usage statistics.

Today's cutting–edge technology paves the way for providing excellent library services to billions of prospective library patrons worldwide without needing to have a huge multi–billion dollar library building and without requiring patrons to physically walk into those buildings. Tilke proposed four possibilities: subscription services on the Internet, library web page, web–based library catalogue, intranet and e-mail.

According to Bryson, there were nine R's in strategies to achieve a customer focus in a library: retention, requirements, refined segmentation, reach, response, relationship, receptiveness, regular consultation, and review. Added value, such as additional advice on the best pages to access and tips on better searching strategies, can help to retain customers. Since different patrons have different information requirements, the best practice is to use tailor–made services to meet their requirements: for example, personalizing the reply e–mail.

## Analytical Comments

It is noteworthy that the Digital Library Federation emphasized the importance of having specialized staff for digital library projects. Firstly, the qualifications of the staff are a combination of library skills and information technology skills (or more precisely, digitization of information skills). And secondly, the staff should possess excellent customer service skills (*i.e.* the "people" aspect hidden or latent in the personality of the librarians) to be communicated to the patrons via the Web. We suggest that the IT skills and human skills of a librarian are distinguishable. A librarian may possess plenty of IT skills, but lack human–oriented customer service skills. On the other hand, the reverse might be true as well. The ideal situation would be to have librarians who might be rated "excellent" on both aspects and dimensions.

Such specialized staff differs from those in the traditional physical library setting because in a digital library setting they are also required to have expertise in the digitization process, which includes computer skills and telecommunication skills. At the same time, they must understand what makes information retrieval via the Internet faster and more precise with less connection/connectivity problems. They should be able to predict and provide a quick response to any technical difficulties that may result in the loss of valuable information. They should be able to keep track of the traffic, number of hits, number of web page visits, number of information downloads and feedback by customers. They also should be able to produce daily, weekly and monthly reports of these statistics within minutes, if not seconds.

Information needs vary according to the customer's level of education. It is more difficult to predict information needs in this digital era. It is not easy for librarians to meet and exceed customer expectations with regard to information retrieval. The main problem, as stated by Tan and Foo above, is the intangibility of service. Different people may have different perceptions, expectations and preferences. However, when it comes to library services, they might have one thing in common: the library should be able to provide the information that the patrons need. It does not matter whether the information need is met via the Internet or via the physical library collection or via interlibrary loan. The patrons must get the information they are looking for at minimum cost (to them) and within the shortest possible time.

The existence of a digital library can merely be considered a value–added library service if the digital library content is too basic (*i.e.* too simple or too little); and hence the patrons still need to go to the library physically to meet their information needs. In contrast, a digital library service can become the main library service to the public if all the information is made available and accessible via the Web with extensive hyperlinks to important and pertinent/relevant sites. Customers, regardless of their geographical boundaries, then can access the library's collection by a few simple clicks of a mouse.

The second problem mentioned by Tan and Foo regarding providing better digital library service was the level of library user demand. We would consider that the demand for a digital library depends on the availability of a telephone connection, the type of Internet connection and the availability of computers. The monies spent on developing and maintaining a digital library cannot be justified if the benefits cater only to selected urban communities. Librarians and libraries will not be able to enjoy the "economies of scale" benefits (the economics principle/concept which states that firms are able to enjoy lower unit cost through mass production and over the long term) through such a small user community.

The motivation to provide excellent digital library service largely depends on the degree of librarian and user involvement. The digital library project must have strong support from all levels of library management. Substantial budgetary resources must be put aside for developing and maintaining a digital library project. Adequate training must be conducted/carried out to ensure the smooth running of the project. There must be extensive marketing so that the public can be quickly aware of and feel the presence of the digital library. Users can play their role by providing continuous feedback and suggestions, and can indirectly promote the digital library website as well.

## Recommendations and Suggestions

The more the staff understands customer preferences, the more a refined segmentation can be achieved. Try to offer different information access and delivery mechanisms, such as networked CD–ROMs, video-conferencing and downloading via the Web, etc. to the customers. Though the digital library may function perfectly, some customers may still prefer to go physically to the library. Therefore, keep the options open for them that will allow them to do so. Ensure that the library catalogue is readily and easily accessible via the Web (not just via the Intranet). Provide more and more value–added services, such as the renewal of borrowed materials, reservation of books, etc., automatically delivering overdue/fine notices, delivering a list of newly added materials (books, print/electronic journals, databases etc.) directly to patrons' emails and conventional postal addresses. The new material should also be listed under the popular "What's new?" link. Deliver the right message to the right customer at the right time in the most courteous and professional manner. Build strong customer relationships by knowing their details and preferences. Librarians and staff must be receptive to feedback and suggestions from customers. Use newsgroups and online forums to discuss and consult customers. Librarians should also continuously review and improve the digital library system. Last, but not least, remember that digital library technology is there to assist human librarians, not to totally replace them or render them useless. The centre of attention should still remain the same: the client and not the technology.

## Conclusion

Qualified library staff coupled with excellent customer service will boost the overall customer satisfaction and confidence in using the digital library. It will make a core contribution towards a higher level of digital library usage among the communities.

## HAROLD LANCOUR AND WEST AFRICAN LIBRARIANSHIP

Harold Lancour's monumental report on "Libraries in British West Africa" has had far-reaching consequences. Much has changed in the region in the subsequent thirty years: the colonies he visited have become independent, and their populations have grown enormously. For example Nigeria has grown from 34 million to over 100 million persons. Considerable economic growth has also come to pass, and the library movement has made significant advances. However, some of the problems identified by Lancour still exist. Despite good supplies of natural resources, prosperity has not reached West Africa; societal polarizations remain intractable; various degrees of political turmoil are found throughout the region, with the possible exception of Gambia.

West Africans, Lancour observed, shared with Americans a high value placed upon education. But in terms of libraries, if the 1950's African was fascinated by them, the 1990 counterpart would appear to be largely indifferent to them. And the fascination with European/American culture, which he found to be typical among Africans of the 1950's, is rare today. Yet, all things considered, the tale of West African librarianship since 1958 is largely a success story. Lancour could hardly have imagined that by 1982 there would be 24 university libraries in Nigeria, 29 polytechnic libraries, 28 college of education libraries, 19 public library systems, and 61 special libraries. Holdings are in some cases substantial: public libraries range from 57, 000 to 500, 000 volumes; universities range from 25, 000 to 700, 000 volumes. A directory of libraries in Ghana, published in 1974, comprised 62 pages; it included seven public library systems, 12 academic libraries, and 32 special libraries. In the Gambia there is a national library and an academic library; in Sierra Leone there are three public libraries, 11 academic libraries and 18 special libraries. But it is in library education-the focus of the Lancour report-that progress has been most remarkable.

In the belief that the advancement of libraries depends upon professional leadership, Lancour recommended the creation of a postgraduate programme in librarianship. He pointed to the University College at Ibadan as a suitable home for that programme. And in 1960 that College (now a University) began a training course to prepare candidates for the (British) Library Association registration examinations. This evolved into the Institute of Librarianship in 1963, offering an independent diploma. Not without considerable opposition within Nigeria, this curriculum became a postgraduate Master's programme offered by the Department of Library, Information and Archival Studies. Graduates of Ibadan have played decisive roles in the Nigerian library movement. The requirement of advanced university education for librarians is no longer in dispute.

With that said, it must also be acknowledged that in the face of recent economic hardships library growth has halted, and indeed there is difficulty in sustaining existing libraries in the region. Economic policies, set up in response to the foreign debt problem, have devastated currencies, impoverished most of the educated middle class, and reduced the ordinary populace to a level of near destitution. For many elements of the population, survival needs rank first. In the libraries, there has been a struggle to pay staff in the past few years, and book funds have virtually disappeared.

It may be that the mission of public libraries in such circumstances needs to be reconsidered. I have examined elsewhere the need for African libraries to articulate their purposes, and other writers have written of the need for library service to address the needs of large rural and non-literate segments of African societies. However, it should not be supposed that Africa should ignore the technological advances available to libraries in order to throw all resources into service to the rural population. Africa needs information technology for development; library automation should facilitate access to knowledge that may bring national economies out of their backward, primary-producer stage into healthy modern forms. Both rural and urban populations have a stake in the success of that transformation. The underlying theme of the Lancour report, that librarians should have the most advanced education so that their libraries can keep pace with those in any part of the world, is to be cherished now, in times of recession, as much as it was in periods of growth.

## RURAL LIBRARIES IN CUBA: EXPERIENCES IN CAMAGUEY

### Introduction

In his *"Recuerdos de mi viaje a Puerto Principe"* [Memoir of my trip to Puerto Principe], published in the Havana journal *La siempreviva*, between 1838 and 1839, Antonio Bachiller y Morales wrote: "I saw a large city, civilized and magnificent in the middle of an island, bordered by arid lands; I saw the second city of my homeland as a mystery in the history of the people." It is interesting to once again read through the memories recorded by the "father of Cuban bibliography, " because, without a doubt, the well–known scholar was trying to bring to life an image of the city and the surrounding land, which he described in minute detail, from the first moment of his arrival, highlighting not only the physical aspects of the area, but also its unique vocabulary and architecture. Historians and specialists on Camaguey agree that Bachiller's descriptions of the interiors of the houses of Puerto Principle are among the best ever written.

Many travellers from distant places passed through the old city of Camaguey years ago on their journeys, and they, too, recorded their impressions, describing the special make–up of a region so different from others on the Island.

Legend has it that the city of Camaguey, whose official name was Puerto Principle, was founded in 1514, although historical sources available today give us a slightly later date, somewhere between the end of June and the beginning of July of the year 1515. For various reasons, in 1516 the city was relocated towards Caonao, on the banks of the river of the same name, and in 1528, it was moved further inland, between the Tinima and Hatibonico Rivers, where it finally remained, definitively established as Villa de Santa Maria del Puerto del Principe, a name which was shortened over time to Puerto Principe. Camaguey, its official name since 1903, is a colonial city that conserves much of the charm of its past, and has gone down in history as a legendary city, birthplace of patriots, and producer of beautiful women.

Within a short time, cattle ranching had become the principal source of wealth in the region. By the beginning of the nineteenth century, with the increase in the production of cattle, and a developing sugar refining industry, Puerto Principe was enjoying a high level of economic growth and prosperity.

By the seventeenth century, Puerto Principe was known as a city with its own unique culture and style. Around 1608, *Espejo de paciencia*, the first work of Cuban literature, was written here. It has been attributed to Silvestre de Balboa Troya y Quesada, a native of the Canary Islands who lived in the city.

The *latifundio* system–in cattle–ranching at first, then in sugar refining–endowed Puerto Principe with a certain cultural profile and a special way of life, typified by a close attachment to the land, and to art and culture in general. These conditions facilitated the creation of special cultural characteristics, such as the use of traditional elements in the city's architecture, and the preservation of Spanish customs, especially those of Andalucia.

The city's celebration of the festival of St. John, which dates from the end of the eighteenth century, marks the end of cattle sales for the year, and has continued to be a part of our traditions today, albeit with profound changes.

Cubans active in intellectual and literary endeavours of the nineteenth century included:

- Francisquito Aguero Velazco, considered to be the first martyr for Cuban independence (1826)
- Gaspar Betancourt Cisneros sponsored railroad construction, and fought for the economic modernization of the area, as well as for improvement in public education
- Ignacio Agra Monte y Lorna, Salvador Cisneros, Bernie Boza, and Eduardo Agramonte, among others, illustrious Camagueyanos outstanding in their fight for independence during the Ten Years' War (1868–1878)
- Gertrudis Gomez de Avellaneda, one of Iberoamerica's most important lyrical voices, whose homeland is reflected in works such as the legend *El aura blanca* and her novel *Sab*

During the neo–colonial period, certain people and groups attempted to achieve some progress for the region. Among these, the scientific research of Carlos J. Finlay, and the work of Luis Casas Romero as bandleader, composer, and radio pioneer should be mentioned. In the field of fine arts, there was Fidelio Ponce de Leon, symbol of the pictorial avant–garde of Cuba.

The literary culture of the nation has been nourished by Camagueyanos such as Nicolas Guillen, Emilio Ballagas, Felipe Pichardo Moya, and Mariano Brull. During the 1950s, the figure of Rolando T. Escardo created a literary environment which fostered the development of authors like Raul Gonzalez de Cascorro, Luis Suardiaz, and others whose work has enriched Cuban literature.

The triumph of the Cuban Revolution allowed a great enrichment of the nation's culture: the literacy campaign, the preparation of and attention to the amateur sports movement, the consolidation of the system of artistic training—all of these programmes helped to begin to erase the differences between urban and rural areas, and to make cultural activities available to all citizens. In order to provide this description of Camaguey summarizing the most important historic and social facts about the city from its founding to the present day, I consulted the Cultural Programme of the Biblioteca Provincial.

The province of Camaguey occupies an area of 16, 000 square kilometres, and is home to a population of 781, 815 inhabitants, of whom 595, 393 live in cities, and 196, 422 in rural areas. Following the political and administrative re–districting of the country in 1974, the province of Camaguey was divided into 12 municipalities; the principal cities are Nuevitas, Florida, y Guaimaro. The economy of the region centres around cattle ranching, the generation of electrical power, and sugar production.

Today, the city of Camaguey occupies 70, 500 square kilometres, the largest urban area in the country, after Havana. Its population of nearly 300, 000 is exceeded only by that of Havana and Santiago de Cuba. Historically, as the city kept moving, its area and boundaries kept changing; the present configuration of Camaguey's city boundaries was established only in the middle of the last century. The *tinajon*, a large earthenware jar used for collecting rainwater, is the symbol of Camaguey, an image so deeply rooted in the history and culture of the area that the city is often referred to by its symbol rather than by its geographical name. For this reason, Camaguey is known throughout all of Cuba as the "city of water jars." The Camaguey area boasts a vigorous education system, with students assigned to particular school centres throughout the province offering varying levels of instruction ranging from elementary grades to high school.

## A BRIEF HISTORY OF PUBLIC LIBRARIES IN CAMAGUEY

The province of Camaguey has been known for having libraries since the nineteenth century. The first public library was inaugurated in 1831, under the sponsorship of the *Sociedad Economica de Amigos del Pais*. Other libraries were established during this century as well, although they served the patrons of private schools or educational and recreational societies, rather than the public.

Also worthy of mention is the public library founded at the beginning of the twentieth century by the *Circulo de Trabajadores*, and operated by the workers themselves. They were able to count on support from the government, sporadic though it was, which enabled them to continue providing services up until 1959. Libraries of the upper and middle classes had a better chance of survival, since they served a much smaller circle of patrons.

The March 1950 issue of the *Boletin de la Asociacion Cubana de Bibliotecarios* notes the existence in Camaguey of 18 public and 36 private libraries. With rare exceptions, these libraries performed poorly, and lacked the dynamic character of our modern libraries.

In 1959, educational and cultural opportunities opened up for the Cuban people, opportunities accessible to all without regard to sex or race. Along with other basic programmes, the Cuban government successfully oversaw the *Campana de Alfabetizacion*–the campaign for literacy–and in 1961 created the National Library Network, an action which assured the development of libraries in Cuba.

Although a public library was opened in Camaguey in January of 1960, it lacked a sophisticated organization, and there were no qualified professional staff members to maintain its operations. As a result, a short time later, its collections were merged with the holdings of the *Biblioteca Publica "Isabel Esperanza Betancourt"*, located in the Ignacio Agramonte Provincial Museum. These institutions were subjects of risky popular debates, which called for official endorsement of both the library and the museum in order to assure their continued operations at a high level. The Isabel Esperanza Betancourt Library remained in a formative stage until the Cuban Revolution, and opened shortly thereafter, in 1960. But it was with the opening on June 1, 1963 of the Julio Antonio Mella

Library, the very first library established in our province by the National Library Network, that our goal was finally realized of having a truly modern cultural centre to meet the needs which had emerged in a moment of enormous cultural growth.

The Juan Antonio Mella Library has a well–structured and functioning organization, with trained professional staff members who serve the library users at the highest levels, making it an effective institution for raising the cultural level of the community. Beginning in 1963, municipal or town libraries were also established. Camaguey's public library system consists of thirty–one libraries: one provincial, twelve municipal and eighteen branch libraries, with thirteen of the branches located in sugar refineries, and five in communities.

The public library system in Camaguey in rural areas and cattle–ranching communities.

The growth of public libraries in the province can be divided into four basic stages:

1963–1969. During this stage, three libraries were created, including the Biblioteca Provincial, on June 1, 1963; and two others in the towns of Nuevitas and Florida. The *Bibliobus*, or travelling library, was also started that same year.

1970–1977. The province's own socioeconomic and educational development during this period promoted the creation of municipal libraries in Esmeralda and Cespedes, and two branch libraries in Santa Cruz del Sur and Florida. In addition, agreements between the Ministry of Culture and the government office of sugar production fostered the creation of libraries in sugar mills, refineries, and communities near these industries.

1980–1989. This was the period of greatest growth, bringing the number of libraries to twenty, consisting of eight in provincial capital cities, nine branch libraries in areas of sugar production, and three in cattle–ranching districts. For the most part, the libraries located in sugar producing areas were defined as small towns, because of the small number of residents–under 10, 000–and the limited radius of service. Libraries in cattle raising areas were considered strictly rural, with fewer than 2500 residents.

1990–1997. The close of the twentieth century saw the creation of four new libraries: two in cattle areas, two in sugar refining areas.

At the present time, the number of registered library borrowers exceeds 10, 475 in the thirty branch libraries. Some of these libraries are located in remote areas such as Minas, Santa Cruz del Sur and Sierra de Cubitas. However, the library staff, in conjunction with those promoting cultural activities, work together to carry out the mission of a modern–day public library, which is to contribute to the development of the people of a community, and to their sense of identity; as well as to serve as a bridge between accumulated stores of culture and free and open access by the community to information, knowledge, and entertainment.

With the creation of the public library system in our province came an ongoing interest in promoting reading to children and teenagers, and along the way improving the cultural and educational formation of the community in order to forge the ethical characteristics of our nationality.

***Figures in the following table summarize the results of these activities to promote reading:***

| | | No. of activities with children | Nos. of participants | No. of activities with teenagers | Nos. of participants |
|---|---|---|---|---|---|
| **Biblioteca Provincial Provincial Library** | | 1494 | 12039 | 400 | 4417 |
| **Bibliotecas municipales** | Nuevitas | 247 | 6120 | 62 | 1820 |
| | Esmeralda | 80 | 436 | 43 | 190 |
| | Florida | 190 | 2637 | 102 | 6740 |
| | Guáimaro | 113 | 2691 | 48 | 1172 |
| | Céspedes | 171 | 3068 | 55 | 1257 |
| **Municipal libraries** | Sibanicú | 393 | 5979 | 204 | 3575 |
| | Jimaguayú | 175 | 2770 | 78 | 876 |
| | Najasa | 166 | 2977 | 36 | 548 |
| | Minas | 193 | 4428 | 164 | 4232 |
| | Sta.Cruz del Sur | 255 | 1619 | 24 | 510 |
| | Vertientes | 40 | 1678 | 8 | 298 |
| | Sierra de Cubitas | 111 | 7220 | 75 | 983 |
| | TOTAL | 2134 | 41623 | 899 | 22201 |

We cannot leave this panorama of the library system without mentioning the attention paid to handicapped people: nine municipal libraries have special areas for the blind and visually handicapped. In addition, libraries provide activities in old age homes, maternity homes, hospitals, and family clinics.

Library service to farm cooperatives, sugar cane factories, and work centres located in rural zones is made possible through the creation of mini–libraries and home–libraries. By 1999, there had been a sizeable increase in this type of service which offers effective ways to bring books to people who, for various reasons, are not able to use the library, usually because it is too far from their homes. In the first quarter of this year, the number of rural mini–libraries rose to sixty–seven, and rural home–libraries to twenty–six, together offering a total of 879 activities to promote reading.

The *Sistema de Informacion de la Education* of Camaguey province, with which the libraries maintain close and productive working relationships, offers travelling collections which provide service to 317 schools in rural areas without libraries. This service is operated by librarians who transport their collections to these schools, organize activities to promote reading, and insure that local teachers have the resources they need to educate the children. Books and other documents—bibliographical and audiovisual—are deposited in the schools, which become operating libraries. Borrowing is done on a weekly basis. The public libraries support this effort by participating in inter–library loan projects, or through the Library Extension Department, which organizes mini–collections to be used on loan for consultation by teachers and students.

The application of new technology to library operations has placed in the hands of librarians valuable tools which increase information and knowledge. The web page of the provincial library includes a complete directory of the thirty municipal and branch libraries; and at the same time, the libraries are listed on the web pages of the municipal offices of culture, which are periodically updated. The web pages have been received with great enthusiasm by people interested in knowing important events and services of Camaguey's public library system. The local organization of the Cuban Association of Librarians offers summer courses in July and August for library staff, aimed at improving their cultural and professional training. Some of the courses which have been offered include: initiatives to promote reading; public relations and communication; and an origami workshop. This year, a "hands–on" course is being prepared, which will include technical assignments, and a special programme on organizing and administering community projects.

Also worth mentioning are the consulting services–part of an overall community health initiative—offered to the staff of the library network by a specialist in the Children's Division of the Provincial Library on the appropriate application of early childhood bibliotherapy to school—age children who experience behaviour problems as a result of poor parenting. The municipal and branch libraries in Esmeralda have seen satisfactory results in children with respiratory problems using reading and stories as part of their therapy. These results have been presented at scientific and community conferences, as have the efforts of the Children's Division of the Provincial Library, which were noted at the Convention of UNESCO Associated Libraries in Cienfuegos in 1996.

## Here Comes the Library!

Our best and most rewarding experience in rural areas has been with the bookmobile, the *Bibliobus*. Those of us who have had the opportunity to work witl. the *Bibliobus* regard those memories with great respect and admiration. Today, for technical and economic reasons, the *Bibliobus*is used mainly for reaching neighbourhoods on the outskirts of the city of Camaguey; whereas the efforts of municipal and branch libraries, which have been working together for more than thirty years to promote reading, have been focused on the most remote areas of the province of Camaguey.

The Julio Antonio Mella Library's *Bibliobus* began operating in 1963. From the beginning, it offered services to specially selected rural areas on a bi-weekly basis, and the response was so favourablc that its route was expanded. When conditions permitted, the *Bibliobus* carried with it photographic exhibits furnished by the provincial office of the *Instituto Cubano de Amistad con los Pueblos*, or documentary films provided by the *Empresa de Cine*, which were shown in schools, grange halls, and small towns. Book borrowing was direct: patrons registered in the *Bibliobus* and were able to take out the books they requested. Children were accompanied either by a teacher or a parent. The bus made 40 official stops along the route, an indication of the extent of the support it offered to the school library system as well. The *Bibliobus* that provided service to the eastern part of the province of Camaguey eventually had more than 3000 members, both children and adults, and made 112 stops on a route which covered more than 60 zones.

By 1971, the mini–libraries had begun to operate. The *Bibliobus* provided service to all those who happened to be situated along its route: it accepted patrons' requests at the stops along the way, and delivered the materials to them on the return trip, two weeks later. In contrast, the collections of the mini–libraries were carefully chosen so that all types of materials were easily and immediately accessible to patrons, and, furthermore, were able to satisfy the specific needs of that patron group.

Clearly, the *Bibliobus* provided services to a very wide public. Its route covered the most remote areas, where people had never before had direct, immediate, tangible access to culture. The arrival of the *Bibliobus* was a great event in the lives of these people. As soon as they caught a glimpse of it, they began to shout, "Here comes the Library! Here comes the Library!" They would line up, and enter the bus in small groups, where they would receive the books they had requested. The excitement which the arrival of the bus brought to life in these distant places was the subject of an article which appeared in *Bohemia*, one of the most important journals published in Cuba.

The study "Dynamics of reading in rural areas of our province, " written by two staff members of the Provincial Library at the end of the 1990s, summarized the work of the *Bibliobus* and its relationship with its registered users, taking into account socio–demographic factors (sex, age, occupation, and level of education) along with the number of visits and number of books borrowed. The hypothesis presented by the authors was that "in rural areas of the province of Camaguey, the greatest number of adult readers would be housewives." In order to examine this hypothesis, 287 registered users, chosen from 10 different rural locales, were interviewed, and other data was assembled based on information from readers' cards, and the type of books borrowed. The results described in the study regarding the use of the *Bibliobus* and its collections prepared the way for other projects in rural zones administered by the public libraries, which we will mention in a moment. The conclusions of the study showed that *Bibliobus* users included adults between the ages of nineteen and twenty–five, and children between the ages of ten and twelve. Of those who had some years of schooling, most fell into two groups: those in the economically inactive sector, who had completed sixth grade; and those in the economically active sector, who had a basic high school education. Most users were housewives, students, or workers in the cattle industry. Students and housewives accounted for the greatest number of subjects consulted. The most popular subject areas requested were foreign literature, national and social politics, Jose Marti, history, and Latin American and Caribbean literature.

### Community Intervention Projects

Community intervention projects, which illustrate the interest in improving the cultural level of people living in rural areas, and in developing good reading habits in children at a very early age, include two studies undertaken by members of the provincial branch of ASCUBI.

The National Programme for Reading that is being carried out in Cuba establishes general objectives, one of which is to consciously and creatively include both the community and the family in the activities of the programme. The "Reading for a Better World" project, which has been run by the Municipal Library of Jimaguayu in the Los Dolores neighbourhood since 2001, is the result of a careful study of reading programmes, and is based on the idea that the individual and his community should appropriate the material and spiritual resources of his environment, in order to satisfy his own necessities, interests, and expectations. The barrio of Los Dolores, a rural area of 896 residents, where the chief economic activity is raising livestock, lies about two kilometres from the town of Jimaguayu. There are no other economic or recreational enterprises anywhere in the area. Because there are no sources of entertainment for the community, the Municipal Library "Gertrudis Gomez de

Avellaneda" decided to launch a programme to promote reading among very young children in their spare time, which would be led by a staff member of the library.

To make the "Reading for a Better World" project meaningful, it was necessary to consider different research methods and techniques, so that the people's perception of the quality of the services offered could be evaluated at the end of the project. The project ended up developing joint activities with cultural and health institutions aimed at capturing the interest of three–year–olds: reading activities, traditional games involving literature, and book presentations, etc. This year, the International Festival of the Book, aimed at municipalities, also benefited rural populations.

The National Programme for Reading also showed the high quality of its programming and the possibility of successfully creating a reading audience, by focusing first on young children and teenagers. A staff member of the Municipal Library set up a casa–biblioteca or "home library" in her own house for greater access by readers, with a collection primarily made up of books for children and young people to be used there until such time as another place for reading could be built.

Another community intervention project that focused on housewives had its antecedents in a study of its patrons conducted by the Biblioteca Provincial in 2000, the results of which showed that this social group was poorly represented among those who used the library and its collections. It was decided to investigate two pre–selected and stratified groups in order to learn about their informational, cultural, and thematic interests: first, housewives residing in the historic city centre; and second, housewives who lived in a rural zone on the outskirts of the city, in this case La Belen, a target area in the Programme for Social Prevention that the Library has been developing since 1991.

The results of the survey were important because they revealed not only the interest of the women in learning skills such as decorating, cooking, hairdressing, and handicrafts, and their desire to understand more about family relationships in particular, and human relationships in general, but also the reading preferences of housewives under 65 years old.

With all of this in mind, the programme directors made a careful selection of assignments or activities which would satisfy the expectations and interests of this group of readers. Because of the distance of La Belen from the Provincial Library, a communication strategy was devised to attract this particular patron group, beginning with activities coordinated with a reading initiative. At the present time, the project is in its experimental stage.

Even though we have emphasized the experiences of rural libraries in the province of Camaguey, it is appropriate and important to point out that the National Network of Public Libraries also provides similar experiences for readers in difficult–to–reach areas in the eastern and central parts of the country, as part of the Turquino–Manati Plan.

Libraries in Guantanamo, Santiago de Cuba, Granma, Sancti Spiritus, and Villa Clara–all provinces containing mountainous areas–have organized a special programme for the people of the highlands through the creation of municipal libraries, branches, mini–libraries, and centres. In the city of Trinidad in the province of Sancti Spiritus, the bookmobile offers its services in mountainous areas, and in Matanzas special attention is given to the rural locales of Cienaga de Zapata. In other libraries around the country, special programmes are being carried out in logging zones, coffee plantations, and mines.

## Conclusions

Although there is more to say on the subject, the short time allotted for the presentation has forced us to summarize both basic and new aspects of rural libraries in Camaguey province. This report, a synopsis of public library development in Camaguey up to the founding of the Biblioteca Provincial, has been preceded by an introduction describing the region from a socio–historical point of view, a necessary preamble to the main topic of discussion. I am grateful to the organizing committee of this event and to the chairmen of these prestigious library organizations for extending an invitation to me, since it has given me the opportunity to exchange experiences and to represent my province at this international conference.

## THE PIONEERS

Asa Don Dickinson, an American librarian, served in the University of the Punjab for a year during 1915-1916. He was the third foreign librarian in British India, preceded by John MacFarlane, who served as the librarian of the Imperial Library, Calcutta, from 1903 to 1906; and William A. Borden, who was employed by the Baroda state in 1911. Dickinson's sojourn, however, was in several ways unlike that of his predecessors. Anis Khurshid views this difference as follows:

Some of the developments emanating from British rule were significantly different from the practice then existing in Great Britain itself. For example, the commission of Asa Don Dickinson in 1915 specifically required him to organize a library training class at Punjab University in Lahore. Such training did not exist at all in any British university at that time. The Calcutta University Commission Report (1917-19) stressed the need for the appointing of a trained librarian with the status and rank of a professor at Calcutta University; this practice was uncommon in British universities where preference was given to those with academic qualifications. All writings published in India and Pakistan repeat these facts without explaining why such events did take place. We shall try to look into these events only in relation to Dickinson. Was the British Indian Government involved in the "commission of Asa Don Dickinson" in any way? This is the key question.

The British tradition of placing the library under the charge of a scholar was very much in force at the University of the Punjab. Dr. A. C. Woolner, who was the principal of the University Oriental College (1903-1936), was also working as the honourary university librarian since 1903. His status in the University can be judged from the fact that he later on became the vice-chancellor of the University (1928-1939). It was quite natural that Woolner was managing the library in the traditional British fashion. A change, however, took place in 1910, which laid the foundation of modern librarianship in Indo-Pakistan.

In 1910, Professor James C. R. Ewing, principal of Forman Christian College, Lahore (1888-1918), was appointed as the vice-chancellor of the University of the Punjab (1910-1917). Ewing, an American national, had been educated in the U.S. His appointment was the beginning of the penetration of American influence in the academic aspects of the University of the Punjab. During 1913, Ewing submitted certain proposals to the Syndicate of the University for the improvement of the functioning of the University. One of his suggestions was to recruit "A trained librarian to thoroughly arrange the library and to train a class of young men for such work." The vice-chancellor's suggestions were approved by the Syndicate.

It seems that Ewing prevailed over Woolner and got the position of a temporary university librarian advertised in the United States. The following paragraphs appear in the May 1915 proceedings of the Syndicate.

# 3

# Role of Library in Modern World

## INTRODUCTION

Globalization is emerging as a major issue in the world today, affecting both "have" and "have-not" countries in many significant ways. In the library world, interactions between libraries in developing countries and organizations assisting libraries are not new: provision of information, resources, and expertise has been ongoing for much of the second half of the last century. Some of the issues raised by renewed concerns about globalization, however, stimulate inquiry into the efforts of developed countries assisting libraries in developing nations. Despite questions being raised in the literature of other disciplines about the impacts of globalization, it appears that very little research has appeared in the library literature that examines the impact of this phenomenon on the practice of library aid.

The concept of "globalization" carries considerable political baggage: whether one views the term positively or negatively depends on one's social and economic view of the world. For Held and McGrew, globalization is a "re-articulation of international space, in which the notions of sovereignty and democracy are being prised away from the traditional rootedness in the national community and the territorially bounded nation-state." North American information-related companies view this "re-articulation" as an opportunity to expand their customer base into developing countries with technology-driven products, and most articles on globalization reflect this commercially-oriented, North American focus. Peter Evans, in "Trends,

Pressures, and Realities in the Library Systems Marketplace, " speaks of the need for LIS companies to develop a different "corporate, cultural, and design philosophy" so they can compete and survive in countries with different languages and cultures. David Dorman, in "Taking Library Services around the World, " reports on library service companies such as OCLC, Blackwell, and EBSCO, whose globalization strategies are designed to increase their share of the international customer marketplace and place their products in developing countries. Some librarians note that globalization can be a "very positive force for cultural and social and economic development...provid[ing] the opportunity for a much greater understanding and interaction among the various peoples of the world." But this view, also expressed by Dorman, relates primarily to the opportunities and advantages realized by North American libraries whose access to information becomes more global as national barriers fall.

David Korten, former faculty member at the Harvard Business School, expresses a more pessimistic view of globalization. He gives evidence of increasing social and environmental disintegration in developing countries, and documents the negative human and environmental consequences of the successful efforts of international corporations to reconstruct values and institutions in developing countries to serve the company's own narrow ends. According to Korten, the convergence of ideological, political, and technological forces behind this process of economic globalization shifts power away from the local governments who should be responsible for the public good (including funding for libraries) and shifts that power toward a handful of corporations and financial institutions driven by the quest for short-term financial gain. A negative view of globalization is also voiced by Alan Scott, who notes that increasing cross-national flows of information tend to make "nations, nationality, and national boundaries less important to people's lives, " resulting in a loss of local identity, control, and responsibility.

This review of literature pertaining to library aid and globalization was prompted by the authors' vacation visits to libraries in various countries, conversations with librarians in developing countries about the "double-edged sword" of donations, and by the authors' admiration for those librarians who continue to deliver very important services in developing countries despite limited resources. The review will focus on two questions: what are the major needs of libraries in the developing countries? And, what are some of the ways those needs are – or are not – being met? Despite anecdotal evidence gathered by the authors during visits to developing countries that globalization has affected the type of library aid now needed, no research could be found that linked these two phenomena. It is the contention of the authors, however, that lessons learned from the existing research about more traditional "book" aid remain very relevant to library aid relationships affected by globalization, and that these lessons should be used as the basis for further research that incorporates this new phenomenon of internationalization.

The phrases "Third World" and "developing countries" are essentially Western in origin and use; they are used to describe less affluent countries in Latin America, the Caribbean, the Middle East, Africa, Asia, and the Pacific. These descriptions are considered to be ethnocentric by most outside the Western world who do not characterize themselves in this way, nor divide the world into two camps – developed and developing. However, in the context of the literature to be discussed, these terms will be used as they are in the literature.

"The phrases 'Third World' and 'developing countries' are essentially Western in origin and use; they are used to describe less affluent countries in Latin America, the Caribbean, the Middle East, Africa, Asia, and the Pacific."

Because a wide diversity of political, economic, cultural, historical, and geographic factors affect libraries in different countries, it is impossible for a single document, or even a suite of documents describing specific needs, to serve as a detailed blueprint for all. As a result, the literature chosen for Part One of this review was selected for its ability to provide general overviews of library needs in developing countries. Essays and books are included that provide a philosophical overview of issues and attitudes for both "givers" and "receivers, " an understanding of which is essential in developing successful programmes. Although published in 1966, Lester Asheim's classic, Librarianship in Developing Countries, remains an excellent explanation of the philosophical underpinnings of culture and libraries, knowledge of which is central to developing successful aid programmes. Asheim's book will form the starting point for Part One of the review.

In Part Two, the focus is on articles that describe an array of different programmes that have assisted Third World countries with library development. There are many different past and present aid programmes to libraries all over the world; it is impossible to review all of them. Therefore, we have selected articles that represent both positive and negative examples of different types of projects, while also highlighting a variety of donor and recipient countries.

One further point regarding literature selected: not surprisingly, much of the literature written in recent years about both the needs of libraries in developing countries and the projects in place concerns technology. While not discounting the importance of technology in this field, we have chosen to focus our attention upon more traditional areas of need, such as collection development and preservation, literacy, indigenous book publishing, and staff training initiatives. Despite the attention being diverted to automating and connecting libraries in both developed and developing countries, traditional areas of need still exist and, perhaps, are in danger of being overshadowed. As Lucinda Zoe explains in her thesis on women's information centres in developing countries:

While library scientists and information specialists praise the abilities of the new technologies developed for information management – computerized online catalogues, commercial online database services, CD-ROMs, laser printers, FAX machines, and electronic networking to name a few – the small information centres in the developing nations of Asia, Africa, and Latin America struggle with fugitive materials that do into fit neatly into traditional classification schemes. ... Furthermore, however impressive the new information technologies and communication systems appear, use is difficult, if not impossible in areas where the infrastructure is not solid: the telephone system is unreliable or erratic; power supplies are often interrupted or non-existent for days, if not weeks; equipment, maintenance costs and access to continued materials (disks, paper, ribbons, etc.) are beyond the financial resources of organizations; and privacy, confidentiality, and protection of information is difficult...

## LIBRARY NEEDS IN DEVELOPING COUNTRIES

### Asheim Still Relevant

Lester Asheim wrote his brief but compelling book, quoted from below, after he spent five years (1961-1966) visiting libraries in Africa, Latin America and Asia as Director of the American Library Association International Relations Office. The quotation provides his basic premise for appropriately serving the cause of librarianship around the world. Although written nearly four decades ago, many of Asheim's observations about library operations in North America and developing countries still hold true, but his opinions must, of course, be taken in the context of the times – the early 1960s. You may remember that I began with a reference to Culture Shock, which I said occurred whenever the system of logic in which we believe is challenged by a logical system to which we do not yet possess the key. It is not the other system that must be corrected, but the absence of the key. There are usually reasons for what people do, even if they are not our reasons. Before we condemn out of hand a pattern of behaviour which happens not to fit our preconceptions, we should try to find out what the reasons were that led to it. We may still not accept the reasons as valid for us, but we may discover a different context of validity for evaluating the behaviour pattern and its use by others.

### Lester Asheim, Librarianship in Developing Countries

Closed shelves, lack of extensive reference or circulating services, differing or absence of classification schemes, limited children's service and, above all, an emphasis on the primacy of the book over the reader are characteristics of Third World libraries as observed by Asheim. These characteristics are still prevalent today.

In his book, Asheim looks for the "key" he mentions above. He describes how economics, education, societal structure, attitudes towards authority, the impact of colonization and its (supposed) overthrow, the predominance of the English language worldwide, religious beliefs, attitude towards work, low prestige assigned to librarianship, and even climate have affected the development of libraries in these countries, and have resulted in libraries which, to Western standards, may appear to be below the mark. Asheim urges us, however, to avoid making that evaluation because:

> *... the difference between two concepts of a service, an objective, or a procedure can be measured by the gap that exists between what each faction sees as the essentials. The essentials are determined by the goals each side wishes to attain, whether overtly stated or not. And the goals reflect the system of values each party holds, determined by its history, its tradition, its culture. We are as much victims of our heredity and environment as they are of theirs...*

Despite the "chasm" between cultures Asheim describes, he believes librarians can establish bridges. According to Asheim, the first question to answer is the hardest: "Does anyone really want the help we offer?" To provide background for one's decision, Asheim then discusses many of the negative ways that Americans and Europeans have used libraries as propaganda agencies for political reasons (for example, donating books reflecting an anti-communism ideology) that in some cases led to the retardation of local development, an opinion shared by others: "[In the past, ] ... the establishment, growth and decline of donation programmes were more closely related to changing American foreign policy objectives than to the success or failure of... [the programmes themselves]." Despite possible negative elements, Asheim concludes that six characteristics of American librarianship are worthy of export:

1. the conception of the library as an organization of books,
2. the evolution of a library profession,

3. the attitude of service,
4. the function of the library as an education institution,
5. the role of the library in the advancement of intellectual freedom, and
6. the conception of organized information as a public resource and responsibility.

Simply put, aid programmes that support one or more of these functions and have the support and cooperation of local authorities are desirable. Attitude is everything, according to Asheim: "...we must begin to see ourselves as an equal partner in an exchange rather than as a condescending Lady Bountiful. We must... develop an Ear of America as well as a Voice. We must listen as well as tell, learn as well as teach, receive as well as give." To further this interactive rather than autocratic viewpoint, Asheim favours programmes that acknowledge the need "...to adapt rather than to adopt the methods and procedures that we happen to favour for our own purposes." Finally, quoting "an old India hand" [Ranganathan], Asheim encourages those wishing to advance librarianship in developing countries – "a daunting task" – to substitute the word "problem" with "opportunity."

"Despite the 'chasm' between cultures Asheim describes, he believes librarians can establish bridges."

## Donor Objectives

A thorough search for reports or theses reporting research results focused specifically on library aid revealed little scholarship in this area. The research of Jesus Lau, however, provides excellent information necessary for understanding the economic and political complexity of well-intentioned but sometimes ill-advised donor objectives. His assessment of the relationship between information growth and social development in 31 countries from 1960 to 1977 revealed that the information gap between developing and highly developed countries is widening faster than the social gap (life expectancy, food consumption). His results also suggested that increased information development as shown through library indicators is associated with positive change in social development.

D.E.K. Wijasuriya, International Federation of Library Associations (IFLA) Representative for Asia and Oceania in the 1990s, echoes Asheim's and Lau's recommendations in a framework for development adopted by IFLA and described in "The Advancement of Librarianship (ALP): IFLA's Core Programme Orientation to the Third World." Much of this document concentrates on facts about developing countries, terms of reference, and time tables, but the author also outlines general objectives and programme areas:

The main objectives of the ALP Core Programme are to contribute, within the framework of IFLA's programme structure, to the progressive improvement of library and information services within the developing countries so as to enable them to contribute significantly to national development. At the same time, programme objectives shall place special emphasis on the creation of conditions likely to contribute towards national initiatives and a systematic progression towards self-sufficiency.

Wijasuriya acknowledges that the advancement of librarianship (ALP) "can be conceived in the most infinite terms, " but maintains that for practical purposes, the primary goals in 1990 were:

1. the establishment and development of public library systems with particular attention to the needs of rural and urban marginal areas,
2. greater identification of libraries with literacy programmes, and
3. greater attention to education and training.

According to Irene Norlund, Scandinavian aid agencies (SIDA, NORAD and DANIDA) have specified support of culture through library/archival aid as a primary objective since the early 1980s. In "Culture and Institution-building, " Norlund outlines both the problems and benefits of aid programmes designed to support cultural heritage. Major obstacles include the reticence of aid organizations to support such programmes, combined with the ambiguous attitude to cultural aid funds held by governments in some recipient countries, who may favour programmes that show a direct economic benefit. She promotes providing assistance to 1) set up new archives and libraries, 2) collect and organize documents, and 3) train librarians to maintain access to historical materials as the key components in preserving of indigenous cultures. "Support to culture will also lead to the building up of enriched and renewed institutions and by that means increased capacity, " observes Norlund. The fragile nature of important cultural and religious documents in developing countries makes more compelling the need for collection and preservation. Many are held in private collections and religious temples or monasteries, where maintenance is not secure. "There is limited time to save these irreplaceable heritages, which are a key both to enlarging knowledge and self-confidence and to building institutions which can link up to the world at large, " concludes Norlund.

Carolina L. Afan, Library Director-Cultural Centre of the Philippines, agrees with Norlund's point of view about the importance of preservation, but from the perspective of an aid recipient, not a donor. She sees a need for support beyond written forms of communication: "The librarian and other cultural workers should have the skills and knowledge in documenting prints, tapes, photographs, films, videos and others." Expertise in preservation regarding these different media is necessary as audiotape, video, film, etc. are more "natural" media for oral cultures to record their stories, history, etc., rather than in the Western tradition of print. Afan speaks strongly and persuasively in favour of repatriating rare historical and cultural materials that are in European and American archives since "colonizers had their share in looting and taking away the resources of their former colonies." In the same vein, she cautions her colleagues:

[Developing] countries should guard against the intellectual and cultural exploitation being done by some foreigners who in the guise of doing research are actually taking advantage of our natural and human resources for their own use and interest. Cultural agreements, donor contracts and exchanges should be carefully studied and analyzed before going into them. Any agreement should benefit both countries and must not be a one-sided affair.

Other librarians and educators have voiced the same concern – that aid to libraries not be a form of "neocolonialism...to perpetuate cultural and economic dependency" on donor countries. Mary Niles-Maack believes that donors' goals must be examined closely: initiatives based on the aim of spreading Western culture have caused "intellectual consequences" for developing countries, as a dependence on foreign books prevents the promotion of local publishing initiatives. As well, donor objectives may be tied to larger global alliances – for political and strategic reasons the donor country may want to strengthen ties with the recipient country. Afan concludes her report by noting that the central government of the Philippines has embarked on a decentralization process for both cultural centres and libraries, which she describes as "the democratization of access to libraries and other learning centres, insuring the provinces and regions that their cultural treasures will be left to them to be utilized, conserved and appreciated."

Rosario Gassol de Horowitz also writes about donor objectives from "a Third World perspective" (the sub-title of her book *Librarianship*). Like Asheim, she observes that library development has taken place from "the Anglo-Saxon tradition" and has been "propagated, consciously or unconsciously, by Western librarians travelling abroad on consultant missions and through library literature, much of which has been produced in the United States." Paraphrasing Ivan Illich, she states that "the nations of the West are packaging their services to contain their views of the world." Rather than rejecting the contributions of the West, Horowitz (in terms she herself identifies as more closely related to liberation than development), calls instead for innovative leadership from librarians in developed countries and an enhanced communication process to assist those countries in breaking free from their inherited mantle of dependency and oppression. "The new orientations confirm the calls for a new type of professional and for a bold and non-traditional library service which cuts across the compartmentalization imposed by tradition and organizations, to meet the circumstances and conditions in which people find themselves." She urges that isolated library workers in developing countries seek support through strengthened ties with other workers throughout the country—as well as the continent—by creating active and cohesive professional associations.

## LANGUAGE CHALLENGES

Language issues are problematic for many developing countries—as well as for donor agencies. In *The Bookseller* (11 April 1997), Caroline Horn notes that South Africa and Ethiopia each have eleven language groups, and she identifies language as a prominent concern for library/literacy projects in these countries and others. Her article also supports the fact, often mentioned in the literature, that libraries are foreign to the way of life for many traditional, oral societies in Africa. As a consequence, governments may be unaware of the purpose and benefits of libraries and reluctant to support them financially.

The issue of language and library development also surfaces in Asian countries where oral traditions have predominated. From a Malaysian perspective, Diljit Singh notes that the "...reading habit is still not fully ingrained in the Malaysian public." He attributes this partially to the fact that Malaysians (East and West) speak many different dialects, creating difficulties for library clients seeking service and materials in their local language. This problem highlights the need for support of local publishing initiatives so people can have access to literacy programmes and to relevant materials in local libraries and bookstores-in their own language.

### Need for a Cooperative Approach

With its long history of apartheid, South Africa serves as an interesting example of "have" and "have-not" communities within one country. *The Use of Libraries for the Development of South Africa; Final Report on an Investigation for the South African Institute of Librarianship and Information Science* proposes a plan for development consistent with the views expressed by Asheim. The report states: "Librarians should familiarize themselves with the psychology and the sociology of the underdeveloped. In particular they should not expect persons bred in the culture of the subordinate to act according to the cultural and psychological patterns of the dominant." The report is also reminiscent of Asheim's observations regarding assumptions about the "apathy of the underdeveloped, " a phenomenon that Zaaiman describes as a psychological state induced by subordination and a dependence on "the dominant group" as well as the overwhelming battery of problems that disadvantaged individuals face. Skepticism on the part of recipients and frustration and discouragement on the part of librarians from donor countries can result. This report says that a cooperative approach to development is absolutely necessary to counteract creation of a cycle of apathy and donor disappointment:

Developing communities should always be fully involved in the planning, development and execution of development projects that concern them... Community involvement means exploring the people's basic needs with them, and designing and developing methods with them to fulfil those needs. It should be remembered that the underdeveloped cannot relate to a concept such as "libraries" of which they have had no experience... Key groups of opinion makers within the developing community should be identified and their views and approval sought at all stages of the investigation, design and implementation of library services... Librarians, should, however, guard against the danger of accepting the views of elites in developing communities as representative of all the needs of that community.

One of the strongest supporters of this cooperative approach is Carol Mills, librarian from the University of the South Pacific in Fiji. In "Aid for Libraries: Should One Look the Proverbial Gift Horse in the Mouth?" she criticizes blanket donations given without prior collection management assessment work done by recipients, saying that this lack of joint responsibility institutionalizes aid and causes an "aid dependent mentality."

## Special Needs of University/Research Libraries

In her article "Filling Bare Shelves, " Carolyn Sharples laments the fact that as aid organizations and governments of developing nations have focused on literacy and books for children, academic institutions have suffered. Cancellation of journal subscriptions has been common as prices have increased, mostly in the area of medicine. Specifically, she notes that books on "tropical medicine, primary health care, women in development, and intermediate technology are...priorities" for her agency, Book Aid International.

Sharples also discusses the difficulties that academic librarians in developing countries encounter when they try to obtain information about newly published material. It is a "Catch 22" situation if library staff are expected to indicate what they need when they do not know what is available. This situation makes bibliographic and selection tools high on the list of desirable materials.

These concerns are reinforced by Yogendra P. Dubey, Professor in Library and Information Science at Banaras Hindu University in India, who describes in his 1986 conference presentation the problems that Indian librarians encounter when they try to meet professors' and scientists' demands for scientific and technological information. Although widespread use of the Internet now makes some of Dubey's observations about information needs outdated, many of the problems he mentions still exist in academic libraries. These include heavy reliance by developing countries on scientific books and journals from the West, in the absence of "home-grown" publishing; supply and currency problems; high prices for subscriptions; copyright restrictions that limit the free-flow of information; constraints of multiple indigenous languages; educational systems that foster rote learning and do not promote individual research; low demand for library services due in part to lack of awareness of their role; and passive attitudes of librarians. Dubey confirms Asheim's observation that when resources are very scarce, service may not be a priority, and "the book" is more important than the person: "they [librarians] are more product than service oriented, *i.e.*, more toward production of bibliographies, catalogues, etc. than toward services directly oriented to users (such as question-answering)." He concludes with a recommended strategy to alleviate these problems that will result in the development of information distribution industries (publishing, libraries, scientific and technical services), knowledge production industries (research and development, education) and information technology industries.

### Importance of Local Publishing

Mills and Priestley both emphasize the key role played by aid or assistance to support indigenous publishing: they maintain that such help is essential if developing nations are to gain true autonomy and supply relevant materials to their citizens. Priestley breaks down the book needs of Third World African countries into six categories: capital funding; the need for textbooks to support education; distribution and marketing knowledge; paper; the need for local language translation, co-publishing, and licensing; and training. Her support for local publishing is strong, but she cautions that poverty and inexperience may be the catalysts for corruption within projects: misappropriation of paper stock and "mismanagement by cumbersome, bureaucratic procedures and unqualified officials" are often significant issues to consider. She concludes that for local publishing to succeed, business management training in areas specific to publishing is crucial, to ensure that grant monies are better managed, overhead costs are considered, and marketing plans are developed. Donor countries need to shift from facilitating the dumping of unwanted materials, such as surplus print runs, to supporting indigenous publishing.

## SPECIFIC AID PROJECTS

### Research Reports

Investigations on the efficacy of library aid projects in specific countries or to particular institutions appear to be very scarce: no research case studies or analyses were located. However, studies that focus generally on library services in one developing country or to one client group in such countries provide informative contextual background. The most relevant research projects that discuss some aspect of library aid are those of Al-Hanari, Bouri, Stander, Floren-Romero, and Zoe.

Abdulaziz Mohamed Al-Hanari's Ph.D. survey research revealed the important roles that national libraries play in developing countries, and resulted in a list of recommended functions for a proposed Saudi Arabian national library. Elizabeth Bouri examined Egyptian public library development in her doctoral research, revealing the positive influence of international agencies such as UNESCO in the 1960s and subsequent public policy choices of the Egyptian government that led to the decline of public libraries.

How to formulate standards and guidelines for school libraries in developing countries was the central question in Cecilia Stander's research, based in South Africa. Stander concluded that basic school library principles can be applied, but that the diverse perspectives of users make adherence to universal standards problematic. Two theses focused on information needs/services of special groups within developing countries: Maria Floren-Romero examined the difficulties that pharmaceutical researchers in the Dominican Republic encounter when trying to obtain information, and their reliance on colleagues' resources outside the Republic, while Lucinda Zoe explored the growth of women's information centres in developing countries – their relationship with and reliance on the international library community.

## Book Donations, Publishing and Distributing

In many cases in the past hundred years, libraries and publishing companies shipped off surplus materials to well-intentioned organizations that "dumped" those items in developing countries, notably those in Africa. As described by Mills:

> *First came the missionaries who propagated their faith by direct action, religious and social; their return being souls and the pacification of the area. In more recent times, governments have largely replaced the churches, aiming to spread the word of their friendly intentions. At times, aid to libraries has had little to distinguish it from the 19th century 'books for heathens' syndrome.*

Donors paid little attention to the language, currency, or context of the material, and the recipient countries were rarely, if ever, able to choose their own books. And even if the recipients could choose, they had little knowledge of what to request. In her article for *The Bookseller*, Seaton gives a list of "unhelpful books donated" to Book Aid International's Africa book drive, which includes the *AA Road Map of Bristol*, and *The Garth Brooks Scrapbook*. This problem of inappropriate giving is frequently noted in both research articles and opinion pieces on library aid, with poor communication between donor and recipient cited as the primary cause.

According to Margaret Bywater, libraries in Cambodia receive some material from overseas that is useful, but they have also received material "which is totally irrelevant to [their] needs now or in the future." Filling library shelves with this irrelevant material discourages rather than encourages use, thereby thwarting the donors' intentions. As an alternative, Bywater recommends the donors consider giving monetary grants that allow staff in libraries to select their own books: this will ensure relevancy and support local publishing. Carolyn Sharples agrees with Bywater regarding "problem" donations and the need to support local publishers. She notes that since 1990, Book Aid International (BAI) has been "refining [their] work to become far more targeted and responsive to the needs of partners overseas." This resulted in project development that specifically targets subject areas where materials are scarce. One project – BAI's Africa Book Collective – purchases African books published locally and then distributes those materials throughout the region, thereby helping to establish a local book market. Sharples acknowledges, however, that despite the increasing output of small local publishers, sufficient "suitable" material is difficult to find, especially children's books, which are in high demand.

"Bywater recommends the donors consider giving monetary grants that allow staff in libraries to select their own books; this will ensure relevancy and support local publishing." E.A. Mwinyimvua of the Tanzania Library Services Board also discusses the measures that Book Aid International has taken in his country to provide suitable books, promote local book production, and ease the administrative burden on recipients.

Three members representing recipient libraries now sit on the BAI Council, facilitating information flow and influencing policy regarding donations to Tanzania and other African nations. As well, all recipients fill out detailed evaluation forms each year, which enables BAI to select books according to library requirements. BAI also invites librarians from recipient countries to spend three months at BAI Headquarters in England selecting books. To stimulate local book production, BAI provides funds for Tanzanian librarians to purchase books published in other African countries. Mwinyimvua believes that Tanzania will continue to need book aid for many years as currency devaluations make purchase of expensive foreign books even more difficult and as rising literacy rates cause demand for books to outstrip the supply, even with increased local publishing efforts.

The IFLA/UNESCO "Books for All" initiative is another international library project. As project coordinator Lioba Betten explains in "Foreign Aid for Children's Libraries: 25 Years, " its aim is to fight illiteracy through providing children in developing countries with books. Betten notes that Books for All seeks to provide long-term aid to libraries and to local booksellers, authors, and publishers by purchasing books in local languages.

Caroline Horn also is critical of those overseas publishers who donate irrelevant materials and encourage "librarians in developing nations to send their orders outside the country." Speaking specifically of African aid projects, she reports that in Senegal "some 80% of books are imported, but are too expensive for the indigenous population. Once students leave school, they are unlikely to pick up a book again." Local efforts are the best means to ensure literacy and relevancy. In her opinion, "book aid programmes can, where properly targeted, help to overcome some of the shortages [of materials], but while libraries remain dependent on aid they are not supporting local publishing initiatives."

S.M. Made, speaking of African aid projects in the early 1980s and Zimbabwe in particular, notes that "low literacy and purchasing power and high unit costs necessitate small editions [of locally produced material], which in turn necessitate small markets and limited distribution." Local printers in developing countries may lack the capital required to purchase paper stock, which often needs to be paid for in advance. Made adds that various local languages and dialects can pose challenges as they may not translate well into the Latin alphabet required for printing. Aid organizations may assist local publishers to solve these problems by encouraging and funding regional associations or consortia of publishers: combined purchasing power to buy bulk paper stock and combined expertise may help to overcome difficulties.

Carol Mills from Fiji is one of the few voices in the literature with a "recipient" perspective. She examines the reasons why developing countries in the South Pacific are not getting what they need from donors:

Donor agencies tend not to set explicit targets, fail to evaluate their donations, and do not properly manage their aid. Books sent at cost may simply sit there if they are not appropriate, making the uninformed donor feel good while creating a burden for the recipient. Sometimes the recipient accepts simply to avoid giving offence and to keep communications open, or else accepts donations with a peripheral value because they are better than nothing.

Mills' comment is crucial to understanding the complexity of library aid in specific countries because her words concern the power relationship that exists with donor/recipient relationships. Many recipient libraries and information centres are reluctant to express their needs firmly for fear of being cut off entirely. This fear, in turn, is reflected in the collections, as it causes library staff in developing countries to be hesitant about weeding irrelevant material. They do not wish to offend donors by throwing out "gifts" and they are anxious that little would remain in their library if they culled all irrelevant material– collection "starvation rather than poverty." As Margaret Bywater notes in her article on Cambodia: "[there is] a reluctance to dispose of anything... because people still feel strongly the loss of personal possessions during the Pol Pot period." Peter Brush, a consultant at the National Polytechnic Institute in Laos, also writes about the reluctance to weed. He observed that many titles in the Laotian collection were in foreign languages—Russian, English, French and Vietnamese—which presented a cataloguing dilemma because no translation services were available. The library could offer little material in Lao, as Laos has a small population and a very small publishing industry. The Institute had no collection development (or weeding) policy, and the Institute Director was reluctant to dispose of any books, even those outdated, irrelevant, and uncataloged because all had been donated.

Scandinavian countries have a laudable history of providing aid to libraries and other cultural institutions in developing countries. This support is documented in a 1995 issue of Scandinavian Public Library Quarterly that focused entirely on Nordic aid initiatives. The articles report on the purpose and progress of projects in Tanzania, Kenya, Uganda, Botswana, South Africa, Nicaragua, Vietnam, Laos, and Cuba. A typical project is one focused on Africa and funded by SIDA, the Swedish International Development Authority:

The SIDA project "Words-Books-Democracy" is one example of an attempt to get a holistic perspective within the literature area. The objective is to create and maintain a literate and reading environment and to protect freedom of expression. This requires access to books, newspapers, magazines and so on. The development cooperation shall strengthen the documentation of oral storytelling traditions, author organisations, independent indigenous publishing, the printing industry, distribution channels, libraries, and so on—all links in the complete chain.

An annotated list of current and recently completed library aid projects where Nordic funders are involved concludes the issue. Children's books are in great demand in most developing countries, particularly in Africa, but the cost of a book, even one locally published, is beyond the price range for most people. Rebecca Knuth in an *IFLA Journal* article revealed how five international organizations are seeking to redress this situation. An innovative joint project by the International Board on Books for Young People (IBBY) and UNESCO involved the production of 2000 kangas (Kenyan cloth pieces used as clothing or baby carriers) that were "imprinted with words and pictures as a child's first text book." In another project, the International Youth Library (IYL) supported "cross national publication and translation" of books from Africa and Europe, while the IASL (International Association of School Librarianship) and UNESCO cooperated to provide books for school libraries that focus on "local needs" in their collections. Citing a UNESCO project in Croatia as an example, Knuth stresses the special need for children's libraries in war-torn or famine-stricken countries as these libraries help refugee children who are "coping with stress and trauma."

Carol Mills provides the best overall assessment of different aid programmes, based on her experience at the University of the South Pacific (Fiji) where donations form the basis of the collection. Her evaluation includes the book aid models of 1) clearinghouses, 2) twinning (mentor/sister-city programmes) relationships, 3) interest groups, and 4) unsolicited donations. She concludes that clearinghouses have varying degrees of success, providing "unbalanced donations of discarded surplus materials, " and indeed may impose a burden beyond useless books, as recipients may have to pay some or all of the freight costs in shipping materials. She is more supportive of twinning relationships because of the personal element involved, but cautions that these arrangements often cannot be sustained.

## Academic Libraries and Archives

Academic libraries and archives in developing countries have garnered less attention in the past decades as aid organizations focused on literacy and books for children; however, several important initiatives are mentioned in the literature. The International Campus Book Link Project (ICBL) was created in 1992 by Book Aid International to support African university libraries through donations of current and back issues of academic journals, particularly in the area of medicine where the shortage is acute. In describing this project, Sharples notes that journals are particularly difficult materials to supply because of sustainability problems: many aid programmes are short term—three years at the most—and are dependent on fluctuating donations from institutions, not an ideal way to build a journal collection.

The Overseas Library Committee at the University of Calgary, Alberta was very active in the 1980s and early 1990s coordinating shipments of donated materials. As detailed in the *Canadian Library Journal* by King and Matheson, volunteer librarians gathered, sorted, boxed, and shipped scholarly and professional books and journals to universities, colleges and research corporations in China, Central America, Yemen, Bhutan, the West Indies and Africa. These volunteers clearly recognized the importance of communication between donor and recipient institutions. In this case, as in others identified in the literature, the motivating force for the volunteer librarians was a "feeling of professional solidarity, such as from one library to another." Books were not sent "on spec" to libraries in developing countries. Instead, "inventory lists of donated materials [were] maintained and circulated to interested libraries, where selections were made by librarians. Only those items selected from the inventory list were sent." The project relied on the generosity of the Calgary corporate community, which provided free storage and sorting space, and arranged for free shipping of boxes. However, an economic downturn in the 1990s jeopardized corporate sponsorship, resulting in cancellation of the project.

Jan Lyall focuses on the preservation crisis in research archives and libraries in her *IFLA Journal* article. She cites the need for funding projects to preserve the audiotape and film that historians used to record the oral traditions of many South Pacific nations. Given the general lack of written cultures in this area, these media were very appropriate for information gathering, but their short life span in a tropical climate makes them an archival/library nightmare. Palm leaf manuscripts are another medium of concern in Southeast Asian countries: the leaves themselves are disintegrating, along with the disappearance of the skill to write and read the traditional script of most of the manuscripts. Lyall notes further that the political climate, as well as the physical, is an important factor in this crisis. Governments in many developing countries are coping with cash shortages, health emergencies, and political strife and instability. As a consequence, they allocate a very low or non-existent priority to libraries, making the largesse of donors to fill this gap crucial. An example of such assistance is the "Preservation of Lao Manuscripts" project, funded entirely by the German government through the "Memory of the World Programme" launched by UNESCO. Its purpose is "to focus world attention on the need to safeguard endangered and unique library and archives collections, and to improve their accessibility to people of the world."

**Expertise, Education, and Training**

The practice of importing of experts from afar is also discussed in the literature, with most authors stressing that this approach neglects to address the problem of self-sufficiency, and does not promote long-term commitment and sustainability. Kari Gulbraar in the *Scandinavian Library Quarterly* emphasizes the importance of high caliber and accessible library education programmes within developing countries as the alternative to the visiting expert.. She relates the story of the Grace Lema Foundation, started in Tanzania by the Norwegian Library Association, and named after an untrained but experienced library assistant who was unable to enrol at the University of Botswana because she lacked financial resources.

A member of the Norwegian Library Association International Committee supported her cause and through donations financed Lema's two-year programme. Building on this initial success, the Association established a continuing fund to support library training within a developing country. This initiative was recognized as a model for library education aid at a 1994 IFLA Conference. Gulbraar also explains the other methods by which Scandinavian library agencies support education: supporting in-service training courses in Asia and the Pacific, funding scholarships to African, Asian and Latin American librarians for short-term visits to Swedish libraries and cultural institutions, and subsidizing librarians from developing countries to attend international workshops and conferences.

Brush reiterates the importance of indigenous training programmes geared to specific situations and the use of locally relevant methodologies when he relates his experiences as a library consultant in Laos. He attributes most errors in the bibliographic records to cultural and language misinterpretations caused by the librarians' attempts to apply cataloguing systems that are rooted in American culture – Dewey Decimal Classification and Library of Congress Subject Headings – to radically different situations. Brush believes that "visiting experts" would be well advised to promote British librarian Ronald Benge's philosophy expressed in his Cultural Crisis and Libraries in the Third World: "Librarians in developing countries would be better advised to follow the spirit of our librarianship, rather than our cataloguing rules..."

## Recommendations for Further Study

This review has highlighted research reports and descriptive articles that address two questions: what are the major needs of libraries in developing countries and, how effectively are those needs being met?

It is apparent from these reports and articles that there are varying degrees of success regarding library aid projects: some address the problems and issues inherent within library aid initiatives and the general donor-recipient relationship, while the effectiveness of others is questionable. The literature indicates that when donors place a high priority on good communication; seek to understand and respect the indigenous culture, language and customs; and learn about the climatic, economic and political challenges that local librarians and publishers face, projects are more likely to succeed. Reports by those in the field show that when donor agencies follow Book Aid International's new slogan: "Give us what we need, not what you don't want" when providing demand-led services to developing countries, the match between donor largesse and library need is much closer. Another recurring theme in the literature is the problem of short-term aid. Too often, financial and materials aid is "single-event, " with no prior communication, no follow-up, and no opportunity for the recipient librarian to do long-term (or even 2-year!) collection management. To ensure that developing countries really benefit from assistance, commitment for long-term support is necessary.

This literature review reveals that globalization of information has created a double-hook for developing countries:

library clients are aware of cultural sources from around the world, but these resources are often less relevant than indigenous ones. Continuing reliance on donated international resources hampers creation of a local publishing industry and precipitates loss of the local culture. There appears to be a gap in the literature regarding the impact of burgeoning globalization on library aid – how has this phenomenon affected the relevance of donations? How has it affected communication between donors and recipients, a crucial factor in the success of library aid projects? How can the negative aspects of globalization be minimized and the positive aspects increased within the donor/ recipient relationship?

What is most lacking in the literature, however, is a corpus of in-depth research on this topic. As evident from this review, a wealth of articles exists describing Third World library needs from the point of view of the recipient and the objectives. Many articles also detail individual projects and the fund-raising efforts behind them. Missing are the research surveys and case studies that evaluate library aid in terms of a set of identified needs, and research that examines the changing needs of libraries as cultural and economic globalization advances. The forces of globalization that move us ever closer to a single world society – mass communications, increased ease of travel, commerce, the Internet, popular culture, and the increasingly widespread use of English as an international language – must be included as variables in future research projects.

Without these projects, we will not move knowledge in this area beyond opinion pieces to the reliable research results that will better inform the relations of donors and recipients. According to Lester Asheim (whose words introduced this review), "foreign relations are, after all, only human relations complicated by some geographical and some psychological distances. I think, with patience and understanding, we are equal to the challenge – and the opportunity – they present." Clearly, in order to develop effective programmes that make a difference within the new global economy and information world, further research on the challenges and opportunities of library aid is needed.

## PROFESSIONAL COMPETENCIES AMONG LIBRARIANS AND INFORMATION PROFESSIONALS IN THE KNOWLEDGE ERA

***Introduction:*** Past is an indication of future. Present connects the two. Given this, the 21st century is all set to be a 'knowledge century' where it will neither be the 'labour' (as in the agricultural era) nor the 'capital' (as in the industrial era) but 'knowledge' and 'information' that will act as a critical resource for socioeconomic development of a nation. This being so, generation (creation), processing and use/application of knowledge will be the hallmark of the new century. Professionals engaged in all these three primary tasks of the 'knowledge cycle' will be required to play a more pro-active role (rather than passive one) as equal partners/collaborators with the scholars. A closer understanding of the available skills/ competencies of the professionals engaged in the information sector reveals that they have miles to go if they have to discharge their roles as expected of them. Course curricula imparted at all levels in the discipline of Library & Information Science need to undergo a sea change to incorporate newer approaches/ concepts. Existing professionals need to be provided with state-of-the-art exposure in art and science of the profession through various in-service (continuing education) programmes. All, existing as well as upcoming professionals, will need to be groomed to take on the role of 'knowledge managers'.

***Competencies of LIPs:*** To take up such a role, Library and Information Professionals (LIPs) will be better off, if they pay serious attention towards developing and enhancing their core competencies. Core competencies in the case of LIPs are: (i) Personal; and (ii) Professional.

Competencies have been defined as the interplay of knowledge, understanding skills and attitudes required to do a job effectively from the point of view of both the performer and the observer. The unique competencies of the librarian include in-depth knowledge of print and electronic information resources in management of information services that meet the strategic information needs of the individual or group being served.

At the dawn of the 21st century, LIPs are experiencing the consequences of three major paradigm shifts. These are:

- The transition from paper to electronic media as the dominant form of information dissemination, storage and retrieval, is the first shift. Convergence of different media, such as text, graphics, and sound, into multimedia resources, has direct impact on this transition.
- Increasing demand for accountability, with focus on quality customer services, performance measurement, bench marking and continuous improvement, is the other shift. Shrinking financial resources for providing quality library and information support services have direct bearing on this shift.
- New forms of work organization such as end-user computing, work-teams, downsizing, re-engineering, outsourcing etc., is the result of the third shift.

Given this backdrop, LIPs can enhance the productivity of those engaged in knowledge creation and its dissemination by playing a more "proactive" role rather than "passive" one. In this changed dimension, LIPs will have to assume the role of analyzers, synthesizers and interpreters of knowledge/ information, rather than be content with acquiring, organising and providing information when asked for. Further, the role of traditional librarianship is changing into cybrarianship to include the tasks of scanning, filtering, selecting, organizing and packaging the flood of information. In keeping with their changing role from 'gatekeepers' to gateways to 'information, ' LIPs should be performing such tasks as information audits, training in information, literacy, information of best practices/ competencies and helping their users to navigate through the world of information, more meaningfully.

## Collection Development Skills

Collection development is a highly challenging task for information professionals. The situation demands that professionals entrusted with this task respond to this situation in such a manner that collections developed by them not only meet the current needs of their clients but also the future ones.

To do so, LIPs must be groomed on the following lines to devise ways and means to constantly update the collections:

- Develop proper knowledge of the organisation, its mission, goals and objectives;
- Develop proper assessment of users' diverse needs;
- Have thorough knowledge of full range learning resources: documentary, non-documentary;
- Develop thorough knowledge about the library personnel: their job profiles, strengths / weaknesses, area of specialisation etc.;
- Develop thorough understanding of the vendor profile;
- Be thorough with Web browsing *i.e.* relevant search engines, meta search engines, methods to find web resources, appropriate list servers, databases, directories and other E-information resources;
- Have subject degree relevant to the field of work;
- Devise ways and means to constantly update the collections.

## Collection Processing Skills

Results of 'Knowledge Capture' will be effective if post capture steps are carried out as follows:

***Knowledge Analyses:*** LIPs require information skills for analysing the quality of information. These skills comprise filtering out noise and focusing on special needs. Hence, LIPs should be able to:

- Understand that information differs in its level of quality;
- Apply evaluative criteria to both print and electronic resources, such as, author's credentials, peer review, and reputation of the publisher, to assess the authority of the source;
- Assess the relevancy of a source to an information need by examining publication date, purpose and intended audience;
- Recognize omission in the coverage of a topic;
- Recognize and evaluate documentation for the information source, such as research methodology, bibliography or footnotes;

- Distinguish between primary, secondary as well as tertiary sources (print & non-print) in the requisite discipline/s and evaluate their appropriateness to the information need.

***Knowledge Synthesis:*** Having selected and acquired the material, the next task is to organise and synthesize it and make it accessible for the users. The recent developments in the Internet and World Wide Web have brought new challenges to information professionals and consequently a number of researchers are now engaged in organising web-based information. Machine readable (on-line as well as off-line) public access catalogue has totally eliminated the tedious task of making 5-10 cards per document, being too much concerned with punctuation marks and other such parameters, and so on. Although the availability of large catalogue databases on-line and several classification schemes on CDs has provided much needed relief to the professionals, yet to accommodate local requirements, systematic recording of all local additions/updates/ variations etc., for use by others in the system will be in order. Here also, constant interaction with the users of the system helps the professional concerned to develop a rich (and practical) knowledge base on the users' information seeking behaviour. LIPs should be able to organise, synthesize, integrate and apply the information in the following ways:

- Use appropriate documentation style to cite sources used;
- Summarise the information retrieved (*e.g.* write an abstract or construct an outline);
- Recognize and accept the ambiguity of multiple points of view;
- Organize the information in a logical and useful manner;
- Synthesize the ideas and concepts from the information sources collected;
- Determine the extent to which the information can be applied to the information need;
- Integrate the new information into the existing body of knowledge;

- Create a logical argument based on information retrieved.

***Knowledge Repackaging:*** Consolidators were filters who will make sense of the world for managers. Few managers have enough time to spend gathering, processing and interpreting all the information they need. The system has become more sophisticated, enabling people to process greater amounts of information. But the very process of development that enables the systems to become more sophisticated also has the effect of increasing the volume and complexity of the information available.

For these reasons there will always be scope for division of labour and the creation of posts for information professionals to reduce the burden on managers. They should be very vibrant at collecting information by way of searching databases and other secondary sources. Further consolidators should be able to see the patterns and make the connections in the information they process. They should be able to interpret the information in the light of the circumstances faced by the organisation for which they work. Also they should be able to develop specialised information products for use inside or outside the organisation or by individual clients.

Hence, to locate and retrieve relevant sources in a variety of formats from the global information environment; the consolidator should be able to:

- Understand the organization of materials in libraries and use locally produces location guides;
- Understand how to use classification systems and rationale for their existence;
- Use location information in the bibliographic record to retrieve locally owned resources;
- Use local resources to locate information sources in the global information environment;
- Understand that libraries have developed methods for locating and sharing resources not owned locally and use the appropriate resource sharing system, such as interlibrary loan or document delivery, to retrieve information;

- Understand that the Internet may be a useful resource for locating, retrieving and transferring information electronically.

***Knowledge Retrieval:*** Retrieval support means assisting users in the proper use of information technology to access the available knowledge. Examples of tasks covered in this area of responsibility include the following:

- Identification of new and emerging technologies to be assimilated and integrated into the organisation to impart competitiveness.
- Develop manageable technological skills, *i.e.*, know how to use available technology creatively in order to achieve the greatest benefit and pleasure from their work;
- Ability to train users to navigate the knowledge base competently themselves;
- Competency in search skills specifically for bibliographic databases, using various permutations and combinations of search terms with boolean operators;
- Competency in IT skills, which can be used for researching sources, accessing information, connecting to experts, communicating ideas and results and packaging the knowledge for reuse;
- Ability to develop user-focused/oriented service skills *i.e.*, linking catalogue searching and other databases to document delivery service.

***Collection Service Skills:*** LIPs have been delivering a wide range of information products and services to meet the needs of their varying clientele. These range from simple issue/ return services to most complex and value added information products and services, in both, on-line as well as off-line manner. What goes on in the planning and launch of these services is:

- Understanding the user *i.e.*, information-seeking behaviour and information needs of the clientele, which is based on survey;
- Understand the library system *i.e.*, resources, tools, techniques, service and people where resources include; Documentary and Non-documentary;

- Match between the two, *i.e.*, in discharging his duties an effective information professional has to be equipped with thorough understanding of users and strength and weakness of the library/ system.

LIPs aim to provide the right information to the right user at the right time and at the right cost. Documenting each and every step in the planning as well as launch/implementation of each and every information product/service will go a long way towards not only standardizing and further improving upon these services, but preparing others concerned to shoulder such assignments, should an opportunity come their way. Hence, to deliver efficient, innovative and just-in-time services, LIPs will have to keep themselves updated in Internet and information technology skills.

### User-education Skills

User education aims to equip users with the needed skills to enable them to make use of libraries and their resources in a use-friendly manner. User education often includes library orientation, induction and information skills training. Hence LIPs should:

- Use wide variety of methods to help users in information skills through lectures, practical 'hands-on' sessions, workbooks, printed guides, videos, and demonstrations;
- Adopt approaches to user education which can reach non traditional students such as part-time and distance learners through information technology support via computer mediated communication;
- Use the web for teaching through linking to ready-made training packages or developing in-house products;
- Use computer-assisted learning (CAL) and hypertext in creating flexible learning packages for developing web library guides.

## EDUCATION AND TRAINING OF LIPS

Clearly, an aspiring professional in LIS needs to know the basics of IT, particularly in the area of computer, communication and networking technologies. The professional also needs to know the principles and techniques of how one structures and organizes information and knowledge so that the right information can be retrieved and so routed at the right time. This would include all the traditional core skills of library and information science, specifically indexing, cataloguing and authority control, and the creation of synthetic structures to reach the information. The Internet, in particular, as an information service/system will have a multiple impact on several areas of LIS as an educational programme. Hence present curricula of LIS should specifically be updated with:

- The impact of the Internet on society and Libraries.
- The Internet as an information sources Channel of communication
- Organisation of information through Internet.
- Information retrieval through the Internet.
- Design of information services using the Internet
- Internet databases and interfacing
- Web page design and authoring
- Compilation of directories of subject documents on the Net.

## CONCLUSION

From the above, it may be summed-up that LIPs equipped with the competencies as outlined in this paper will be fully geared to discharge their role, not only as gatekeepers of knowledge, but managers of the same. Thorough revision of course curricula as suggested will no doubt be instrumental in creating a breed of professionals with a positive mind-set in so far as their role in the knowledge cycle is concerned.

To take care of existing (in-service) professionals, a need is felt to expose them to newer concepts/dimensions/approaches through the organisation of multi-tier short-term/continuing education, teaching and training programmes. Examples of such programme can be found in plenty in India. In particular, present as well as prospective professionals need to be given thorough exposure to various information literacy skills. Need-based and tailor-made short-term training programmes need to be developed for existing professionals, for honing their skills and developing their expertise.

# 4

# Libraries after the Civil War

The decade–long war, which erupted on March 23rd 1991 east of the country, was a spillover from Charles Taylor's NPFL war in neighbouring Liberia. It arose as a result of unchecked corruption, bad governance, deprivation and the elimination of a vast majority of the population especially those in rural areas, the systematic dismantling of democratic institutions, social injustice and a culture of impunity in plundering state resources. It, however, ended with the disarmament of over 70, 000 ex–combatants and the subsequent destruction of arms and ammunition in January 2002.

The war was traumatic for the people of Sierra Leone. Many people lost their lives; properties were destroyed, thousands displaced while others were forced to seek refugee status in the sub–region. Coupled with its aroused objective of wiping out corruption, political and social ineptitude, underdevelopment and widespread poverty, was its attendant problem of human rights violation and the break down of law and order. Progressive voices were silenced by brute force, thus resulting in a culture of silence.

*"... the literacy rate fell sharply below 32 percent, since there was no schooling in most parts of the country."*

The civil war severely hit the socioeconomic and political order. The economy remained precarious; agriculture was seriously undermined while prices of goods escalated and unemployment dominated the labour force. Poverty became widespread as living standards fell especially among the poorer segments of society. Against this backdrop, smuggling, especially of diamonds, remained pervasive and debilitating. Similarly, the country's physical and social infrastructure was affected. Road networks were destroyed and lack of maintenance resulted in a deteriorated power supply system. Human resources development was neglected while the literacy rate fell sharply below 32 percent, since there was no schooling in most parts of the country. In the civil service, the quality of service declined as the majority of the middle and lower level staff lacked adequate education and were preoccupied with second jobs due to poor salaries.

The public health sector was left in an appalling state: hospitals, health centres and clinics were looted and left unguided, understaffed and riddled with corruption. Health services were limited in many parts of the country and access depended entirely on how much one could afford to pay. So much devastating effects did the war cause that by 2003 the country was ranked 175th in the UNDP Human Development Index, with a life expectancy at birth of 34.5 years (2001), while the adult literacy percentage stood at 36 percent of those aged 15 and over (2001).

However, the euphoria that greeted the outbreak of the civil war could only be overcome with the creation of a need for a new set of priorities that would address such pressing issues as peace and reconciliation, health, education, infrastructural development, unemployment, agricultural inefficiency and an effective price control system. The provision of adequate, relevant, timely and accessible information is a precondition for development as well as the outcome of development. Postwar reconstruction cannot take place without the ideas and notions embedded in documents which form the basis of our informed knowledge. To this end libraries are crucial.

## Information and Post–War Reconstruction

As the country is in the throes of post–war reconstruction, rehabilitation and resettlement, the desperate need for sustainable peace and security should not be overemphasized. The struggle and challenge for peace and its enhancement should be the responsibility of both the state and the citizenry, even though the former is expected to play a leading role in ensuring that all the necessary and requisite mechanisms for achieving peace are firmly in place.

In building peace all over the world and in Sierra Leone in particular, there is a need for accurate, reliable and helpful information. Information is an essential resource for development, human rights promotion, conflict resolution, peace and security. The availability of information is, at the level of governance, a major yardstick to measure accountability, transparency and predictability in a democratic society besides its impact on the economic sphere. Regular and smooth communication channels through which healthy and sound information flows can lay the foundation for the effective functioning of a democratic system. Information promotes and empowers citizens' participation in the democratic process; it maintains the Rule of Law and creates a viable outlet for the injection of public opinion. Information informs the policy–making process of political leadership, all of which nurtures the building of sustainable peace for the enhancement of the State.

No nation can progress significantly without the availability of sound information networks such as the media, libraries and information services, educational institutions at all levels, and vibrant and relevant professional bodies. The unique and inestimable role of these information agents for learning and information dissemination for the achievement of lasting peace should not be ignored in any society. Rather, they should be seen as crucial for effectively supporting research, advocacy, and awareness raising and as a means of attracting appropriate support from the international community. In particular, this will no doubt accelerate the speedier implementation of the provision of the Truth and Reconciliation Commission (TRC) as essential requirement for building peace and reconciliation and postwar reconstruction as provided for in the 1999 Lome Accord in Sierra Leone.

> *"If the country's hard–won democracy is to be nurtured... librarians should collaboratively and assiduously work for lasting peace."*

A state of peace involves the practice of democratic norms and values, justice, universal economic and social well– being.

Sierra Leone is going through a period of transition with the implementation of innovative peace building and peace education activities. The rationale behind these is that since wars begin in the minds of men, it is in their minds that the defence of peace must be constructed. Sierra Leoneans, therefore, must not only participate, but should also be proactive to enable the government and policy makers to adopt robust policies and strategies to finally attain a lasting peace.

In this regard librarians and their respective institutions have a role to play in the dissemination of information. If the country's hard–won democracy is to be nurtured, if its socioeconomic, educational and cultural sectors are to be developed, and if indeed Sierra Leoneans are to prevent another such deadly and meaningless conflict, librarians should collaboratively and assiduously work for lasting peace. They should pool their collective strengths, share the national burdens and labour symbiotically for progress.

## Library Scene in the Country

Libraries are derivative agencies. They rise from particular needs within a society and their types and functions reflect the diversity within that society. In Sierra Leone, however, libraries form an important part of the country's information services. Their general aim is to collect and store whatever information that is likely required and to provide access to information as speedily as necessary and to arrange its supply in the most useful manner. The principal types are public, special, academic and school libraries.

The public library (The Sierra Leone Library Board), which also doubles as the country's national library, was established in 1959. Its functions as outlined in the 1958 Government White Paper on education development are as follows:

a. To support and re–enforce programmes of adult and fundamental education.

b. To provide effective service for children and young people including requisite services for schools.

c. To provide much–needed information and reference services.

d. To promote and stimulate reading for pleasure and recreation.

e. To provide, where needed, adequate services for special groups, that is, women, language groups, the disadvantaged, etc.

In addition to the Lending, Reference, Cataloguing and Children's Departments at the headquarters library in Freetown, the library also runs a primary school service concerned mainly with the provision of books in areas where there are no libraries. There is a branch library in the capital city, Freetown, and regional libraries in the district headquarters towns although most of these have ceased operation due to the war. "Experience has shown that a country's educational system could be as strong and as weak as the library resources that support that system." Also, there is a wide variety of special libraries concentrating on limited subjects. Their organization falls into three major categories:

i. *Special libraries,* which are associated with professional and learned societies, government departments and research centres. Some of these contain not less than a hundred and fifty textbooks plus a handful of periodicals as at the Sierra Leone Parliament and the Ministry of Foreign Affairs and International Cooperation libraries. At the extreme are those like at the Bank of Sierra Leone which have the best collection in their specialties

ii. *Documentation centres* such as the National Agricultural Documentation Centre (NADOC) and the Development Documentation Centre (DDC) at the Ministry of Economic Development and Planning which process the literature in their respective fields

iii. *Information centres,* which are principally associated with government departments and research and industrial establishments which provide specific information like Shell (Oil Refinery) library and the Gender and Research Documentation Centre (GRADOC). Access to most of these institutions is sometimes restricted.

*Academic libraries* are those libraries of the university and teacher training colleges which have the predominant function of servicing the teaching and research activities of their respective institutions. The size of these libraries, especially university libraries, exceeds over seventy–five thousand volumes excluding periodical publications. Their organization, subject coverage, acquisition policies and services reflect the responsibilities of their parent institutions. Facilities are limited to bona fide clientele, that is, faculty, students, researchers, scholars, and the administration while lending facilities to individual members of the public is exceptional.

*School libraries* give the children their first exposure to information resources and mould their information behaviour for the future. Their services are limited to a few textbook and magazine collections. In addition to pupils, they serve teachers and provide service to parents and the public as well. Librarianship is a professional activity concerned with information—its acquisition, storage, organization or use and its supply to the inquirer. In Sierra Leone, however, the physical formats of the contents of libraries are mostly books. While books and journals represent the accumulated record of mankind's knowledge and information, librarians believe that change is the keyword in society. Supporting postwar reconstruction requires an environment rich in learning stimuli. Experience has shown that a country's educational system could be as strong and as weak as the library resources that support that system.

The progress of education is dependent on the progress of the country's economy. This in turn depends on agriculture, technical, medical, commercial, and industrial change. Similarly, if a more sophisticated culture should emerge institutions such as libraries have a vital role to play. This was the rationale behind the Sierra Leone Association of Archivists, Librarians, and Information Scientists' (SLAALIS) hosting of their fourth annual conference on the theme "Information for peace building in the 21st century, " on 21st–23rd March 2001. At the close of the conference it was resolved amongst other things that:

- SLAALIS should strengthen its advocacy and lobbying strategies with government, the Parliamentary

Committee on Education, Civil Society Movement, the National Commission for Democracy and Human Rights (NCDHR), Disarmament, Demobilization and Reintegration (DDR) and other organizations dealing with peace building in implementing its programmes and activities.

- SLAALIS should provide a forum/base for activities relating to peace building, peace education and conflict resolution in the country.
- SLAALIS should work in collaboration with relevant organizations like Government, NCDHR, DDR, Civil Society Movement, Freetown City Council (FCC), and international organizations on networking, partnership and linkages in peace building.
- SLAALIS should organize talks, discussions and public lectures for schools and colleges and the community on peace building.

## Librarians and Post–War Reconstruction

The refrains in the country today in conference, workshop and seminar halls and on radio and television discussion programmes are exclusively democracy, good governance, human rights and peace building. On these depends the attainment of sustainable peace for the survival of the nation. Similarly, a noticeable trend in the activities of librarians to date is the growing interest in the role their institutions should play in postwar reconstruction. This switch in professional direction is not so much a change in direction as a change in emphasis following on a reappraisal of traditional library goals and practices. But how much dedication have librarians to successfully transmit the required message for postwar reconstruction? Very little. True, indeed, that information is power and power belongs to the people; that information leads to understanding and this in turn generates sound judgment and decision–making; the benefit of this is productive action. Precisely these ingredients are missing in librarians' efforts in postwar reconstruction. Apart from the unavailability of adequate funds, librarians have not been able to identify the issues at stake, their target groups and the necessary channels to get on to their targets. Sierra Leone is a poor country with a high level of illiteracy and limited high–tech communication facilities almost entirely confined to the capital city. Librarians, therefore, should start to identify and utilize the basics of information dissemination channels and agents the citizens are familiar with, such as religious occasions and gatherings where pastors, imams and other religious leaders are powerful information agents. Also trade fairs, periodic markets, sports, secret societies, court sessions and trade unions to cite a few, are indispensable to information dissemination.

Besides, the very concept of service in postwar reconstruction is in itself testimony to many divergent interpretations of the nature of library service. To date discrete groups of readers, such as ex–combatants, war amputees, women, children and young people, the traumatized, and the old, are emerging as targets for specially oriented library service. This brings librarians to adhere to the concept of outreach. In reaching out to these clientele groups, librarians will be operating in an area of activity already occupied by other public service departments, like Health, Education, Agriculture, Labour and Social Welfare, where efforts are being made commensurate with community demands. The old passive role of libraries as minority service will start to diminish. In its place, libraries would be viewed as part of a group of several institutions working within society whose overall aim is the improvement of social conditions and the development of human resources in postwar reconstruction. Librarians, therefore, should begin to hold talks, organize seminars, conferences and meetings to sensitize themselves about these new and challenging issues in order to gain a new direction if their services in postwar reconstruction are to be worthwhile.

Information has become such a vital raw material in the country today that the increasing expense of obtaining and exploiting it should stimulate librarians in postwar reconstruction. As professionals it is incumbent upon them to not only support and promote the rebuilding process; it is their responsibility, as purveyors of information, to ensure that they facilitate that process through provision of resources at their disposal to policy makers and citizens alike. They should regard themselves of being in a position where they can make an impact, but, at the same time, the onus of the level of impact is not solely theirs. Users should recognize their worth within their midst, especially since they are entrusted with the task of collecting, storing and disseminating such resources they may have in their charge.

Libraries are service institutions and librarians the world over are emphatic in making their materials available to the public. Librarians in Sierra Leone should realize that printed formats, which largely dominate their institutions, are not the only means of storing and disseminating information. Consequently they should have a choice to house and make available new media technologies, such as computers, CD–ROMs, facsimile, telephone, reprographic facilities and Internet services. Besides, they should integrate their institutions in large networks with information centres within and outside the country, using computers and tele–links for information processing and transmission for advanced information systems. In addition to their traditional services, they should offer customized services of relevant literature, provide bibliographic services, offer Selective Dissemination of Information and Current Awareness Services culling relevant material from current literature for the attention of their users, with minimal fees charged for their work.

It is the place of librarians to provide the public with the full range of services, book and non–book materials alike. Equally certain is their duty to add their expertise to the struggle against poverty, bad governance, democracy, inequality, crime, discrimination and illiteracy, especially as the UNDP Human Index has ranked the country as the least developed in the world for 2002. To this end librarians should bring their skills and training and begin to discover where they will not have effect. In other words, they must seek recognition by the public if their libraries are properly placed in the overall schemes of community service. They should, therefore, go out to the country and seek out the social problems of the day; they should identify those suffering from these problems and endeavour to bring them into contact with total community resources through the resources of their libraries.

> *"... the UNDP Human Index has ranked the country as the least developed in the world for 2002."*

Librarians, especially those in the public library, should broaden their concepts of library service and build up relationships within their community. These should be built with existing groups like Non–Governmental Organizations, both local and international, community development workers, social workers, teachers, youth workers, medical teams, child guidance workers, trade unionists, Peace and Reconciliation Commission officials, Civil Society Movement and community lawyers. Librarians should encourage these groups by making their rooms and services available for seminars, conferences, workshops and community development meetings.

There is every justification for librarians to get involved in eradicating illiteracy in the country by providing space, materials and guidance in developing the reading skills of adult learners. It is a truism that the only significant activity of librarians, especially those in the public library, is book lending.

As this view is becoming obsolete, provision should be made in the form of non–book materials like cassettes, films, tape and video recordings, reading kits and pamphlets. Not only should librarians strive to maintain a high degree of responsiveness to clientele seeking help but they should liaise with development committees, adult education committees and animators for voluntary service. These public–spirited people should be encouraged to use libraries as a means of introducing their profession, explaining what they hope to achieve and what they can meaningfully contribute to overall community education and development.

Librarians need to work with community agencies and professional persons to develop programmes that will promote good health principles. It helps to have librarians assist medical professionals in an analysis of ongoing programmes to see exactly the repercussions of such issues as drug abuse, child abuse, teenage pregnancy, maternity and HIV/AIDS. To be effective, librarians should develop an awareness and understanding of the range of health–related problems. Where possible, they should function as members of community health teams and should use their institutions as publicity centres for health programmes by displaying posters, advertisements, community radio programmes and media publications on health related issues in their libraries.

Sierra Leoneans are faced with broad issues like environmental pollution, democracy and good governance, peace and reconciliation, trauma healing and counselling, awareness raising, and agricultural development in postwar reconstruction. Librarians, therefore, should modify their provisions and services towards this goal.

Libraries should not only be seen as places to study for examinations and leisure purposes, but also as information centres for key national issues as outlined above. These institutions, in addition to the provision of relevant materials, should also promote the aforementioned programmes by creating special collections, such as newspapers, flyers, and brochures, posters and radio/television interview documentaries.

If possible, exhibitions and displays on these activities should be organized while personnel involved in these programmes should be allowed to hold talks, seminars, conferences, workshops, and meetings in the library. The provision of mobile library units could be essential; the public library can play a crucial role in this direction.

Librarians should also pay attention to the information needs of women, most of whom are less educated and have fewer employment opportunities and suffered the brunt of the civil war heavily. Currently, women in the country are advocating for their civic rights and the role they can play in postwar reconstruction. Hence, there is the formation of such groups as "50–50" which advocates for equal rights with men; they are also deeply involved in civil society movement activities and the campaign for good governance, the rights of the girl child and against female circumcision.

Librarians can make their institutions access points for this vulnerable group by providing relevant and timely information as essential support for coping with life crises and the changing concerns of everyday life. Such information could come from books, magazines, guides, directories, newspapers, special reports, educational group programmes and audiovisual materials. Many women could be encouraged to use libraries as sources of information and for individual and group leisure. Librarians should provide well–designed programmes for specific information so as to bring women together with their peers to discuss topics of common concern like health–related issues, gardening, cooking and their civic rights.

However, the attainment of these programmes is centred on the availability of adequate funds and the determination and devotion of librarians to effectuate them. Librarians and their institutions do not function in isolation; they depend on their parent organizations and other funding agencies for financial support. Incidentally, the country is going through drastic financial constraints and under such circumstances libraries are not a priority.

But with the limited funds availed to them, librarians should find ways of raising income like charging for services rendered, sales, sponsorship, support from friends of the library groups, and soliciting external financial support. In addition, they should be research oriented to be able to identify those services that society needs and can provide. Together, they should be able to market their provisions and services through the creation of public relations offices. Any service designed to reach out to people in postwar reconstruction should have high visibility, both inside and outside the library and those in charge of such services should use available avenues to promote their services.

## Conclusion

It is apparent that the culture of librarianship in the country tends to be responsible only to itself. That is to say, the structure of its work, its commitment and loyalties are defined institutionally and professionally rather than in relationship to the community which is the focus of its work. It is a truism that the country's libraries are what they are because society has perceived them as negligible. But, aspirations to redirect librarianship from what it is can be a powerful lever for change, especially in postwar reconstruction. In order for librarians to attain their goals in this era they should provide quality service tailored to the immediate needs of their respective communities and sensitize people to the availability of such services. To this end, they should cooperate with government and other community development agencies to acquire legislation and financial support so that relevant and needed services for nation building could be provided. Only through this can librarians contribute meaningfully to postwar reconstruction.

## EDITORIAL: LIBRARY SERVICES AND INDIGENOUS IDENTITY

*World Libraries* is proud to present this theme issue on Indigenous Library Services to mark the Third International Indigenous Librarians Forum hosted by the American Indian Library Association November 9-12, 2003 in Santa Fe, New Mexico. The theme of the Forum is *Closer to the Fire: Ensuring Culturally Responsive Library Practices*. This is an opportunity to make a wider audience aware of recent developments in indigenous librarianship both locally and, especially, globally since the Maori Library Association Te Ropu Whakahau ("they who encourage and incite ") took the initiative to invite the world's indigenous librarians to the First Indigenous Librarians' Forum on the Waipapa Marae in Auckland, Aotearoa/New Zealand in November 1999. The Sami of Scandinavia followed their lead and organized the Second Forum in Jokkmokk, Sweden, two years later, and now, after a further two years, the Third International Indigenous Librarians' Forum is about to get underway, hosted by the American Indian Library Association (AILA) and the Smithsonian's National Museum of the American Indian (NMAI).

To celebrate this event, two of the participants in all three of the Forums, Loriene Roy, a Professor at the School of Information in the University of Texas at Austin, and Peter Sarri, Library Counsellor or Consultant to the Sami Parliament in Sweden, were invited to be guest editors of a special issue of *World Libraries* on indigenous librarianship. They have enlisted the aid of native colleagues from both northern and southern hemispheres. Each guest editor has also graciously provided prefaces to their sections with background information on their authors and the special situation of the indigenous peoples they represent. A world map has been added to Loriene Roy's preface to show an approximate distribution of indigenous peoples around the world, and a map of Scandinavia and the Kola Peninsula illustrates Peter Sarri's account of the Sami.

Concern for library services to indigenous people goes back much further than to the turn of the millennium. Until well after the Second World War, however, much of that "service " was more to the benefit of the encroaching colonizing civilizations as they moved in to convert and assimilate the "primitive savages " to their dominating and pervasive culture. Gordon Hills outlines the process from missionary-invented orthographies through the development of printing and literacy instruction (though without mentioning the destructive effects of residential schools) and provides some documentation of its effects for the native peoples of Arctic North America, in part from his own experience in Alaska and Yukon and partly second-hand from the accounts of Russian writers.

But Hills also conveys the evolution of other, more positive attitudes in providing access to information for indigenous peoples, arising in the late 1970s, not only in North America and Europe, but also in Australia and New Zealand. Two extensive, selectively annotated bibliographies, one mostly to 1990, the other a supplement through 1995, undergird his assertions for the circumpolar north, with a cursory side glance at conditions south of the equator. At the same time, though, a more pessimistic note rings through Hills' account of the situation in professional library organizations where the "compartmentalizing effect of having 'roundtables, ' 'special committees, ' 'interest groups' or sections on multicultural and Native/Indian library services... tends to relegate such progressive, client group-oriented and socially responsible aspects of the profession to 'fringe' or even, in the early going, to 'cult' status." Library education does not appear to offer much hope, based on questionnaires Hills' own survey data from 1987, to the extent that the author claims that "the education of Native librarians on all fronts is scandalously short-changed, and the education of non-Natives in multicultural and Native librarianship has been, until very recently, identically treated."

Much of the malaise to which Hills refers can be said to be compounded precisely because there are so few Native individuals involved in library services to their own people. A distinctive feature of the International Indigenous Librarians' Forums originated by the Maoris and continued subsequently at their request, though perhaps a little less stringently, is a factor that can contribute to reversing this trend, namely the fact that participation has been reserved to a great extent for indigenous peoples only. Te Ropu Whakahau are right to make this assertion in my opinion and experience, for the e reason that indigenous librarianship is so much more than merely providing access to materials in the native language of the clientele one serves.

This is the message of Hills' book, and it was also the clearly expressed consensus of the delegates present at the 1998 IFLA Satellite Conference in Tromsø, which may have been the first global seminar on indigenous librarianship. Asbjørn Langeland, then director of Norway's Public Library Directorate *Statens bibliotektilsyn*, invited me to have the privilege of providing the closing remarks as a summary of the proceedings. The burden of the discussions at the closing session was a message of the need for more indigenous staff and training and a need to make libraries more accessible to indigenous peoples. Jackie Huggins wrote of library services to Australia' Aboriginal and Torres Islander people: "We offer our clients the opportunity to get acquainted with their roots again." Leading people back into their roots is in large measure only possible if the guide is himself or herself well acquainted with these same roots. Few non-Native librarians are prepared to perform this service adequately.

A personal interest and concern for indigenous library services and their impact on indigenous culture and identity that was awakened while working in Norway as the Associate Director of Southern Nordland Regional Library in Mo i Rana from 1994-97 has confirmed the conclusion that Native librarians should have primacy in service to indigenous people. The South Sami cultural centre in Hattfjelldal, *Sijti Jarnge*, fell within the purview of the Regional Library, and part of our services included consultation for library services.

Perhaps the most important service that was inaugurated during that time was *Gærjah Sijti Jarngeste*, the South Sami bookmobile, which was intended to serve the South Sami on both in Norway and Sweden, from Mo i Rana south and west to Umea on the Gulf of Bothnia. The dedication of the bookmobile was an experience very different from the familiar ceremonies of a more Western Christian nature—and yet with an inherent serene spirituality, calmly proclaimed by the words spoken in blessing before the vehicle by Anna Jacobsen, an elder among her people. Here was a community whose culture is very different from that of the North Sami showcased by Nils-Aslak Valkeapaa at the opening of the Winter Olympic Games in Lillehammer in 1994, just a year before.

The language of the South Sami is very unlike its northern counterpart (about as different as Norwegian and Icelandic), and even the *joik* (pronounced *yoik*), the characteristic chanting of the Sami exhibits great variance between north and south. Manning the "book bus" (a direct translation of the Norwegian *bokbuss*, a term also used in Sami, *gærjahbusse* in South Sami, *girjebusse* in North Sami) were the two Kappfjell brothers, who happened to be the nephews of Anna Jacobsen. This was no accident, as I very soon learned. Neither Tom nor John has any extensive formal library training—Tom has some college studies in law behind him; John, by his own admission, is a "Jack-of-all-trades. " But together, they have something that is rare among their library-educated counterparts, even if the latter had learned some of the South Sami language: as members of the quite extensive Kappfjell family, they have a bond with the entire South Sami nation that gives them entree anywhere their people gather.

Their uncle, Gustav Kappfjell, Anna's brother, has been called the South Sami culture's "foremost poet, " whose work was at the time of his death "still the only work written entirely in the South Sami language, and contains some of the most beautiful poetry that have [*sic*] been written in any Sami dialect." Gaebpien Gasta (his Native name) was also an accomplished *joik* artist who performed with Nils-Aslak Valkeapaa. Both Gustav Kappfjell and Anna Jacobsen were among the founders and longtime board members of the South Sami theatre group *aarjelhsaemien teatere* (Anna even acted in the group) and the South Sami Residential School *Gaske-Nøørjen saemienskovle* in Hattfjelldal. Another relative of Tom and John was Thor Axel Kappfjell, the legendary BASE jumper who became world famous for parachuting from some of the world's highest skyscrapers, only to die when jumping off a fog-enshrouded cliff in southern Norway in July 1999. This may seem irrelevant to library service, even nepotistic, but it is everything to the South Sami. Knowing what family you belong to, who you are related to, gives you a bond and a sense of belonging with other South Sami you meet, because you know where you fit in the scheme of things.

The South Sami have a word for this: *laahkoeh*. Tom published a book about this kinship system in 1991, illustrated by his niece, Lena, John's daughter. It is this kinship system that makes the arrival of *Gœrjah Sijti Jarngeste* in town more than just another stop to lend out some books (and, of course, the bookmobile brings not only books, but other materials and cultural artifacts as well), more a family reunion, a time to meet the folks and chat over a cup of special Sami coffee with the compulsory hunk of smoked reindeer meat to dunk as well. Tom explained the goals and objectives of the bookmobile at the Barents Library Conference held at Ajtte in Jokkmokk a few days after the 2nd International Indigenous Librarians' Forum:

***Goal:*** The goal is to help clients become more secure in their identity in order that eventually they may dare to live as the Sami people they define themselves to be. It is not easy to revitalize a Sami culture when one lives in a community where the majority culture largely defines the environment.

***Objectives:*** To create a permanent identity factor, a "town square " which can contribute to increasing the understanding for the Sami culture and language for the Sami themselves and equally important for those who have the Sami as their closest neighbours.

That, in a nutshell, is what indigenous library services are all about. And that is why the involvement of indigenous librarians is crucial to successful indigenous librarianship. Non-Native librarians can be little more than doctors who strive to keep the patient comfortable but can't really understand where it hurts or why it hurts. We can do our best to provide access to materials we think will satisfy the needs of our indigenous patrons, even to the extent of pietistically preserving all we can collect that has any relation to the situation or the language of the people we are working with. But without the heart that listens and resonates to the same drum, it is very difficult to be able to reach the goal of helping our patrons "become more secure in their identity in order that eventually they may dare to live as the... people they define themselves to be. " Ripping slivers from a cut of smoked reindeer meat with a sharp long bladed Sami knife and dunking it in a mug of strong coffee is not to every taste, although there is a certain appeal to this strange blend of flavours once you have experienced it.

We are approaching the close of the United Nations Decade of Indigenous Peoples, 1995-2004, "proclaimed by the General Assembly in its resolution 48/163 of 21 December 1993 with the main objective of strengthening international cooperation for the solution of problems faced by indigenous people in such areas as human rights, the environment, development, education and health." The theme for the Decade is "Indigenous people: partnership in action " and among the goals, as set out by Indian and Northern Affairs Canada, are the following:

- Raise international awareness of the contribution of, and problems faced by, indigenous people throughout the world;
- Empower indigenous people to make choices and enable them to retain their cultural identity while participating in national economic and social life, with full respect for their cultural values, languages, traditions and forms of social organization;

- Educate indigenous and non-indigenous communities on the situation, cultures, languages, rights and aspirations of indigenous people

The initiative of Te Ropu Whakahau in instigating the 1st International Indigenous Librarians' Forum, response of the Sami in taking on the 2nd Forum, and now the continuation by AILA in hosting the 3rd Forum in New Mexico together with the Smithsonian's National Museum of the American Indian will further a focus on developing strategies that will ensure that these goals may be met through culturally sensitive guidelines that "send a clear and consistent message to library providers around the globe that library policies need to be strengthened so that they acknowledge the cultural needs of their native users." Our hope is that this issue of *World Libraries* may make its own contribution to the furtherance of these goals.

## LIBRARY SERVICES IN CUBA

This special issue of *World Libraries* has been several years in the making, and *World Libraries* is indebted to many people for contributing and making suggestions for contributions. Its origins are in themselves international, when curiosity was aroused in an editor not cognizant of the situation by a posting by Robert Kent in the fall of 2002 on behalf of his organization, The Friends of Cuban Libraries, to Biblioteknorge, the Norwegian librarians' email discussion list. Kent wrote that he wanted to draw the attention of the list's subscribers to the plight of Juan Carlos Gonzalez Leiva, "a blind activist and independent librarian" after his arrest by Cuban authorities. The background to these events would be very much within the purview of the journal, and Kent was invited to write an article about the Cuban situation for *World Libraries*. However, he was enjoined to write in broad, general terms, in order to provide our readers with an overview of the situation.

Further investigation on the web during this fall of 2002 revealed the existence of another organization, the Cuban Library Support Group, which provided a very different picture of Cuban libraries, suggesting that there was freedom to read and very little censorship in the country, if any. That group was founded by a British librarian, John Pateman, Head of Libraries and Heritage of the Borough of Merton in London, England. An article was requested also from Pateman, in order to provide a balance.

It was becoming clear from ongoing discussions, both in the American Library Association and earlier at the IFLA meeting in Boston that this was a divisive issue, and one that was more complicated than Robert Kent's repeated missives to library discussion lists might suggest. A delegation from ALA under the leadership of then President-elect John Berry had visited Cuba in May of 2001. Among the delegates were some who had close ties with our publisher, Dominican University, so that there were several who might be willing to write an article. John Berry very graciously agreed to write an article as soon as he was contacted, an account that provides a very helpful background to the history of ALA's relations with Cuba (click here). Attendance at an International Relations Committee meeting at ALA Midwinter in January 2003 brought another promise to write from Rhonda Neugebauer, who had made several visits to Cuba. Her article, "For Services Rendered, " shows a picture of the independent libraries and librarians that contrasts sharply with that of Robert Kent.

But, at the same time, the suggestion was made to include articles that illustrated other aspects of Cuban librarianship and US relations with Cuban libraries. Dean Prudence Dalrymple was aware that Jeanne Drewes had been involved with a preservation project in Havana. Jeanne Drewes is Assistant Director for Access and Preservation at Michigan State University Library, and her website shows that she has made a number of visits to Cuba or arranged workshops for Cuban librarians. When asked about the possibility of writing an article for a special issue on Cuba, Ms. Drewes suggested a novel approach: formulating the article as advice to readers who may be interested in being involved in some kind of service project abroad, using her experiences in Cuba as an illustration. The result is a very interesting article which can be read here.

The memorable joint annual conference of the American and the Canadian Library Associations in Toronto in June 2003 brought the prospect that as many as five articles could be added to the growing issue. When asked if he was aware of possible authors, the Director of ALA's International Relations Office, Michael Dowling, mentioned that there would be a delegation of librarians from Cuba who would be making presentations in Toronto, and suggested that we might consider publishing translations of their papers. This exciting opportunity became reality with oral permissions secured from all five at the seminar during the conference. Robert Kent was also present, together with Ramon Colas, who launched the independent library movement in 1998, but who now resides in Miami, Florida.

In keeping with theorganizers' expressed desire to present Cuban librarianship in the specific areas of "library education, library associations, outreach to the community, service to rural areas, and collections, " four of the five papers present a wealth of information about everyday library work, both urban and rural, and suggest that, despite the difficulties that have resulted from the political situation, library services have continued very much as they have in other countries. *World Libraries* has attempted to provide as broad and informative a presentation as possible, so that the reader may make up his or her own mind. For additional information and perspective on the changing views on Cuban libraries, the reader is referred to the websites of the Friends of Cuban Libraries and the Cuban Libraries Solidarity Group. Ultimately, perhaps, only a visit to the island can give a surer idea of what exactly is happening there, as Gretta Siegel shows in her article, "A Tale of Two Conferences." At the same time, however, there is more than a little suggestion that where one comes down on this question will be coloured by a prior political stance.

## CUBAN LIBRARIES

***Eliades Acosta Matos:*** A real flesh-and-blood librarian in Cuba is almost always a woman, a fact that is rarely of any interest to the ever-growing number of journalists and writers who say they are presenting the "real" Cuba in their articles. But since the true nature of life on the island is seldom presented in an objective way in major newspapers—the so-called "free and professional" press—then it shouldn't come as a surprise to us that little or nothing is really known of the 12, 000 or so information specialists who provide an important social service in Cuba, a poor country besieged and embargoed by the greatest world power in history as if it were a criminal nation, or one which harbours a disease fatal to the rest of the world: that of showing that a different world is possible.

It is ironic that, in spite of this vile criminalization of an entire nation, this sinister persecution of a social enterprise which profoundly revolutionized the old structures of exclusion and injustice under which the vast majority of Cubans lived and suffered, Cuba boasts the highest rate of school attendance in the entire Third World, higher even that in many developed countries. Nor does Cuba suffer from illiteracy: it has the highest per capita number of teachers, and is recognized by UNESCO as having one of the best school systems, capable of preparing its students with the highest quality education.

But none of these facts would seem to have any real importance for those who criticize and accuse Cuba.

It doesn't matter that no Cuban child has to beg in the streets in order to survive. It doesn't matter that education in Cuba, from preschool to university, is free and universal. Or that health care is available to all as well. Or that Cuban children and teenagers don't shoot each other in school, or murder their teachers in their own classrooms.

In fact, all these things seem to be irrelevant.

It doesn't matter that since September of this year [2002], Cuban schools employ one teacher for every twenty students. Only Denmark, where there is one teacher for every twenty-five students, comes close to achieving such a ratio.

It doesn't matter that there are 6, 000 school libraries serving students in our educational system. Or that in the year 2002, 50, 000 computers, televisions, and VCRs were installed in our schools—even in the almost one thousand rural schools which operate without electricity, and which were provided with solar panels as well, even in the 173 schools in remote areas which open their doors each day to teach only a single student.

None of this really seems to be important. It doesn't matter that we have more public libraries here in Cuba than there are in Italy; that these libraries meet the standards set by UNESCO of being able to provide each citizen with at least three books; that last year our library system served more than eight million people—eight million from a total population of eleven million; and that book prices in Cuba are among the lowest in the world. It matters even less that all of these resources and services are provided to each and every Cuban citizen, down to the very last one, not only to the privileged elites, or to those with the greatest purchasing power; just as it is of no importance that all these successes, of which we Cubans are the most proud, were achieved in the middle of a war which has been going on now for 43 years.

The recent restrictions imposed by the U.S. government on the exchange of academic ideas and projects only confirm that the embargo doesn't recognize borders, and that the protestations of the U.S. to the contrary are purely rhetorical. The prohibition by the American authorities preventing Cuban librarians from travelling to Puerto Rico and to U.S. It is clear to us that as long as the embargo laws remain in effect, we cannot live a normal life; we cannot escape from this reality.

As a matter of fact, we Cubans have been living under extraordinarily difficult circumstances for almost half a century now. Those of us who, like me, are younger than fifty years of age, were born and raised with the embargo; and now our children and grandchildren are living under these same conditions. The threat of experiencing first-hand the aggression of a foreign military power has never left us for a moment during this time. And all the while, much of the so-called "liberal and objective" press has devoted itself to poking around in the corners of our lives, relentlessly hacking away at the great work of social justice which we have achieved under such adverse conditions; and creating in its place a virtual Cuba which they make out to be the worst of all possible places on this earth. Recently—with notable cunning and using a surprising new onslaught of scandalous lies—these vile forces have focused their efforts on the work of Cuban libraries and librarians. What are they accusing us of? What are these terrible mortal sins which we have committed, and which have earned us the harshest condemnations of these implacable judges?

Cuba is the only one of the almost 200 countries in the United Nations which, in the eyes of the IFLA committee on Free Access to Information and Freedom of Expression (FAIFE), warranted a separate analysis, and two special reports, one in 1999, the other in 2001.

And this year, we had the honour of welcoming a large delegation of representatives from ALA and FAIFE who travelled around the country, visiting our libraries—both real and false—and interviewing anyone they wanted, including writers, librarians, booksellers, and ordinary citizens. While Mrs. Susan Seidelin, director of FAIFE, checked our libraries, list in hand, and ended up finding all the "censored" works she had erroneously been led to believe would be missing from our shelves, an English fellowship student, Mr. Stuart Hamilton, roamed the streets of Havana "incognito"—like a character from a Graham Greene novel—interviewing those people euphemistically referred to by the agents of propaganda and psychological warfare against Cuba as "independent librarians."

In spite of this suspicious fixation with Cuba—as if Cuba were the country where intellectual rights and liberties were most threatened; as if Cuba, and not the United States, were the nation most often condemned on FAIFE's own website for outrageous violations of these rights and liberties; as if Cuba, and not the United States, were the country where, in some places, books by Mark Twain, Alice Walker, and Isabel Allende were prohibited and burned, and where national debate raged on whether or not "Harry Potter" belonged on library shelves—in spite of all this, the resolution on Cuba was approved with more than 86% of the votes cast by the delegates to the IFLA General Assembly, which met during the summer of 2001 in Boston.

And it's also worth noting that this resolution, supported by both Cuban and North American librarians, unequivocally established the position of the worldwide information community towards the so-called "independent librarians", urging the

United States government to "broadly share information resources with Cuba, especially with Cuban libraries, not only with those independent non-governmental individuals and organizations" who represent the political interests of the U.S.

To the delegates who voted in Boston for the approval of this resolution, it's clear that one cannot be "independent" while representing the political interests of a particular country, whether it be the United States or the Kingdom of Tonga.

In fact, with regard to Cuba, what is being emphasized when the adjective "independent" is used with the noun "librarian"?

In the first place, it assumes that all other Cuban librarians are "official", simply because they are paid by the government; that is, the thousands of librarians who studied for years and passed exams in order to practice the profession, and who have worked every day under very difficult conditions, displaying an admirable creativity and spirit of sacrifice so that our country could become, as it has, one of the most cultured on earth. Following this same logic, what would we call the great majority of librarians in the world who work in the public sector of their respective countries, and who receive salaries from their respective governments, when they are able to pay them and are not forced to make budget cuts, as is happening right now with the libraries of the richest country in the world?

On the other hand, if the decisive criterion for calling some librarians "official", and others "independent" is who pays their salaries, then the "independent" librarians in Cuba cannot be called independent. Although they don't work for the Cuban state, they do, in fact, work for the American government, as has been incontrovertibly shown; they themselves have admitted it to visiting foreign librarians. The evidence is undeniable and well-documented, including the fees they charge for their services, the equipment they receive, the books which are delivered directly to their homes in vans belonging to the *Oficina de Intereses de los Estados Unidos en La Habana*, the Office for the Interests of the United States in the province of La Habana, and the generous emigration visas which they and their families are given as rewards for services rendered.

Secondly, if the criterion for distinguishing between the two groups depends on their respective ideological affiliations, then the matter becomes even more complicated. The vast majority of the Cuban people support the Revolution. If they didn't, they would not have been able to endure so many years of siege, embargo, and aggression, from terrorist attempts like the one in Barbados in 1973, to invasions like the Bay of Pigs in 1961, the nuclear threats in 1962, and the introduction of epidemics and disease. Cuban librarians and their professional organizations support the Revolution, and we are proud to say this loudly and clearly; it is a right we claim in the light of day and of which we are not ashamed. Not a single important intellectual or information specialist or writer has been successfully recruited for this subversive campaign. Can the so-called "independent" librarians prove that they are not working to undermine the Revolution? That they do not receive political orders and millions of dollars of financing from those agencies of the American government whose mission it is to sabotage the institutional order of Cuba, such as "Freedom House" and USAID, to mention only those organizations who act publicly, and who, more than librarians, act as conspirators, violating Cuba's laws in the service of a hostile foreign power?

Let it be said in passing that Section 180 of the U.S. Code provides penalties of ten years in prison for those who work for a hostile foreign government within United States territory, as James Petras has shown in a recent article. "Professional intrusion, " a punishable offense under both Cuban and American laws, is proclaiming oneself "director" of a library, entering a profession under false pretenses, and receiving monetary compensation for it. These "brave and dedicated freedom fighters"—as their defenders like to call them—earn in one month, in the comfort of their homes, without lifting a finger, 2.2 times more money than I earn each month as director of the National Library of Cuba, in charge of providing services to some 400 users every day and preserving a collection of more than three million documents.

Are we facing a professional problem related to the general principles of librarianship which all of us share in our noble profession? Or, on the other hand, are we having a political discussion having to do with the actions of political agents in the service of the all-out war which has been waged against the Cuban Revolution by the administrations of ten successive U.S. presidents? If we agree that we are not discussing applications of the Dewey Decimal System, or metadata, or preservation issues concerning national bibliographic and digital patrimonies, or ways to strengthen collaboration between Cuban, Canadian, and North American librarians, then what, in fact, are we talking about, when, in spite of the resolution approved in Boston, "independent librarians" continue to be labelled as such, even when they obviously are not? When, in the name of principles which are not demanded of the United States, a country that attacks the free flow of ideas and information with its own laws concerning Cuba, the victim is condemned for being small and weak, not the executioner, who is big and powerful?

There is not the slightest doubt that in fact we are dealing with a political agenda rather than a professional issue. As a result, I wonder if professional groups such as those who have organized this conference ought not to distance themselves from their professional objectives of taking political positions toward one side or another. And furthermore, I wonder if they are capable of taking a position based on Cuba's internal situation without regard for external factors, especially the embargo, and the relentless harassment which the island suffers at the hands of the American government.

Based on this decision, would these organizations be willing to issue statements and take clear positions on the innumerable political problems which today plague the modern world? Would they agree to do this, for example, concerning the conflict between Israel and Palestine, or the ongoing war with the Iraqi people? Did they condemn a war like this one, which resulted in not only thousands of innocent civilian victims for the benefit of the military-industrial complex, and transnational oil interests, but also caused the looting and destruction of the National Library, the National Museum, and dozens of other important sites which were the patrimony of all mankind? The campaign that continues even today seeks ultimately to create a climate conducive to isolating Cuba and ruining her international reputation, in order to mount a military attack on the island. The most reactionary groups of Cuban exiles in Miami have worked frantically—and quite successfully—to create the slogan filled with hatred and frustration, which they unveiled when they gathered for the only public demonstration in the world in support of the Iraqi war: "Iraq now, Cuba later." Military aggression against Cuba, they say, is the only possible way to "resolve" the Cuban problem, thus following the examples of the American government, which has reduced the already-reduced academic and cultural exchanges with the island, and the European Union, which has virtually prohibited them altogether. It is the tacit recognition of their defeat in the exchange of ideas with Cuba, in the exchange of ideas country-to-country. What do they have left, then, after having exhausted completely, without success, all possible means short of bombings and invasion, even when this will result in the loss of hundreds of thousands, perhaps even millions, of human lives, and not just Cuban lives, but those of citizens of other countries as well?

Since the early days when Cubans fought for their liberty during thirty long years, practically alone, we have been a country that expects nothing from other governments, but much from other people. We know very well that throughout history we have received much support and solidarity from the people of the United States and Canada. And this is what we hope for in these tragic moments filled with danger, when the destiny of humanity once again is played out on an island in the Caribbean. This is what we hope for from our colleagues attending this conference. This is what thousands of Cuban librarians believe and desire as well, those who have never been, or will ever be, interviewed by the big information media, but who, at this very minute, are introducing our children to the unforgettable pleasure of reading their first book.

## What Caribbean Librarians Want from Caribbean Publishers

This article provides an overview of Caribbean Libraries, discusses some issues of selection and purchasing as well as bibliographic requirements of interest to publishers and, finally, makes some recommendations for collaboration between publishers and librarians. Specific country and language issues will be highlighted wherever possible.

The Caribbean can be defined in various ways. The one used in this article is that of the Association of Caribbean University, Research and Institutional Libraries (ACURIL), which includes those countries in the Caribbean basin, mainland countries including the Guianas, and the States of United States of America, which border on the Caribbean Sea or the Gulf of Mexico. In ACURIL, the countries number over forty. ACURIL's membership reflects about 110 institutional members, 10 association members and 80 personal members. This is different to the Caribbean Publisher's Network (CAPNET)'s, which includes mainly those countries in the Caribbean Basin.

Libraries in this area represent a population of over 40 million people. Unique to the area are the multi-lingual (Dutch, English, French, and Spanish) and multi-cultural aspects of a people who have a rich and diverse history and development. The Caribbean Library Market reflects the types of libraries that exist everywhere—academic, school, special, national and public libraries. Each type of library has specific acquisition and collection characteristics, which reflect their purchasing ability and needs.

In the Caribbean, academic libraries tend to have better funding than other types of libraries. Purchases are often made in bulk from international publishers and agents. There are normally acquisition departments, usually, with at least one professional librarian. The larger well-funded academic libraries will be automated and have Internet access for both users and for library administration. Purchases are made based on the curriculum and recommendations from faculty and librarians employed at that University. The subject areas taught are an indication of the type of material needed by the institution.

School libraries in the Caribbean tend to have the lowest funding. Their needs are for a specific age range and level. Though with a specific curriculum, school libraries need a wide variety of books and periodicals. However, they often cannot afford these purchases because of low or minimal funding. Some secondary school libraries may have a professional librarian, but more often than not a library assistant or teacher-librarian would manage the school library at either the primary or secondary level. Use of information technology is often not very high in these libraries at this time. Even if Internet access is offered to users, library automation or use of the Internet for library administration is to a large extent non-existent.

Special libraries buy to satisfy their niche clientele. These libraries have collections in a specific subject area like law, business, health, economics, government, etc. These libraries have varying levels of funding and can be a good market for publishers who cater to their needs. Often their requirement for very specific information related to the Caribbean is not met due to a dearth of local publications. Special libraries usually have at least one qualified professional. The level of implementation of information technology can vary widely, often depending on funding, and its use varies with the level of expertise of the library staff.

National and public libraries also have varied levels of funding. Usually, a technical services area with at least one professional librarian manages central purchasing for several branch libraries. This often calls for multiple copies of materials, so that to be cost effective, libraries may have to seek international publishers. The application of information technology varies widely from country to country, based on funding and the level of training of library staff. Internet access may be available but library automation is not always implemented. Directors of public libraries in countries with small economies sometimes have to share a computer with staff and may check e-mail once a week or so. One fact remains and it is that all Caribbean libraries buy Caribbean material. Caribbean materials can be defined as follows:

- books published within the Caribbean. (Caribbean origin)
- books on the Caribbean regardless of their origin. (Caribbean focus)
- literary works by Caribbean authors published outside the region. (Caribbean authorship) [Bandara 1994]

Caribbean librarians will buy from local bookstores, directly from local publishers as well as international publishers—wherever they find the material available.

There are a number of issues which affect what libraries purchase in the Caribbean. Librarians do not just buy books; they are building and developing collections. Many Caribbean libraries are trying to fill gaps in their collections. Thus, apart from the collection needs of the libraries, problems with selection, other major areas requiring further discussion are purchasing and bibliographic standards.

Some selection difficulties involve the fact that libraries must be aware of what is published in order to select for purchase. One major problem with selecting Caribbean library materials is that there are few reviews and regular title listings. Many, if not all, librarians want a review, a synopsis or even a title list of what is published locally. Librarians need reviews to justify publications. French Caribbean librarians claim to have money to purchase, but cannot identify what is available around the Caribbean. A professional approach would be to use catalogues, but it is acknowledged that producing one is costly for publishers.

Librarians have made attempts to strengthen the book industry by doing book review projects or producing extensive bibliographies. There was a project for a *Caribbean Books in Print* embarked upon in the 1990s. A *Caribbean Review of Books* was published 1991-1993 (Bandara 1994). There are national bibliographies being attempted in a few countries. However, these are irregular and often not quite up-to-date. There are several Caribbean Bibliographies in print and online, including Mitchell's West Indian Bibliography, which is posted on the Internet (Mitchell 2003).

With few reviews and abstracts, an actual physical assessment of the items is appreciated and, if possible, some librarians buy on the spot. For special collections, placing titles in the bookshops and notifying relevant librarians can work. Librarians appreciate visits to publisher houses to collect material that may not be available at the bookshops. Another way publishers can reach customers is to develop a selective dissemination activity similar to the ones that libraries use for their clientele. If publishers maintained profiles of libraries and their collection's, they can service the libraries better, and the profiles will give an idea of the subject areas, topics, even keywords for material which specific libraries and librarians need to build collections. Publishers may more easily come across titles that are in the process of being published and can assist librarians in filling gaps in their collections.

Also part of the selection process is the question of what is published. Audience-appropriate publications are needed. There is a need for local topics to be addressed in a simple manner; for example, with children books, where authenticity of illustrations and content is desired. Older readers may require large print formats. The Dutch Caribbean librarians feel neglected, as the scope of what is published is not always relevant to their users. Publishers usually know when there is little information on a subject; they can be pro-active and publish a work knowing that there is a captive market that will purchase it. Publishers have a role to play in stimulating writing as well. There are insufficient materials on the Caribbean by Caribbean people. This may be to a large extent because of a lack of self-appreciation among Caribbean people as a result of their Colonial past—a feeling that what they have to say is not worth documenting. Of course, Naipaul and similar writers who are held in high esteem discount this idea, but more books are needed that build self-esteem: more biographies, more books that put achievements by the Caribbean people on the world stage and show that they are comparable if not better in some areas. The mix of cultures and genes are the basis for their "Caribbeanness" and their achievements should be celebrated by being recorded. Publishers need to address the issue of out-of-print material, which is sorely needed by Caribbean libraries. One suggestion is small runs with more than one item. India, for example, produces cheaper formats for internal distribution. There is also a need for multimedia materials, *e.g.* talking books for the visually impaired.

Language is a very interesting aspect of selection. The Dutch Caribbean librarians want publishers in the English-speaking Caribbean to know that they speak and want materials in English. They would welcome promotional material, reviews and title listings in English. All librarians want translations into their own language and, probably, because of the dominance of English, some librarians in non-English-speaking territories want books in English.

There are several issues related to purchasing. Libraries, because of their funding and traditionally bureaucratic administration, tend to use purchase orders and not cash payments. If publishers are to capture this market they have to accommodate this type of purchasing. Some libraries with funding usually want to purchase all that is published on a specific listing or catalogue, so this should be facilitated via purchase order rather than having to obtain them singly.

Regarding purchasing power, recent monetary devaluations (as in the Dominican Republic) and other economic problems besieging Caribbean countries have affected libraries. Budget cuts mean that the more expensive science and other specialty books are priced out of the libraries reach. Libraries want library editions for limited budgets and discounts for purchasing multiple copies. For electronic material, libraries want better rates. The French Caribbean librarians want it noted that they have customs and foreign exchange problems, and if publishers can do more to minimise this, they would be appreciative.

Publishers' use of information technology by establishing websites or sending e-mails is useful, but many Caribbean librarians still prefer to order by regular mail. Libraries need prompt confirmation of orders. They need to know all the charges up front, that is, the actual cost of acquiring the items. They expect prompt shipping at the lowest cost, naturally. They require stable mailing and contact information for publishers. Libraries, in turn, can provide information by which they evaluate quotations. Such information can be posted on websites like the "Evaluation Criteria" page on Trinidad and Tobago's National Library and Information System Authority (NALIS) website (National Library and Information System Authority. 2003. Evaluation Criteria). Bibliographic issues involve standards for format, both physical and layout, yet many books published in the Caribbean do not conform to any standards. There may be a title and an author but no date, no information on the publisher or copyright. All librarians want better editorial and bibliographic standards in publications. Some suggestions for books are as follows:

Books must be physically suitable for library use (good paper and binding), should be user-friendly and should include the following information:

- Full title (A title page with basic information is acceptable)
- Imprint (Place of publication, publisher and date of publication)
- Copyright information—if more than one person is involved, that should be stated
- Publisher's address (especially important for small publishers in the region)
- International Standard Book Number (ISBN): An ISBN is a 10-digit code that identifies one title or edition of a title from one specific publisher and is unique to that title or edition. NALIS states that since 2003 it has become the ISBN agency for Trinidad and Tobago. The ISBN is mandatory and can be obtained through a process of registration and paying a processing fee for a block of numbers. These fees may be waived in appropriate circumstances.
- International Standard Serial Number (ISSN): An ISSN is an 8-digit code which identifies a serial publication, *i.e.* a publication issued in successive parts, having a common title and intended to be continued indefinitely (if applicable)
- Table of contents
- Numbered pages
- Index (if applicable)
- Series information (if applicable)
- Cataloguing in Publication (CIP)
- Software capabilities.

Books must generally conform to international standards.

Caribbean libraries are now purchasing more print materials that have non-book accompaniment and multimedia items, such as music CD-ROMs etc. Standards for this type of material maybe as follows:

- Names of the disc's artistes/author(s)
- If applicable, the instruments each artiste plays (we frequently see "J. Jones-all instruments" in the region; this is unacceptable)
- Universal Product Code (UPC): A unique thirteen-digit inventory tracking number assigned to a compact disc by the Uniform Code Council to allow tracking when sold commercially.
- Release number (usually an in-house code),
- The CD logo is mandatory, although many do not include it,
- The title
- Length
- Time of each track
- The name of the copyright agency *e.g.* COTT (Copyright Organisation Trinidad and Tobago).

Acknowledging that the relationship between publishers and librarians should be of mutual benefit, the following recommendations for collaboration are suggested. Publishers could partner with libraries, especially public and school libraries, to emphasise the importance of reading for personal and employment reasons.

Librarians should encourage publishers to support legal deposit activity. Legal deposit is the act of depositing published material in designated libraries or archives. Legal deposit legislation serves a clear national public policy interest by ensuring the acquisition, the recording, the preservation and the availability of a nation's published heritage. (National Library of Wales 2000). This tradition has been well instituted in developed countries since the 1500's. However, it has only recently been introduced to Caribbean countries and is extremely necessary for maintaining a record of who the Caribbean people are and their achievements.

One innovative idea for making librarians aware of what is published is to post a comprehensive website, such as the one under development by CAPNET, so that librarians can visit a central source to determine what books are being published.

Of course, it will be only as good as the publishers who support the venture. Even the list of publishers available on CAPNET's website is extremely useful. One librarian from Florida pointed out that they do not even know who the publishers are in the region, far less get access to their title lists.

Librarians should talk to publishers about what services they believe to be important to their users. Librarians can invite publishers to attend various library association meetings in the region and arrange "focus groups" with groups of librarians. These discussions are useful to librarians for learning about the issues for publishers, as well.

Librarians could encourage publishers to join library associations and exhibit at conferences like the annual ACURIL conferences and those of local library associations. This gives immediate exposure of titles to a ready market and an opportunity to network at the same time.

Users today are interested in having access to electronic full text publications. While this is especially true for journal titles, it is also important for monographs. While publishers may not want current list titles available in electronic full text form, they may consider making older texts available. Some libraries would be interested in working with publishers to digitise their works, thus making older, out of print works again available. Obviously, there are financial issues to consider. Libraries can work with publishers to digitise their materials in cooperative projects.

Librarians support all book promotion activities. Book launches held at libraries inform the librarians of what is published and provides an opportunity to celebrate reading and for networking. Providing information on writers, sponsoring writers' and librarians' awards, planning book fairs and debates are promotional activities, which can benefit all.

Acknowledging that reviews are expensive, library associations *e.g.* national and regional library associations may be able to assist by having training for librarians in "How to do Reviews." If the Associations produce newsletters or journals, they can publish reviews and the librarians would have benefited from continuing education, having acquired a new skill as well as have the required tools for selection purposes.

In conclusion, it should be stressed that, first and foremost, librarians and publishers should have a symbiotic relationship. This mutually beneficent relationship would be rewarding for all concerned as both can help each other achieve their objectives and should see each other as natural allies.

# 5

# Libraries after Civil War Period

This chapter describes how Lebanese librarian coped with the impact of the civil war (1975–1991), and their post–war efforts to rebuild the library infrastructure. Despite damage from bombing, triple–digit inflation, and staff shortages, many libraries functioned throughout the conflict. The American University of Beirut opened for business every day, although badly damaged, and is now moving vigorously to rebuild and renew services. Some new staff have been hired, and an archives department has been established. Automation is underway. Beirut University College, not severely damaged in the war, has taken up new projects, such as indexing of special collections and continuing education for librarians. At the Lebanese University, open only intermittently during the war, there is now a systematic approach to collection processing in the education faculty library. New initiatives are being taken also in the national archives, and by the Lebanese Library Association. Despite the serious impact of the war, the library community in Lebanon is focused on regeneration and progress.

Nineteen–seventy–five was a year of promise for librarianship in Lebanon. The Lebanese University was in the process of building a central library on its new integrated campus; a programme in library science was created at the Faculty of Information and Documentation of the Lebanese University, which was upgraded from the Institute of Information and Journalism; and the Lebanese Libraries Association (LLA) began publishing its Newsletter. It was also the year of the outbreak of the Lebanese Civil War. The tragic events of the decade and a half that followed severely disrupted the country's institutional life, and libraries were not spared. Bombardments damaged and destroyed library buildings and collections; triple–digit inflation effectively cut library budgets; widespread emigration led to a shortage of trained librarians. Despite these many difficulties, the Lebanese library community managed to sustain itself through the years of war, and now that peace has come to Lebanon, it is looking not only to rebuild what was lost, but also to move forward with new initiatives.

While the general conditions of the war were shared, each institution lived the war in its own way. It is instructive to see how they coped with war conditions, and what their plans are now in the postwar period. As an example of a university library one may look to the American University of Beirut (AUB). AUB was established in 1866. Its primary language of instruction is English, and it has a student body of approximately 5, 000. It has four libraries: main (Jafet Library), medical (Saab Library), Science and Agriculture, and Engineering and Architecture. With approximately half a million volumes, AUB is the largest library collection in the country.

According to Nawal Naamani, chief of circulation, the highest priority throughout the war was to keep all library functions operating at some level, even if at times very much reduced. The AUB libraries opened every day, regardless of conditions. Ms. Naamani recalls at times entering the stacks with a flashlight in order to retrieve books for students when the electricity did not work. She said also that in order to support the educational programme of the University (both coursework and research), maintaining acquisitions was a particularly high priority, especially in the sciences where it is vital for materials to be up to date. With mail service to Lebanon often cut for long periods, this was at times very difficult, but she feels that they were successful in their acquisitions programme and that there are now no serious gaps in the collections. Nevertheless, Ms. Naamani commented that it was often advantageous to receive offers of books or serials on exchange from foreign libraries making orders for microfilms of AUB theses or serials, as this enabled them to obtain books that they might have been unable to obtain in the past and which went out of print. Further complicating matters, the AUB libraries lost much of their staff during the war. According to Helen Bikhazi, university librarian, the staff of the AUB libraries now numbers 10 professional librarians and 52 support staff (excluding the medical school library), less than 60 percent of pre–1975 staffing levels.

In addition to serving its student body and faculty, the AUB libraries have also taken on a wider responsibility to the community at large. Already before the war AUB libraries were open to all those affiliated with an academic institution, whether Lebanese or foreign. This policy was maintained throughout the war, although it was necessary to discontinue borrowing privileges for non–AUB affiliates. (It was, however, sometimes difficult for non–AUB affiliates to gain entry to the AUB campus due to tight security.) This open–door library policy was particularly important in light of the fact that the bulk of the collections of the National Library were stolen in 1975.

This policy of maintaining full library services received a difficult test with the November 8, 1991, bomb that destroyed College Hall and seriously damaged Jafet Library, which was located directly behind it. Though none of the collections in the stacks were harmed, the reading room and other public services areas were destroyed, as well as many offices. Today the library operates in the middle of reconstruction, the noise a constant surrounding refrain. Reading rooms were set up in two nearby buildings, with a small reading room set up in Jafet Library for periodicals and non–circulating monographs. Circulation records had to be retrieved from the rubble and reconstructed, a time–consuming process. It is anticipated that the building will be completely finished within a year.

The characteristics of these collections make preservation a high priority. The manuscript collection is being microfilmed in its entirety, to avoid unnecessary handling by researchers, and to avoid any possibility of loss of these unique items. The microfilm lab at AUB is the only one in a library in Lebanon at the present, although commercial microfilming facilities exist. AUB has for that reason at times microfilmed materials for other libraries, in exchange for a copy of the microfilm. This practice has had to be curtailed, as some of the microfilming equipment was damaged in the 1991 bombing, making it necessary to concentrate on AUB needs. Beyond these microfilming projects, efforts are being made to see that materials are housed and stored under the proper conditions to ensure their long life.

Another AUB project in the planning stages is automation; an automation librarian has been hired for the purpose. The AUB libraries were planning for automation in 1988, but had to drop it from consideration due to the resumption of fighting during the constitutional crisis. Only the medical library underwent automation, as this was necessary for the AUB medical school to keep its accreditation. A major consideration in automation planning is the fact that the AUB libraries have considerable holdings in non–Roman script languages, with Arabic naturally being a particular priority.

Beirut University College (BUC) provides an example of a college library. BUC, formerly known as Beirut College for Women, was founded in 1924. Its language of instruction is English and it has a student body of approximately 4, 000. BUC is primarily an undergraduate institution, but it does have several master's programmes. The programmes in education, business, and arts are particular areas of strength for BUC. BUC also has a library science programme administered by library staff. BUC is served by the Stoltzfus Library, whose collections are primarily in English. Stoltzfus Library contains two special collections of note: its Documentation Centre of the Institute for Women's Studies in the Arab World, and its Children's Library. The former contains books and serials in women's studies, as well as clippings files. The Children's Library serves both as a forum for projects of BUC's education students and as a public library for children. During the summer, the library is used in conjunction with a summer camp programme for children sponsored by BUC.

While the Stoltzfus Library did suffer a hit in 1983, there was only minor damage to the building and collections. BUC's major problem during the war was budget freezes. There was therefore a very careful attempt to work with faculty to assure that the book budget was allocated as wisely as possible. Department chairs give approval to book selections, while the library director, Aida Naaman, stays abreast of the literature in order to advise the faculty of available titles. Gifts have unfortunately not been a very important component in the library's collection building. While gifts of books relevant to the BUC academic programme and published in the past decade are very much welcomed, gifts have tended to be of older books. Gifts not retained are passed to the BUC branch in Saida, as its library is still in the early stages of collection building. Aida Hajjar, the acquisitions assistant, pointed out that computer books, to support BUC's new master's programme in computer science, are particularly costly and must be acquired by purchase. Art books represent another expensive acquisitions area.

With a small staff of seven, of which two are professional librarians, allocating staff resources is also an important consideration. The UC library has made judicious use of student talent to provide additional services. Student projects in the library science programme, for example are oriented to be not only instructive, but also of benefit to the library, and thereby the BUC community. For example, library students have created comprehensive catalogues of the library's periodicals and audiovisual materials. A library student prepared an index to the collection's theatre periodicals, of use to BUC's active theater programme. Non–library students have enriched the library as well, for example by creating clippings files for the Women's Studies Documentation Centre.

Despite the constraints on their time, the staff of the BUC library have devoted efforts to the promotion of librarianship in Lebanon. Aida Naaman explained that BUC has a strong tradition of service to the community, and that the library has a commitment to contributing to these activities. For example, library staff periodically conduct short courses in library education. This past summer, they conducted a cataloguing workshop for children's librarians under the auspices of the Red Cross. The previous summer, two workshops were held with open admission, one on general library services, and one on record–keeping for archives. The case of the library of the School of Education of the Lebanese University is an example of a university faculty library. The Lebanese University was founded in 1953 by the Lebanese government; its language of instruction is Arabic. The University has no central library; each faculty (department) has its own facility. The library of the School of Education was formerly the largest of these faculty libraries, with approximately 40, 000 volumes. In 1982, during the Israeli invasion of Lebanon, the library was destroyed by fire and its entire collection was lost. As soon as was possible, two professors were sent to Egypt and France to buy books for a core collection, and in 1984 the Library was re–established in another building. The library now occupies two rooms, one for monographs and one for periodicals.

There are two more rooms available for the library when there is a need to expand. The librarian, Maha Shehade, explained that the library unfortunately was only able to open intermittently during the war, making it difficult to proceed with collection processing. Now that the library is open on a regular basis, it is possible to approach collection processing in a systematic manner. The library's collections now number approximately 10, 000 volumes. These books are supplied to the library by the administration of the Faculty of Education, either purchased by the administration on the request of faculty or received as gifts; library staff are not involved in acquisitions activities.

It is hoped that now that the faculty has resumed its publications programme, the library will receive more publications on exchange. Books are registered by staff on arrival, and are shelved by accession number. There are subject listings, but as these are out of date, students require the assistance of library staff to locate the books they need. A cataloguing and automation project is now underway, using a personal computer supplied by the faculty and CDS/ISIS software provided by the Arab League. Descriptive cataloguing is done in Arabic or Roman script, depending on the language of the work, with subject access provided via keyword descriptors in French taken from UNESCO's Education Thesaurus and the

French index of the Arab League's trilingual thesaurus, JAMIA. Hala Zein El–Abidin, the library's cataloger, explained that initially it had been intended to classify according to the Dewey system. It was later decided to retain the accessions number as the call number, at least for the time being, as she was the only staff member trained in classification and that doing classification would slow down the work flow.

As the collection was completely uncataloged, it was felt that it was more important to proceed with cataloguing as quickly as possible. It is anticipated that the cataloguing project will be completed in two to three years. As the cataloguing project proceeds, paper indexes will periodically be generated from the database. Eventually it is hoped that it will be possible to provide online access to the database by students.

Libraries in educational institutions are not the only ones where new initiatives are being taken. A case in point is the Lebanese National Archives Centre. The archives were created in 1978 to serve as a repository for the documents of all Lebanese government institutions. According to Riad Tabbarah, head of the archives' board of directors (and dean of the Faculty of Health Sciences at AUB), the collection of government documents was systematic until 1982. At that time, the war conditions brought a halt to all regular operations. What began then was the second stage of the center's life, with the salvage by archives staff of materials from government buildings. This included 40 paintings of the 19th–century formerly hung in the National Library, as well as the remaining manuscripts from the National Library's collections.

The archives also received gifts, such as the 5, 000 slides of the historic Lebanese postcard collection compiled by Fouad Debbas, deposited as insurance against the possible destruction of the collection of postcards. The archives now house such items as a collection of 16mm Pathe–Gaumont newsreels of Lebanon, and a collection of first issues of the world Arabic press, among other materials.

The archives are now entering into a third stage of their existence. Early in 1993, a board of directors was created to oversee the future of the archives. Their focus has been on the preservation of the collections. The first step, now underway, is to catalogue and rehouse the materials. Some restoration work was done right away; for example, a Lebanese artist undertook the repairs of paintings that had been slashed. In the main, however, the work so far has been to assure the short–term security of the collections. As that is well in hand, the next step is to address the long–term preservation issues. Of particular concern are the audiovisual materials, which pose special long–term preservation problems. The regular government documents collections of the archives also need attention. Segments of the collection have already been microfilmed, but some of this microfilm is not legible and needs to be redone.

Possible cooperation with institutions outside of Lebanon to preserve the archives collection is being explored. Dr. Tabbarah pointed out that cooperation is being sought both in the area of technical assistance and of funding. At the same time, an effort is being made to raise public awareness in Lebanon of these collections; an exhibition containing a selection of the archives' collections was therefore planned for November 1993 to bring attention to the archives' materials.

The Lebanese Library Association (LLA), which had been dormant for a long period during the war, is also undergoing a revival. Its main project at present is a survey of Lebanese libraries, documentation centres, and archives, which will be published. According to Linda Sadaka, secretary of the LLA and head of the gifts and exchange section of AUB's Jafet Library, the goal is to get a picture of the state of Lebanese libraries, as a base for planning. The original impetus for the survey was a request by UNESCO to LLA for information on the Lebanese library situation in order to evaluate requests for grants by certain libraries in Lebanon. The data collection has been carried out largely by students of the Faculty of Information and Documentation of the Lebanese University, and the project has been financed by UNESCO.

While clearly the war has had a serious negative impact on librarianship in Lebanon, the focus in the library community is on regeneration and progress. It is to be hoped that the situation in Lebanon will remain stable to allow long–term planning to be done.

### The Professional Situation of Librarians in the Rio de la Plata Area

This is the report of a survey, completed in 1991, of librarians in Argentina and Uruguay. Of the 57 persons who replied to a questionnaire, 17 were from Montevideo, the others from various cities in Argentina. The Uruguayans noted that there is full employment for librarians, but that salaries are so low that many professionals need to hold more than one job. Many important positions, for example in the state libraries, have gone unfilled; and smaller libraries do not have any professional staff. Funds for acquisition of materials are inadequate across the Uruguay. There is a lack of governmental interest in libraries— in part because librarians have not been good exponents of their needs — and no national library policy.

In Argentina the salary situation is similar, and librarians often hold several jobs. There is little interest in professional associations and indeed wide discouragement over the dim prospects of libraries. Resources are seen to be inadequate, and there is no national sense of the importance of libraries.

Why was librarianship chosen as a career? The main reason seems to have been shortage of other professional opportunities; but other reasons given were the love of books and a vocation to service. Despite the problems of the library profession, most respondents said they do advise students to become librarians.

The principal satisfaction of library work is said to be the interaction with users. There is also interest in computerization and networking, although not much progress has been made. Library schools are in the process of introducing computer applications, but there remains a traditional emphasis (for example on preparation of catalogue cards) in the programmes. Continuing education for librarians is scarce, and there is not much attendance at international conferences where new technologies are exhibited and discussed. In general, the survey results paint a dark picture of the professional situation in Rio de la Plata. One encouraging sign is the possibility of recognition of librarians as professionals, through legislation being considered by the Argentine parliament. Efforts to have similar legislation enacted in Uruguay have so far met with no success.

## The Effects of the Structural Adjustment Programme on Nigerian Public Libraries

Like many developing countries, Nigeria is engaged in a structural adjustment programme (SAP): a set of economic reform measures designed to achieve recovery and growth. The availability of foreign aid is often linked to progress in a nation's SAP. Nigeria embarked on SAP in 1986, emphasizing domestic production over expensive imports, and a lesser dependence on oil revenues. The government was also committed to reduce expenditures and to stop wasteful spending, and the country's external debt obligations were rescheduled insofar as possible. A balanced budget was sought, and foreign capital investment was pursued. Since Nigerian public libraries are supported by government, they are facing serious financial problems in this period of national retrenchment. But the effects are not all negative.

SAP has definitely brought benefits to the national economy. Libraries have seen a number of favourable impacts:

- Foreign exchange is facilitated;
- Systematic collection development is encouraged;
- Local publishers are supported;
- Greater use of public libraries as rising costs make book purchases by individuals more difficult;
- Use of Nigerian library schools for staff development, saving the costs of overseas training;
- Enhanced interest among librarians in the advantages of interlibrary cooperation and lending; and,
- Greater efforts to secure books through the generosity of such organizations as the Ranfurly Library Services and British Council.

There are also serious negative effects of SAP on public libraries:

- Large price increases for essential services and for books and other materials (up to 400% between 1985 and 1987; a greater percentage of increase since 1987);

- Government appropriations for public libraries have risen very slightly, or actually fallen, since SAP began; for example the subvention to Imo State Library Board experienced a real–currency decline of about 70% in appropriations between 1984 and 1992;
- Building projects have been delayed or cancelled;
- Maintenance of facilities is minimal;
- Binding of newspapers and journals has been abandoned by most libraries;
- Theft and mutilation of materials have increased, as a result of costs too high for individual purchases; and,
- Vacant positions have been left unfilled.

To librarians — and, it appears, to the rest of the Nigerian people (except for the wealthy class) — SAP is proving to be a hardship. Inflation consumes the small salaries that most people earn. Crime, disease, strikes and lockouts, and widespread hunger are the signs of failure in SAP. At the very least, the government ought to remove the import duties on books and other library requirements, so that some flow of materials can resume. It would not involve too great a cost to increase maintenance of library facilities. Key vacancies ought to be unfrozen. Library managers also have the responsibility of finding ways to save money, by seeking supplementary ways to acquire materials.

## Information Seeking Habits of Nigerian Agricultural Scientists

Agricultural research began in Nigeria about 100 years ago, and there has been a steady rise in its output. The country has two universities of agriculture, 20 schools or faculties of agriculture in general universities, and 16 agricultural research institutes. In order to give optimal service to researchers in agriculture, libraries need to know how they use information in their work. The present study attempted to gather some facts by means of a questionnaire sent to seven universities, of which six provided usable responses. Of 205 questionnaires mailed, 82 were returned (45.6 percent). Although the survey dealt with a number of professional activities, such as teaching, only the results that relate directly to research are reported here.

Nearly all the respondents (96.3 percent) were active researchers. With one exception, they stated that their institutional library was the first port of call as they initiated new projects. Contact with colleagues was also a typical step: fellow scientists were involved in the review of research carried out by 87.8 percent of the respondents. Favoured materials in the library were (in order of reported use): journals, dissertations and theses, technical reports, conference proceedings, monographs, abstract/index services, and bibliographies. It is encouraging that 75.6 percent of the scientists stated that the reference librarian was a significant assistant in locating information. As in earlier studies of scientific research behaviour, the use of personal files was also prominent, cited by 74.4 percent of the respondents. Only 34.1 percent reported use of current awareness services — which are not offered by most libraries. Microprint files were also used less than might be expected (24.4 percent of the respondents), considering that they contain important journal files and much of the technical report literature, but in Nigerian libraries the reading equipment is often non–functional. Computer software, CD–ROMs and other electronic resources are generally not available in Nigerian universities.

To recommend the addition of costly equipment is not realistic in view of the depressed economy of the country. But librarians could enhance current awareness activities without incurring major new costs. Another inexpensive aid to researchers would be to offer them convenient facilities for the discussions with their colleagues that are so important in their work. Above all, since they do appear high on the list of resources used by the scientists, reference librarians should intensify their own preparation to deal with literature searches and factual inquiries.

## Library History in India: Historiographical Assessment and Current Trends

The study of library history, for a long time the province of antiquarians, has grown into a distinct field with distinguished authors, especially in the past quarter century or so. The founding of groups for those interested in the history of libraries within national professional associations was crowned by the establishment within IFLA of the Round Table on Library History in the late 1970s. By that time, several journals had begun to assume significance for the field, and since 1973 the *Annual Bibliography of the History of the Printed Book and Libraries* has appeared.

The proceedings of the international symposium, "Library History Research in the International Context, " held in Wolfenbuttel, Germany, in April 1988, marked yet another benchmark on the road toward sophistication in the study of library history. Survey reports on the status of library history research were presented by scholars from 13 nations representing four continents. Though not all the news was uniformly encouraging, in general the participants and the readers of the printed text felt that there was hope for the future. One of the conspicuous omissions from the 1988 Symposium was a report on the status of library history in India — a nation known for its ancient and medieval, as well as more modern, library establishment. Although the history and tradition of literacy and books among certain classes in what is now India is long–standing, the modern library movement has roots in the later 18th century with real growth appearing a century or more later. Programmes for professional library education developed in the principal centres of Madras in the 1930s and Bombay, Calcutta, and Delhi in the 1940s, with others following during the 1960s. A number of relatively short surveys and monographic works dealing with Indian library history have treated various chronological periods, types of libraries, geographical areas, or a mix of these. Since the tradition is so rich, the library education programmes relatively strong, and the interest in pursuing national cultural history keen, questions that recur to the student of library history are: What is the status of library history in India? How can this be explained? What might the future hold?

One of the authors of the present article, Donald G. Davis, Jr., undertook a systematic overview of the situation in India during a five–week research tour in the summer of 1988 sponsored by the American Institute of Indian Studies. The project "aimed to study the current status of library history in India by cursorily reviewing the existing [English–language] bibliography, by surveying present activities, and by describing and evaluating the findings from an international and sympathetic point of view ". In addition to long stays in Calcutta at the National Library of India and in Delhi, the tour encompassed visits and interviews at eight library schools and nine other institutional libraries. The report that resulted was widely distributed in the following two years.

The findings of the survey included description of the literature, the historians, the organization structure, and the general attitude toward library history within the profession. The literature survey enumerated works written primarily as history, rather than description, and accounted for fewer than 100 significant monographs, dissertations, scholarly articles, chapters in collected works, and whole volumes of collected papers. These publications constitute a core bibliography for the field. Strengths include the public library movement, Muslim influence, the national library, and library associations; weaknesses include academic libraries, private libraries, library education, and comparative studies.

In library history, about a dozen persons were identified as productive researchers and writers. Several are in retirement, continuing their research after leaving professional employment; as these cease their labours, the profession will sustain a great loss. On the other hand, there is a good group of widely–scattered, younger historians who are just beginning to assume the responsibility of continuing the work of interpreting the profession to its society in historical terms; some of these live outside India.

The organization structure of research in library history is diffuse, with the best collection of printed materials at the National Library of India. Programmes in library and information science have not given much attention to library history; and even on the doctoral level, most of the dissertations that have appeared have been done in other departments or overseas. There are no identifiable groups that bring persons interested in library history together and not many conferences on the subject. The few historically-oriented articles that are produced appear in the general professional journals, or, more likely, in scholarly journals published abroad.

The general attitude of library historians seems to be discouragement. The elder scholars as well as their junior colleagues usually work in isolation, sometimes with academic colleagues in historical or literary studies. They see little professional recognition for historical research from their fellow librarians, despite the rich sources for explicating the role of libraries and information in the complex culture of a developing nation. •

The survey concluded that despite the pessimism regarding the future of historical studies in librarianship, the outlook for the future is not without hope. The challenge of the coming years will be to find agreement about the nature of the unfinished agenda. Two questions are critical: First, is library history a luxury for a few aberrant and typically elderly members of the profession; or is it a topic that the whole profession, or a significant portion of it, can embrace with pride and enthusiasm? Second, is library history only the province of nations heavily influenced by the West, or it a mark of a maturing profession in any nation that is coming to grips with its role in the cultural life of the country and contributing its part to that cultural record?

Some possible steps envisioned for the future included formation of regional interest groups under the aegis of the Indian Library Association, regular programme meetings, an informal newsletter, occasional publications, and development of a model syllabus for library education programmes. Mention was even made of programmes at the forthcoming IFLA conference in 1992.

Essentially, little has changed since 1988. Yet there is evidence for hope. Some of the younger library historians are completing their doctoral degrees and have published their results. They need to be encouraged and to communicate more regularly with one another. Another major achievement is the splendid, two–volume compilation, *Humanities Information Systems and Centres* (1991), that presents capsule descriptions of 66 specialized institutions in the fields of cultural studies, many of them being archives or rare book repositories. Most of the entries, many prepared by scholars who might form a nucleus of a library history network, contain substantial historical notes on the founding and development of the institutions and their libraries.

The identification of potential research topics and subjects for investigation is a role that library historians can play in their profession. And when contemporary problems manifest themselves, historians can examine the evidence and help to explain their context, offering some insight into possible solutions and alternative courses of action. In the case of India, libraries represent all of the various types known to the human race, including those of the most advanced countries. Yet one must acknowledge that some outstanding examples may serve only as exceptions to the prevailing low status of libraries, and that fine looking organization charts and statistical tables do not always provide a clear picture of what the real situation is at the grassroots level.

Among the many potential contemporary topics that might invite the attention of Indian library historians are the underdeveloped state of public libraries, the lack of genuine library consciousness in the library community, and the role of the profession.

On paper India appears to have a well–organized, functioning system of public libraries that attempt to supply the reading needs of all its citizens. In reality, the condition of most public libraries, large or small, urban or rural, city or village, is exceedingly poor. In fact, a case could be easily made that with few exceptions, genuine public libraries worthy of the name are yet to be established. Modern public libraries that are user–centred, service–oriented, and collection–balanced centres for graphic records are still in the future. The reasons for this extremely slow development, despite efforts in the early 20th century to approximate the kind of service available in Europe and North America, are surely worth exploring.

While the effects of domination by colonial powers, primarily the British, may have produced a lack of concern for the vernacular–speaking and reading populace, local and more recent decisions about priorities are certainly involved as well. Comparative studies of individual states has only begun.

The issue of library and information consciousness in the nation is relevant here. One could receive the impression that a commitment to the value of reading, information, and libraries is not high among professional librarians and sponsoring agencies. Some in the library establishment are convinced that the government is interested in libraries and literacy on only a marginal level. Though individual states differ greatly in their provision of library service, a prevalent idea seems to be that passing library legislation by itself will result in great advances, whereas funding and implementation have frequently failed to support legislation. Studies examining the comparative effect of library legislation in various states could yield some fruitful insights that might provide guidance to future efforts.

Another issue for investigation is the role of the Indian library profession. Judged on its past, the Indian library establishment has been unable to mount an effective effort to achieve some short–term and medium–term goals with respect to library development. The tension between the specialized libraries connected with government agencies and the commercial sector, and public libraries and libraries associated with educational institutions, has been one reason for the lack of success. The historian can examine actions taken, and not taken, by library associations to discover their impact on library progress. One persistent problem has been the creation of professional standards. Another has related to the proper duties and responsibilities of librarians. In his 1987 presidential address to the Indian Library Association, T. S. Rajgopalan rightly remarked:

It is generally acknowledged that our libraries are underutilized in relation to investments being made in them. Non--use and low–use of libraries amount to wastage of facilities being made available. Maybe the literacy rate, lack of reading habits, etc., are the causes for low use from the side of patrons...User education programmes must be organized by libraries in a way that libraries are fully utilized. If library historians would address the roots and trends of library use issues, they would provide a valuable service to their profession and society.

With the centenary of S. R. Ranganathan's birth in 1992, it is an appropriate occasion to reconsider the expression of opinion that he offered in a radio talk in April 1956:

An account of the libraries in the first four periods (the Vedic, the Buddhistic, the Medieval, and the Muslim) must necessarily depend upon the historical research. This has not yet been done. The library profession is too small in India to spare a person to fill up this antiquarian gap. Those trained in the scientific method of tracing history are too preoccupied with dynastic and political history to spare sufficient time for cultural history in general and library history in particular. This statement no doubt reflects the feeling of many colleagues from India, but is it not possible now to fill the "antiquarian gap" in a way that will benefit librarians and those they serve?

**Libraries**

Northwestern University maintains an extensive library system to support its programmes of study and research. This system includes the University Library and a number of special libraries on the Evanston and Chicago campuses. The library holdings constitute a collection of approximately 4.3 million volumes, 4.2 million microfilms, and over 39, 000 currently received journals and other serial publications. Special libraries primarily serve the schools or departments they are associated with and are open to all Northwestern Students. Because of the quality and extent of its holdings, the Northwestern University library system ranks tenth among the nation's private universities.

**University Library**

The University Library offers excellent facilities for graduate study and postdoctoral research. Numerous subject specialists are available to help locate specific research resources. The main library and the adjoining Charles Deering Library contain the Evanston campus collections in the humanities, history, and the social sciences.

### Use of the Library

The University Library is open to students, faculty, and staff of Northwestern University. Guides to the library, copies of the regulations governing use of the library, and the library's lending policy are available at the Circulation, Information Commons, and Reference desks. The WildCARD identification card issued by the University to students, faculty, and staff serves as a library card and must be displayed for entrance to the library during nights and weekends. The Reference Department provides many services to graduate students, including individualized instruction in research methods and assistance in locating print and electronic resources needed for research. Staff members offer special library tours for graduate students each fall. Schedules of these tours are available in the library and in the various department offices. Graduate students may apply at Circulation Services for carrels in the research towers. A limited number of closed studies are available to advanced graduate students. Many other departments offer services to students. The Government Publications and Maps Department has extensive collections of federal, state, and international documents, as well as social science statistical data sets. There is a permanent reserve collection — the 36, 000-volume Core-Reserve — which consists of key books in each discipline taught at the University. The Interlibrary Loan Department makes available books and materials from research libraries in the United States and other countries. The University Library also features MediaWorks, a student multimedia lab, the Marjorie Iglow Mitchell Multimedia Centre, and Digital Media Services. The Curriculum Collection, containing teaching aids and related materials, targets those interested in the field of education.

### Art Collection

Located in the Deering Library, the Art Collection contains books and journals in art, architecture, design, and related visual arts. Collection strengths include nineteenth-and twentieth-century Western art and architectural serials.

**Charles Deering McCormick Library of Special Collections**

The special collections include 225, 000 volumes of first, limited, or special editions and other rare and valuable material. The major collecting areas are nineteenth-and twentieth-century political movements, underground newspapers, the Women's Collection, and the modern movement in American and English literature.

**Galter Health Sciences Library**

The Galter Health Sciences Library on the Chicago campus includes approximately 277, 000 volumes and more than 3, 000 current serials in print and electronic formats. The Galter Library serves the educational, patient care, and research information needs of the faculty, staff, students, and alumni of the Feinberg School of Medicine and the McGaw Medical Centre institutions. Consequently, the collection focuses on basic science, clinical science, physical therapy, prosthetics and orthotics, public health, genetic counselling, clinical psychology and clinical investigation information resources. The Galter Library also has a large and varied collection of historical materials dating back to the 15th century related to these subjects. The library's Health SmartLibrary service allows users to personalize and customize resources to meet their personal and professional information needs.

**Joseph Schaffner Library**

The Joseph Schaffner Library, located on the Chicago campus (Wieboldt Hall, second floor), is chiefly an electronic library. It serves primarily the School of Continuing Studies and the evening Managers' Programme of the Kellogg School of Management and the Medill School of Journalism graduate programme.

**Melville J. Herskovits Library of African Studies**

A rich resource of approximately 275, 000 volumes, plus 15, 000 books in over 300 African languages, 2, 800 current journals, documents, posters, videos, photographs, rare books, and other materials on every aspect of Africa.

**Music Library**

The Music Library, recognized internationally for its collection of contemporary art music, is one of the country's finest academic music libraries. The library holds approximately 250, 000 volumes of books, scores, sound recordings, journals, and rare materials and provides access to numerous online resources. The facility, located on the second floor of Deering Library, also includes the Listening Centre, which holds the library's collection of sound recordings, and a computer lab equipped to support a variety of interests in music technology.

The Music Library's special collections contain many rarc publications and primary documents, including the archives of composer John Cage, conductor Fritz Reiner, and thc publishing firm Ricordi.

**Pritzker Legal Research Centre**

The Pritzker Legal Research Centre, located on the Chicago campus, serves the information and research needs of the faculty and students of the Law School and Northwestern community. The fourteenth largest law school library in the United States, with more than 550, 000 volumes, it has research-level collections in Anglo-American and international law.

Its foreign law collections, are strongest for European law, and its comparative law collections are supplemented by collections for ancient, medieval, Roman, canon, Islamic, and Jewish law. The Pritzker Legal Research Centre provides patrons access to a wide range of electronic resources for Anglo-American, international, and comparative law and the services that make its print and electronic information resources accessible to faculty and students.

**Seeley G. Mudd Library for Science and Engineering**

The Seeley G. Mudd Library (SEL) for Science and Engineering holdings include the principal publications in applied mathematics, astronomy, biochemistry, biology, chemistry, computer science, engineering, and physics. SEL branch libraries — The Geological Sciences Library, in Locy Hall, and the Mathematics and Statistics Library, in Lunt Hall— house additional science collections. Transportation

Library. The Transportation Library, founded in 1956, is one of the nation's largest transportation collections. It specializes in the socioeconomic and operational aspects of all modes of transport. It also has a major collection of materials on law enforcement and police administration, and a large collection of federal environmental impact statements.

### United Library of Garrett-Evangelical and Seabury-Western Theological Seminaries

Located on Northwestern's Evanston campus, the United Library's collection of 325, 000 volumes and 1, 800 periodicals is rich in biblical studies, patristics, Christian art, ancient Near Eastern studies, archaeology, church history, American denominationalism, pietism, Christian education, African-American theological studies, women's studies, Anglicana, and Methodistica.

### Centre for Research Libraries

Northwestern holds membership in the Centre for Research Libraries (CRL), located in Chicago. The Centre operates a cooperative library for less-used but important research materials available to Northwestern students and faculty through interlibrary loan. Detailed guides to the collections are located at the Reference Desk of the University Library.

### Chicago Libraries

Northwestern University has an advantageous location for library resources. The Chicago area is one of the country's most concentrated library centres.

Among the libraries of scholarly interest in Chicago are the Newberry Library, outstanding in Continental, English, and American history and literature, as well as philology, music, and the history of printing; the University of Illinois at Chicago Library; the library system of the University of Chicago; and the libraries of the Family Institute, the Chicago Historical Society, the Art Institute of Chicago, and the Field Museum of Natural History. Students should consult the Reference Department of the University Library about qualifications needed for use of special libraries.

# 6

# Special Libraries

## INTRODUCTION

Although there has been much discussion recently about Cuban libraries, it is quite likely that only a few of the participants have any real knowledge of the subject beyond a passing familiarity with the public libraries they may have encountered during sightseeing tours in Havana, or hasty excursions into the provinces. But the world of information science and librarianship is not limited to this single aspect of library activity. Special libraries, teaching libraries, information centres, and the professionals who staff them are essential components of the professional life of our country, and important providers of information for the scientific, technical, and cultural development of Cuba. Even under the colonial rule of Spain during the eighteenth, nineteenth, and twentieth centuries, Cuba began to see the formation of institutions which, in one way or another, were concerned with education and learning.

The dominant social class, the *criollos*, had access to important institutions such as the University of Havana, the *Sociedad Economica de Amigos del Pais*, the National Archives, and the Academies of Science, Liberal Arts, and History, and were able to use the information these institutions provided to help shape the era, to put down roots, and to establish a tradition of improving Cuban society through knowledge and education.

One can name hundreds of illustrious physicians, engineers, architects, writers, and artists whose work helped shape the Cuban national character and identity, in which science, technology, and intellectual curiosity and creativity all play an important role.

## EARLY SOURCES OF INFORMATION

During the pre-Revolutionary era, the Lyceum Lawn Tennis Club, a well-known and prestigious women's cultural society with an advanced social agenda, was a pioneering institution in the field of library studies in Cuba, and virtually the only public library in our country at that time which made use of modern technical and professional advances.

The professional Colleges of Medicine, Engineering, and Architecture provided their students, faculties, and educational affiliates with access to information resources, in one form or another. The thirteen schools within the University of Havana had their own bibliographic resources, some organized as traditional library collections, others accessed by students and teachers in different ways. The University's Central Library became the home of the first university-level library school in Cuba. In other areas, the Association of Cuban Sugar Workers (*Asociacion de Tecnicos Azucareros de Cuba*) maintained an excellent library which specialized in resources dealing with the sugar industry. Although the library's fine collection of journals on the subject was particularly noteworthy, its professional library staff was inadequate

From its founding in 1902, the National Library of Cuba began its fifty-six year-long pilgrimage in search of a home through garrisons and barracks The second half of the twentieth century saw the founding of universities in Oriente Province, with a main campus in Santiago de Cuba; and the Central University of Santa Clara (now called Villa Clara), each with its respective libraries organized by well-trained and respected professionals of that era.

## THE REVOLUTIONARY PERIOD

Revolutionary activity affected all aspects of Cuba's social, economic, and scientific life, producing profound changes, and in some cases, a sudden new birth. The outcome was the reorganization and growth of the national government bureaucracy, and an expansion of its functions

In order to provide each sector of social, economic, and political activity with the necessary attention, the government institutions, organizations, and ministries of state responsible for implementing the policies and programmes outlined in such fundamental documents of the Revolution as "History will absolve me" were either newly-established, or re-structured.

In order to implement the vast political, social and cultural movement authorized by the Agrarian Reform Law (*Ley de Reforma Agraria*), the National Institute for Agrarian Reform (INRA) was formed. The creation of the National Institute for Urban Reform (*Instituto Nacional de la Reforma Urbana*) resulted from the need to confront new challenges and changes in housing. In order to deal with changes in, and to implement new directions for, the economy, the Central Planning Council (*Junta Central de Planificacion* or JUCEPLAN) was established, as well as the National Bank of Cuba (today known as the Central Bank of the Republic of Cuba), the Ministry of Finance (*Ministerio de Hacienda*), and the newly formed Ministry of Industry. The need for hydraulic development gave rise to the National Institute for Hydraulic Resources (*Instituto Nacional de los Recursos Hidraulicos*).

The former Ministry of Health (*Ministerio de Salubridad*) became the new Ministry of Public Health (*Ministerio de la Salud Publica*), organized around an entirely different concept, ideology, and agenda, in order to comply with the mandate of Moncada to make the health of the nation a top priority.

Educational reform on all levels of instruction, including the literacy campaign of 1961, became the responsibility of a totally re-structured Ministry of Education, a government department whose reputation under the former "pseudo-republic" had been completely eroded, and whose effectiveness had ultimately been weakened by the loss of status and respect. Some years later, the Ministry of Higher Education was organized to deal with the growth, development and specific needs of the university educational system, all of which resulted from the greatly increased access of the public to the universities, and from all of the scientific, technical and cultural development they were producing.

Radio and television would take a new direction under the aegis of the Cuban Institute for Radio and Television (ICRT), while the almost non-existent production of Cuban cinema was addressed by the Cuban Institute for the Cinematic Arts and Industry (INCAIC).

The need to provide recreation and entertainment for the general public through sports, and to channel the abilities of numerous men and women athletes (who performed in many cases under all types of pressures, and without any official sponsorship during the "pseudo-republic") led to the creation of INDER, the National Institute of Sports and Recreation; while the National Institute of Tourism (formerly INIT, now INTUR) began to focus on national tourism for the Cuban people, and then turned its attention to developing international tourism, some of the earliest clients of which were Canadian visitors.

The guardianship and development of the country's cultural values were the responsibilities of the National Culture Council, which, due to a sharp increase in, and broadening of, its functions, was reorganized as the Ministry of Culture in 1977. At this time, the groundwork was laid for the establishment of various councils and institutes that currently nurture and promote the coordinated development of artistic expression in the country. Very soon it became apparent that in order to realize these transformations, it was necessary to have access to information and a knowledge of the rhythm and level of development in the areas of science, technology, and culture in the modern world. In other words, along with all of this political change arose the need and the quest for information.

In their need to implement all of the aforementioned changes, to carry out founding decrees, organizational regulations, and calculations of staff and office space, those institutions—which today are Cuban state institutions—were pulling books off the shelves of refurbished libraries, searching for bibliography, titles of books and journals, and of course, new forms of processing and acquisition.

The fervour of all the revolutionary changes that were occurring also brought about the establishment of the

JUCEPLAN Library; the Centre for Agricultural Information (*Centro de Documentacion e Informacion para la Agricultura*, or CIDA); the library of the Ministry of Foreign Trade (*Ministerio del Comercio Exterior*, or MINCEX); the library of the National Bank of Cuba; the Information Services Centre for Medicine; the library of the Public Works Ministry (known at that time as the Ministry of Construction); the information centre for the Ministry of Foreign Relations (*Ministerio de Relaciones Exteriores*, or MINREX); the INIT (National Institute of Tourism, now INTUR) Information Centre; the INRA library; and the library of the Ministry of Industry. The latter enjoyed the support of one of the figures of the Cuban Revolution most concerned with the value of the book as a source of information, and with the library as a centre of scientific and technical study and discovery, namely Commander Ernesto Che Guevara.

For the first time, we librarians could sit down around a table to analyze the concrete reality of the need for development by trained experts, for the development of library collections, construction of shelving, placement of lights and location of store rooms, and a new emphasis on the formation of trained staff in terms of quality as well as quantity.

Quickly we realized the need to systematize all of these independently conceived efforts and projects, and to coordinate them, in order to achieve our proposed objectives.

## Science and Technology: IDICT

On April 19, 1963, by the authority of Law No. 1107 of the Council of Ministries, the Institute for Scientific and Technical Information—IDICT—was created as a subsidiary of the Cuban Academy of Sciences, which had celebrated its fortieth anniversary, just a few weeks earlier. This legislation called for an Advisory Council made up of representatives of the libraries and information centres of many of the organizations previously mentioned: The Jose Marti National Library; JUCEPLAN; the Ministries of Industry, Public Works, Public Health, Foreign Trade, and Transportation; and INRA. Other libraries and information centres were added to the initial membership throughout the formative stage of this project. Among the earliest advisory reports on developing scientific information in Cuba were those of the Indian professor, Pitiri Kawla, who consulted with the Central Library of the Jose Antonio Echeverria University City (CUJAE), today called the Jose Antonio Echeverria Polytechnic Institute (IPSJAE), and the Soviet specialist from UNESCO, Mijail Kiyaev. We began to hear a c ompletely different language. We were introduced to the idea that scientific and technical publications were considered obsolete five years after publication. These new standards for scientific information were a bit strange to us, having at that point already been mired in the underdevelopment produced by the embargo, where it often took us five years to find out that a certain book even existed, to seek funds with which to purchase it, and then to request that someone agree to sell it to us.

In the early years of the creation of IDICT, there was little or no expertise in Cuba on scientific information resources and delivery systems, regulations, and objectives; and even less on issues in the information world's ongoing debate about methodology and the handling of documents, given the overwhelmingly rapid discoveries and developments that had been taking place since the early 1950's.

The efforts of IDICT were very decisive in synthesizing foreign advisory reports, most of which originated in Eastern European countries, principally the Soviet bloc. These evaluations introduced new ideas on information processing, such as the use of the Dewey Decimal Classification System, consecutive order for shelving books; making a distinction between "documents" and "books"; and the use of abstracts as preliminary sources of information for specialists, among others.

Through agreements established between IDICT and VINITI, we were able to receive abstracts of hundreds of journal articles published all over the world to which we had no direct access due to the limitations imposed by the embargo.

"Since our creation, and for almost three decades, we [IDICT] maintained close ties of cooperation and collaboration with many important information organizations in Eastern Europe, who facilitated our access to the most important human, information, and technical resources of the world at that time."

Perhaps IDICT's most impressive achievement of that era was the way in which it became, practically speaking, a clearing-house for professional information, and a source of information for our country on all the latest information technology.

In 1976, following the principle that even the most remote corners of the country should benefit from the successes and victories of the Revolution, branch centres, known as Multisector Centres for Scientific and Technical Information (CMICT), today called Centres for Technical Information and Management (CIGET), were established in other provinces.

In 1982, for the first time in Cuba, IDICT began using an XT microcomputer for information services, and in 1983, in collaboration with CIICT, initiated dial-up access to databases located in Europe.

By virtue of Resolution No. 16/84 passed by the Cuban Academy of Sciences, IDICT was designated a member centre of the National System of Scientific and Technical Information (SNICT), and shortly thereafter, of the National Centre for the Automated Exchange of Scientific-Technical Information.

The National Scientific and Technical Library was inaugurated in 1988, with a modern focus on giving its scientific and technical patrons better and more direct access to specialized information in their respective fields through automation.

IDICT is now the headquarters for the INFO Congresses, recognized as the most important event in the field of Information Science in Latin America and the Caribbean, attended by colleagues from all over the world. The 1990 Congress coincided with the meeting of the forty-fifth FID Congress and Conference in Havana. That year, the institutional name of IDICT became Institute of Scientific and Technical Information, although the acronym IDICT is still used. Once Cuba gained access to the Internet in 1996, IDICT became the organization that introduced, supplied, evaluated, and popularized this technology throughout the country.

### Culture: Jose Marti National Library

While the creation of IDICT was aimed at developing science and technology, the National Library turned its attention to rescuing the national bibliographic patrimony, and to developing culture for the enormous numbers of people who, through the literacy campaign, were acquiring the ability to read, and to recognize the cultural values of the nation.

To elaborate a bit on the National Library's project of recovering the national bibliographic patrimony: a retrospective edition was prepared, in order to gather together bibliographic information from those years during which the bibliography had not been published.

The foundations for what is today the National Library System were established with the creation of a library in each province that would function as the central organizing agent for the growing number of municipal libraries which were springing up. The first reading incentive programmes were initiated, and the novel concept of the "mini-library" was introduced as a means of bringing books and information resources to many different sectors of the population.

Under its strong influence, the Library Technical Assistants School was founded, which produced mid-rank library professionals with solid training, on whose shoulders rested the better part of the Cuban library system. In addition, the National Library played a key role in the reorganization of library studies at the university level.

Library service for children and young people began with the children's room of the Lyceum Lawn Tennis Club, but it was not until the creation of the Jose Marti National Library that such services were formally instituted and made accessible to all children.

When the Ministry of Culture was set up in 1977, the National Office of Libraries was created, which assumed responsibility for the development of public libraries. At the same time, the Office also recommended the creation of ten basic community cultural institutions for each municipality: library, drama troupe, community chorus, band, film theater, cultural museum, art gallery, and cultural centres as a means of making cultural events accessible to the greatest number of people. Although from the perspective of the public libraries, it seemed that much progress had already been made, this initiative helped to strengthen and complete that which we have now, a public library in each city and territory. In particular, it introduced library organization as described in the Minaz-Cultura agreement, which defined a very special "*sui generis*" type of public library.

During the 1970s, work on Cuban libraries was expanded, scientific and technical collaborations with library systems of the socialist countries were set up, and Cuban professionals participated in various groups set up for designing and implementing political strategies for scientific and technical development of the library profession in those countries.

In 1981, the Cuban Association of Librarians (ASCUBI) was organized with the participation of distinguished librarians from all systems, and soon became part of the International Federation of Library Associations (IFLA), whose sixtieth Conference was held in Havana in 1994.

During this period, Cuban libraries began providing library services for the blind and visually handicapped; initiated library and information science research; and pursued new methodologies for scientific and technical development of the Public Library System, which are still in operation today.

In 1987, the transfer of responsibility for the development of public libraries in Cuba to the Jose Marti National Library brought with it a higher profile for the library, and an organizational restructuring. The first library research department was added, which has carried out important research work on socio-historical and cultural subjects, and has served as the centre for methodology and library development throughout all of Cuba.

New means of automation and transmission of information were introduced, and there was a renewed interest in the study of preservation and conservation concepts, and in the practical applications of these ideas to the collections. A national bibliography was compiled, as well as specialized bibliographies on outstanding figures and events in Cuban history and culture.

The library publication, *Revista de la Biblioteca Nacional*, was once again being published after a long hiatus during the Special Period. Collections became increasingly specialized, and were made available exclusively to students and specialists. As a result of the decree of June 8, 2003, Eliades Acosta, director of the Jose Marti National Library since 1998, ordered that all items acquired by the library must be catalogued electronically, as a first step towards the automation of the library's entire catalogue.

"Reading is an activity which expresses and sustains the culture of a nation, its spiritual motivation, and its values, its ability to persevere and develop." Guided by these principles, Cuba carried out an enormous programme to promote reading, which culminated in the annual "*Leer a Marti*" competitions, in which more than 500, 000 children and young people from all levels of education participated. At the present time, the system maintains 392 libraries located in Cuba's provinces, districts, and towns.

**Education: School Libraries**

In the last five years of the 1950s, with the establishment in Cuba of the UNESCO Regional Centre for the Western Hemisphere, a pilot school library in the Teacher Training School in Havana was set up for the dictatorship's Ministry of Education, under the administration of UNESCO library specialist Carlos Victor Penna. This pilot project helped to spur the development in Cuba of school libraries, which are so necessary for the complete education of children and young people. At the same time, the Office of School Libraries was created within the Ministry of Education. Dra. Olinta Ariosa, a pioneer in many areas of Cuban post-Revolutionary librarianship, was selected, under Minister Dr. Armando Hart, to establish and direct the Cuban Network of School Libraries, one of whose goals included the continuation of the literacy campaign begun in 1961.

This network connects the Colleges of Medicine in each province of the country, offering them e-mail services, and access to other information services. INFOMED, the National Centre for Medical Sciences Information, and the National Library of Medicine form an information network for public health in Cuba, which, for forty years, has made information accessible to medical professionals, collaborated in the training of doctors, and helped to further the study of medical sciences in Cuba.

## Other Institutions and Libraries

Between the earliest years, to which we referred at the beginning of this paper, and the present time, other powerful information institutions and libraries have arisen that form part of the spectrum of libraries and library services in Cuba.

The first library established in Cuba, the library of the *Sociedad Economica de Amigos del Pais*, second only to the Jose Marti National Library in its collections of the bibliographical patrimony, today operates under the aegis of the Ministry of Science and Technology, and is the central office of the Institute for Literature and Linguistics.

*Casa de las Americas*, a cultural institution which focuses on the study and dissemination of Latin American and Caribbean culture, has one of the most complete libraries in the area. The universities have tripled their offices, libraries, and information systems.

The huge strides of progress in scientific and technical research which have determined the discoveries and advances made by our scientists in many areas are greatly supported by the information centres of LABIOFAM, BIOMUNDI, and *Polos Cientificos*, which provide information and consulting services.

Many of those early organizations to which we referred were developing excellent modern information centres, among which we would include the Centre for Information in the Basic Construction Industry, mentioned earlier.

## Some Observations

In order to show points of development in the different information systems which comprise the National Information System, and to trace the evolution of Cuban library and information sciences, we have chosen to focus on just three of the greatest and oldest systems of the Revolution. We should like to draw your attention to the fact that the systems represented in each of these three cases outlined today exist simultaneously in each province of Cuba, including the special town Isla de la Juventud. In each province there are as many school libraries as there are schools, as many university libraries as central university campuses, as many public libraries as towns, as many Teacher Training Information Centres as towns, including an Information Centre (CIGET), and a Centre for Medical Information.

What we have shown so far might lead one to think that the scientific development of library and information services in Cuba has been carried out in a coherent, sustained, and cooperative manner, without any great impediments. However, all of this development has been marked by the unimaginable confrontation of and struggle against the economic and political blockade imposed by the United States government since January 1959, to which, hidden under the fig leaf of the term "embargo", Cuba has been forced to submit.

The formal imposition of the North American blockade took place February 3, 1962, the date on which the U.S. president, John F. Kennedy, signed Executive Order 3447, which established, from that moment on, a complete embargo of all trade with Cuba. The initial order was reinforced in 1988 by an amendment to the defense spending bill of 1992, introduced by Senator Torricelli, and in March 1996 by the Helms Burton Bill. The collapse of communism in 1990 made the situation even worse, when it deprived us of all material, financial, and commercial assistance. As a result of these developments, in 1992 the Revolutionary Government was forced to initiate the Special Period—*el Periodo Especial*—in our country.

Whenever concerned colleagues and visitors inquire about the effects of the embargo on information access and library services in Cuba, questions centre on the acquisition of books and other materials in order to increase collections and develop services, and the ways in which the embargo might deprive the people of access to literature and information. But this is only one side of the issue.

Undoubtedly, there have been instances in which it has not been possible to obtain materials necessary for the continued development of these information institutions which we have described above, hindered as we have been by the many obstacles imposed on us by prevailing U.S. legislation. We have been compelled to develop many different types of initiatives on our own: for example, *Ediciones R*, the immediate response to the abrupt cut-off of the supply of materials from the large specialized North American publishing houses, and/or from their subsidiaries in other countries, opened up a new phase of development for the government press, *Imprenta Nacional*.

The large printing runs demanded by the cultural and intellectual development of the country were initiated with *Ediciones Huracan*, and today are continued by the *Biblioteca Familiar*. Meanwhile, other editorial houses were established in Cuba to fill important gaps in publishing for the sciences, technology, and the humanities: Editorial Academia, for subjects of great scientific importance; *Pueblo y Educacion* for school texts; and the publishing houses which comprise the Institute for the Book (*Instituto del Libro*), namely: *Editorial Arte y Literatura*, dedicated to the publication of the great works of world literature; *Editorial Gente Nueva* for children's books and young adult literature; *Letras Cubanas* for Cuban literature, both traditional and contemporary; *Editorial Oriente* for literature of the eastern provinces; *Editorial Jose Marti* for literary works in foreign languages; and *Editorial Nuevo Milenio* for works of social science and technology.

As an example of the publishing output of the ICL, in 2001 more than 5 million copies of books were produced, a figure which does not include the output of the other 136 existing publishing houses. This was how we dealt with the difficulties of buying books abroad: we created our own publishing industry. However, given the impenetrable nature of the embargo, we still faced many obstacles; we have to use all of our skill and cunning just to buy paper, ink, and printing equipment, and to keep up with advanced technologies. Book fairs in Cuba were not held until the beginning of the 1980s, although there had been fairs, expositions, and book sales earlier at different points in Cuban history, in particular those organized in the 1940s and 1950s by intellectuals such as Raul Roa Garcia, later known as the Chancellor of Dignity (*Canciller de la Dignidad*), and other national cultural figures.

Those fairs officially known as the Havana International Book Fairs (*Ferias Internacionales del Libro de La Habana*) were inaugurated in 1982, exactly 21 years ago, when the first was held in the Fine Arts Palace (today, the Museum of Fine Arts), attended by a small sampling of Latin American publishing houses, and which featured the work of Jose Marti and Felix Varela, and other outstanding intellectuals. Its slogan, "The book: bridge of friendship among the countries of the world, " characterized the Fair for many years thereafter. The ninth International Book Fair of 2000, with a new slogan, "To read is to grow", and dedicated to the famous Cuban poet and essayist, Cintio Vitier, winner of the National Prize for Literature, and to Italy, as an invited guest country, was held for the first time in San Carlos de La Cabana, currently still the official site. Growing national and international participation, which accompanied a gradual recovery of the Cuban book, has prompted the Fair to be held annually. The most recent Fair, the twelfth, was held in February of this year (2003), and was dedicated to the winner of the National Prize for Literature, Pablo Armando.

## CHINA, LIBRARIES AND HUMAN RIGHTS

I was invited to give this paper at the Library Associations Umbrella 4 Conference, Manchester, June 1997. The purpose of this paper was not purely academic but to initiate debate. This is it did to a greater degree than I had expected-unfortunately the ensuing discussion was not recorded but I hope its publication will promote further thought and discussion. For another angle on this area see John Pateman's article "Breaking the Information Blockade " (an abridged version of which appears in Focus, 1997 28(2)114-117)-much of which I am in agreement-and my article, "Barriers to technical solutions: institutional, policy and legal barriers to information access. Information Development 1996 12(3), 149-154".

Given the topic of this paper, my first step will be to define human rights. I will use the most generally accepted definitions and descriptions, that of United Nations instruments. A word of warning, these Declarations are not universally accepted-in fact the Chinese government is not a signatory of either

Covenant and personally I actually have disagreements with the very concept of "rights" (more of this later).

Before I start, I must emphasise that I do not consider any state to be perfect in matters of "human rights", whether social or economic. My remit however is China, so I must concentrate my critique there. What is China's record? The Chinese governments response to trade union activists, independent writers & journalists, ethnic/cultural/nationalist movements are well documented. There are other, more comprehensive sources available so I will just illustrate certain aspects-concentrating on information access & dissemination.

17/4/94-Star TV drops BBC news broadcasts to China after pressure from the Chinese government. Reception of satellite TV programmes requires government permission.

16/1/96-Chinese State Council requires foreign news agencies to submit to regulation by the official Chinese news agency and forbids Chinese agencies from purchasing economic information directly from overseas.

11/10/96-Novelist and screenwriter Wang Shuo's publishing house was ordered to stop printing his 'vulgar and reactionary' collected works. November 1996-a state ideological departments announced a quota for the closure of one third of China's provincial and municipal newspapers, periodicals.

June 97-"'Some (internet) address are being filtered, so you are not allowed to enter' the Chinese Internet official said. 'They have too much news and (could) have an influence on things in China'"; Chinese who attempted to access on site on the anniversary of Tiananmen could only access 'Forbidden'.

The Chinese government sees the increase in information revolution as a threat. The increase in cross border data flows, wither by fax or internet, not only enable economic growth but bring with it dominant international, mainly US, values. The Chinese Communist Party attempts to control access to decision making via 'nei-pu' or internal documents, with limited circulation. While this is true of all information within Leninist parties (and many right wing parties & most governments), this shows the danger when the state and the party are confused. Even retired cadres try and retain access to such documents in order to stay informed. How can libraries enable people regarding human rights? Mainly by providing access to information that will allow them to make informed decisions. This could be current affairs / social science information for social rights or economic, scientific & technical information for economic advancement (ie. poverty alleviation). Rather than trying to cover all Chinese libraries I will tend to concentrate on those libraries to which all ostensibly have access-public libraries.

In 1994 China had 2, 596 public libraries with 0.323 billion books & 45, 000 staff members. In 1986 this meant of China's 1 billion population only 570, 000 had access to a public library. In 1984 there were 0.25 public library books per person (compared to 130 university books per student). 1996 figures indicate that there is one library per 0.44 million people. Attempts are being made to improve this situation:-In 1994 public libraries, at or above the county level, set up 17788 service points for circulating books; in 1989 200+ childrens libraries or reading rooms were set up in Beijing; travelling libraries are being promoted, currently 160 are in existence. However, this real situation is worse given that information resources decline from the developed East to the poor West of China, though attempts are being made here also, with 425 ethnic libraries including 5 national minorities autonomous regional libraries. So even before I address the restrictions placed on Chinese libraries, the paucity of access limits their role.

What is the remit of Chinese public libraries? "The main tasks and functions of Shanghai library are publicizing Marxism-Leninism, Mao Zedong Thought, as well as lines, general and specific policies put forward by the party and the state, carrying out situational education concerning patriotism, socialism and our motherland, disseminating scientific information". And what of the professional staff? In 1987 a document promulgated by four Ministries and Committees, including the Propaganda Department of the Central Party Committee, clarified the adoption of the "Director Responsibility System and set out the responsibilities of the chief librarians as follows: seriously implement the guidelines and policies of the Party as well as relevant laws and guidelines of competent authorities.....give full play of the roles of the Party, the trade union and the youth league". "The objectives of CSLS (China Society for Library Science), from its inception, have been to organize all members and unite the mass of librarians to adhere to guidelines and policies of the Central Communist Party and the State".

Even if librarians wish to go beyond the above-what problems do they face? Regarding acquisitions, I have been unable to find references to what is permissible and what is not; so I will infer from the situation with respect to publishing. According to Liu Jernow, there is no formal policy of permitted or forbidden literature-just unwritten boundaries. Going over these boundaries one can be punished and even disappear. These boundaries can also change with the political climate-not an easy road! Further evidence for this informal system comes from Hong Kong librarians, when asked if they would obey a direct request to remove a book from the shelves, the response was that such a request would not be made, the book would simply disappear and if the librarian made a fuss this would affect their careers or even lose them their jobs. The Chinese authorities also distinguish between provision of libraries and provision of information & only some type of information are allowed free dissemination. 'Neibu' (inside) information includes "objective" current affairs, foreign literature, "illegal" Chinese literature. This distinction carries through to library stock. Scientific & technical "information" is no problem for libraries-there are State bodies specifically to promote the dissemination (and historically the copying of) this material. The funding for such material is also much better than for social sciences and public libraries devote much time and effort to economic and scientific document delivery. This is at a time when the funding from the government for public libraries in general is not enough to meet the needs of users.

Even if material is held in a public library, how do users fare gaining access to it? While open access shelving has been put forward as a method to increase the cost efficiency of libraries it is still a minority of libraries that have this facility, although newer libraries are moving in this direction. Why is open access important? China has historically seen the library as storage space for 'cultural relics' as opposed to a source of useful information for the public-so staff "could not imagine anyone would be foolish enough to come into the library to ask questions ". Besides this, asking for material that the state deemed unsuitable "the common wisdom was that it could be downright dangerous ". While these last two quotes are from Tibet, I would argue that given the nationalist sentiments in Tibet this means that people there are confronted with these problems more immediately. Further restrictions on access occur due to charging for information; for example, while many in the West have focused on China's restrictive practice regarding what information may be access on the internet, little regard has been paid to the cost of access for individuals. Given the paucity of telephone access in China (23 phone lines per 1, 000 people), internet access will be public libraries, such as in Tianjin. However-as for SDI services-this is charged for at a price beyond most locals means. Also, many public libraries are becoming subscription libraries, again restricting access. Even the China Society for Library Science's research topics for basic library science are now focusing on markets and the library.

Another, more fundamental restriction, on access to public services is the "hukou" system of household residency registration. While this has been relaxed to allow newly redundant rural workers to gain temporary residency in urban areas, they must still retain their "rural affiliations", denying them access to state welfare benefits (I was not able to discover wither this included access to state facilities such as public libraries). This is conditional on them obtaining non agricultural work and secured accommodation, leading many rural-urban migrants not to register-meaning that they may be denied access to any state facilities-including public libraries. In line with the commercialisation and marketization of Chinese life, residency and other permits are available on the flourishing urban black markets, if one can afford them.

This question of rural-urban migration leads me on to the question of information needs and provision in rural China.

With a 1/5th of the worlds population and 1 1/15th of its land mass, agriculture is a major issue for China. A large proportion of the population earn a living from agriculture with traditional production methods predominating. The rural economy is thus underdeveloped, a large percentage of the population being semi literate or illiterate, agricultural education inadequate and qualified personnel in short supply. The demand in these areas is mainly for economic, scientific and technical information in order for farmers to earn their way out of poverty, ie. access to information to enable their economic human rights. China is attempting to meet this demand in various ways. Information is collected, collated and published on production techniques of planting and breeding. This is disseminated in various ways: village reading rooms borrow from animal husbandry departments of urban district libraries and teach peasants using blackboard newspapers and compiled materials; agricultural libraries and information institutions establish agricultural information networks, publish network journals and provide other information services; provide services for agricultural extension projects; provide clipping services and information reference services via oral, written & telephone forms, carry out SDI services and public lectures. Rural libraries can act as rural information exchanges.

Budget constraints inevitably also operate here. There are problems satisfying the largest user group-the farmers. Research & university libraries close their doors to the public and Although the village reading rooms and technical extension stations disseminate information in these areas, it is still inadequate. Often information is only provided to members of agricultural networks, collective funded libraries are only open to members with market orientated libraries charging for services. With China's reform economy and local officials blocking access to inter-regional trade, the rural rich are getting richer while the poor remain poor. Thus access to information enabling the poor to alleviate their position is by definition out of reach. As rural areas develop, albeit inequitably, there is a rise in rural libraries. Concomitant with this an increase in wealth comes an increased interest in "cultural" consumption; ie. people start to look beyond immediate rights such as economic well being to other their social & political situation. Then we are back to the issues raised earlier.

The picture I have painted is bleak-and I believe it is. In China there is the worst of 3 worlds: a poor developing country with limited funds to provide true access to information; a move towards a Capitalist economy via privatisation and commercialisation thus favouring information access for the wealthy and denying it to the poor; a single hierarchical one party state denying free access to information in order to remain in power. I reject the concept of non individualistic 'Asian values', a la Tung Chee-hwa (Hong Kongs new first chief executive), advanced to justify denial of freedom of expression. Democracy (in its real sense) is hardly individualistic, besides-how can anyone make an informed decision on how they wish to rule (or be ruled) if they do not have free access to information? (My thanks to Ronald Dworkin).

This issue became clear to me on reading the Guest Lecture by Marianna Choldin, at the IFLA General Conference in Beijing. This lecture was specifically related to IFLA's recently initiated Committee on Access to Information and Freedom of Expression (CAIFE). While the paper starts out from the position of endorsing "the fundamental principle of access to information and freedom of expression", it then raises, and often endorses, ideas contrary to this. "I have come to the conclusion that there must be a universal human instinct to censor"; I do not believe that there is biological basis for censorship, nor for freedom of expression-these are historical, cultural, *i.e.* social constructs.

"We need to recognise the very real tensions that may exist between cultural and societal standards and traditions in a given country and a commitment to universal human rights"; while this recognises the social basis for these issues, it imputes a single cultural and societal standard, not recognising that the governing and governed may have very different views on these topics. This is reinforced by the comment "I w ant to stress that I do not believe in any country's model; a country is comprised of many values, and the model referred to is usually the state's model. "We must establish mutual trust and respect "; just because people are fellow librarians, this does not mean that they accept what I consider fundamental human rights, let alone that I should trust and respect them. It is also stated that librarians should not initiate actions without an invitation from librarians within a country. This becomes important when deciding how to view the demands and wishes of the people of a country. It may be impossible for a principled librarian to carry out their job in a country, leaving only the unprincipled; it may only be possible to communicate with "leading librarians " in a country whose interest usually do not coincide with ordinary librarians or users. Does that mean outside professional bodies bow to the judgement of those librarians they can reach as to action regarding that country? Or should they refer to other bodies representing users? While IFLA, being an organisation representing national organisations, may need to tread carefully in order to keep certain countries as members, this should not be justified by watering down principles.

# 7

# Global Reach of Libraries

## Benefits and Challenges for Special Librarians

There is a lot of talk these days about the future-the New Millennium and the role of information and the information professional in the development of a "global village." We also hear references to the creation of the "Global information infrastructure, " referred briefly as "GII"-an interactive, interconnected system that will provide a dynamic means for people to communicate worldwide; allow information professionals to communicate not only as a global community, but also to create a "global information marketplace;" and provide information professionals with opportunities to participate in exchanges not only of information, but employment opportunities worldwide.

During the last fifty years, we have been moving from a world in which society, commerce, technology, and education were defined within the context of nation-states to a world in which they are increasingly perceived as part of a global community In essence, ours is a world of fax machines, email, international TV instantaneous coverage, interactive electronic communications, and rapid travel; a world of academic research interconnected with the work of scholars throughout the world; a world in which people interact with their colleagues around the globe, exchange information and messages, and coordinate activities through a variety of technological and communication means.

It should also be emphasized that one of the most important features of information technology is its universality-its global impact. As new information technologies expand their uses and coverage, the world shrinks; information flows globally, faster, and in more detail; and both personal and business contacts proliferate globally. Accelerating technology changes are creating many challenges globally. Our roles and skills as information providers require us to understand the potentials of continuously developing technologies, the systems they support, the status of technological change, and the types of systems those changes will foster not only nationally, but more so globally. It should also be emphasized that economic developments, as well as technological advancements, are providing the means and increasing the need for the information profession to transcend geographic barriers and enhance the profession on a global scale.

Special Libraries Association (SLA) is an international organization with members in fifty-eight countries and is increasingly becoming involved in promoting international cooperation, exchange visits, and forums. SLA fosters participation in international organizations and conferences and encourages sharing of information resources between libraries worldwide. Numerous programmes and publications also reflect SLA's international focus. In consideration of international readership, summaries of feature articles in Information outlook are provided in English, French, and Spanish. They are also exploring ways to broadcast portions of SLA's annual conference to other countries or 'better yet, create an interactive format." It should also be noted, as emphasized in the February 1996 issue of Specialist, that the Second Worldwide Conference on Special Librarianship will be held in the year 2000 in Brighton, England, 'to bring together information industry leaders from around the world to seek solutions to common problems and to enhance the information profession on a global scale."

Viewing the information profession globally as the predominant profession of the future, it is important to emphasize that at no point in history has there been such a high level of realization about the importance to understand the dynamics of global interdependence and the need to establish and maintain strong and harmonious international relations.

As we have progressed from the age of agriculture to an age of technology and finally into the present informational society, our capacity and the need to build strong relationships with other nations has grown exponentially. Understanding other cultures is becoming more important as we move forward to an increased global exchange in technological and economic productivity. These and other similar global issues are almost certain to have an even greater impact in the future on the information services provided by information professionals-in particular by special librarians-who must adjust and be prepared to meet the escalating demands for specialized information for the changing needs of their user clientele. It is thus logical to conclude that only a dynamic, forward-looking, and globally oriented information professional-aided by up-to-the minute information generated both nationally and globally-can provide quality service in the realm of continuously changing specialized information needs and participate in exchange of information on professional issues and developments globally.

As we travel into the future, our world is becoming more interconnected and interdependent, information is becoming an international commodity, and a critical need for more emphasis on the integration of international issues into library and information science (LIS) programmes is becoming an imperative urgency. More than ever before an "information workforce"-one that is professionally skilled, well-educated, and knowledgeable of worldwide conditions and developments-has become an essential prerequisite not only for the control and growth of an organization and sustained economic growth of a country, but also for the exchange of information globally.

Expanding on the above issues, we are reminded of a critical issue that has been occasionally discussed during meetings at professional conferences: "Are American library and information science schools providing students with the knowledge and understanding to participate and discuss the conditions in countries worldwide and relate to global library and information increased global exchange in technological sues?" A related and equally important !sand economic productivity. These and other sue that has also been raised by several in similar global issues are almost certain to- internationally minded leaders in our profession pertains to internationalizing the LIS curriculums an issue that has become more important than ever before in view of the expected outcome of the New Millennium in making the "global village" a reality and especially in view of social, economic, and technological developments taking place globally. For example:

* world problems have become interconnected;
* every single aspect of mankind's activities, concerns, and crises is presently considered in a global sense, a perspective that is expected to increase in the future;
* an emerging globally integrated society is demanding increased utilization of technology and information obtained through technology;
* information has become the most important ingredient in decision-making anywhere in the world;
* the exchange of information worldwide has become imperative;
* sweeping changes in technology, increase in worldwide communications, and a growing competition in the global marketplace require global knowledge and education and training in all types of information technology and communications;
* *in an increasingly interdependent society information services will increase in the need for networking across national boundaries and across oceans.*

It is thus logical to conclude that if information professionals both in America and worldwide are going to participate in international data flow and exchanges, it will require a greater degree of international knowledge and professional sophistication. Thus, attention to international professional LIS education has become a mandatory issue. In this respect, it should be emphasized that contrary to the belief that every innovation and change requires monetary investment, internationalizing LIS programmes requires no increase in the LIS schools budget. What it does require is an attitude and an initiative on the part of LIS school's administration and faculty and the involvement of the total student body-American and international. To create the most effective means of internationalizing LIS programmes in order to be beneficial to both LIS schools and the international and American students, we may consider: (1) involvement of international students in curriculum planning with information on their home country information needs; (2) study of global issues in appropriate courses; and (3) creation of specialized courses dealing with specific international subject matter. LIS schools would expand their programmes in a positive way by including information on international students' home country information needs and relevant global issues into certain aspects of the curriculum; international students would gain from a more appropriate education to adapt their acquired knowledge and skills to the needs of their home countries; and American students would have a better knowledge of the world and the workings of the information profession worldwide. AU students stand to develop a better understanding of global affairs and world cultures and the universality of librarianship, be motivated by this experience and eventually be more involved in international exchanges, and develop an awareness that actions of one nation deeply affect the rest of the world.

Challenges and benefits from internationalizing LIS programmes are thus numerous. International students would have the opportunity to participate in the design of certain aspects of the programme more appropriate to the needs of their home countries. American students, on the other hand, would benefit from additional courses designed from an international perspective and from the integration of foreign countries' professional issues into the contents of appropriate courses.

In adding global professional issues into the curriculum, there would be a wide choice of issues to select from: information activities of UNESCO and the organization's efforts in bringing to an appropriate level of education worldwide, including education and training for library and information service; information on communication and behavioural aspects of the Third World societies that determine the production, distribution, and utilization of graphic and non-graphic records in contrast to those of the Western Society; situations in lesser developed countries that affect the development of collections in libraries and cultural institutions; issues that are characteristic of numerous countries worldwide, including the issues of illiteracy and semi-illiteracy, resulting in special considerations in building library collections and in providing specialized services; the critical issue of resistance to technology that relates to employment problems in some countries, including the resulting problems for libraries and their potential solutions; the critical question of bibliographic control in numerous countries worldwide.

Diffusing international issues and materials as widely as possible throughout the LIS curriculum in addition to creating specialized courses dealing primarily with international subject matter has also been strongly recommended by E. J. Josey during the International Doctoral Student Conference at the University of Pittsburgh, School of Library and information Science, held during September 23-25, 1988. In response to the question, "What can faculty members do to bring more international perspectives into the curriculums Josey suggests, "Faculty members can take the diffusive approach, that is, diffusing international materials as widely as possible throughout the library and information science curriculum as contrasted with creating specialized courses only dealing with international subject matter.

While we may use the diffusive approach by bringing the international perspectives throughout the curriculum, nevertheless, we would still need specialized courses such as seminars and the introduction to international librarianship. But the specialized courses would only reach a small percentage of the students in library and information science schools, that is, those who opt to take the course. The diffusing of the international perspective throughout the entire curriculum will mean more students will become more in internationally oriented and this will be very helpful to the international students."

Dispersing international materials and relevant global issues-including issues and materials pertaining to a foreign country or countries-throughout the LIS curriculum, in addition to creating several courses and seminars dealing primarily with international subject matter, and having several faculty members with strong international expertise would indeed constitute the characteristics of a strong internationally oriented LIS programme. Since most international students that come to study in LIS schools in the United States come from the lesser developed countries (hereafter referred to as LDCs), we should briefly refer to the information needs of these countries in the context of their economic, social, and professional conditions. While the populations in developed countries-especially in the United States-enjoy a high level of sustained economic growth and technological development as a result of having devoted a large amount of resources to education and training, populations in numerous LACS are simultaneously living in different socioeconomic systems and at several stages of technological development. Numerous LACS continue to be predominantly characterized by illiterate or semi-illiterate populations living in rural communities that are without access to library or other information services. Although the revolution in computers and communications technology offers hope for the LACS to catch up with the developed world, some LACS have been unable to profit to their full extent from the new age of information.

Among the main reasons for this situation are absence of an adequate infrastructure for information storage and processing; absence of an adequate infrastructure for information retrieval, dissemination, and use; and economic, technological, and quite often cultural barriers to an adequate information flow.

It should also be emphasized that the solutions the LACS adopt are often inappropriate. For example, before fully reaching the age of print and literacy, numerous LACS have to face the age of computers and satellites. High levels of illiteracy among the majority of the people are contrasted with high levels of education for a few of the elite who are tied to global information and power networks. Here we have the information-poor the illiterate majority contrasted with the information-rich-the elite minority, and this gap is narrowing slowly, if at all. In this respect, it should be emphasized that the information needs of diverse user communities in the LACS should constitute some of the guiding factors in determining the type of LIS education and training to be undertaken by international students from most LDCs and education programmes abroad should take such needs into consideration. A well-known African library professional leader, Ogundipe, calls for preparation to meet the information needs of the few elite; however in particular, to promote literacy, educate for change, articulate the wants of the rural communities, increase productivity, and improve the quality of life-especiauy in the rural areas where most of the population in developing countries live.

With all these points in mind, we can easily see that the challenge of attracting and educating information professionals for the New Millennium-both for the developed and the developing countries-has become one of the critical issues of the remaining years of the 1990's. The American LIS degree programmes have a special role and an increasing challenge and responsibility in the education of information professionals worldwide. Although these programmes have received acclaim worldwide, there is a need for new ways and ideas to make the education experience for international students more meaningful and transferable upon returning home.

Thus, the LIS faculty needs to realize that international students are an invaluable resource. With their input of information regarding their home countries into the LIS curriculum, as well as other changes suggested recently in professional literature and during meetings at professional conferences, the American education experience for all students-international and American-might become a more meaningful one entering the 21st century. The groundwork for the development of future international network contacts-professional partnerships-would indeed be enhanced when international students return to their home countries. Endless opportunities would open up with communicating globally-colleague to colleague. What better place to begin with this partnership" then in the library and information science classroom situation? Communicating with their foreign colleagues, the challenges and benefits for special librarians of all types are numerous. If CEOs in the corporate world and industry are developing exchange contacts with CEOs in foreign countries, special librarians, as part of the information industry, should also accept such challenges and become beneficiaries of contacts and exchange of information with their foreign counterparts. Through exchanges between special librarians globally, the knowledge of the special librarian/information professional in any country worldwide would be greatly enhanced with updating and keeping current with professional issues and developments around the world.

Through an exchange of information with foreign colleagues, U.S. special librarians employed by corporations with offices worldwide would have a broader and firsthand knowledge and understanding of the conditions, the culture, and the economic situation in a particular country and would most likely become a greater asset to the parent organization. Communicating with their foreign counterparts, special librarians employed by banks and other financial institutions which deal with banks in foreign countries and financial institutions with affiliates in foreign countries would have an excellent source of information for the bank CEOs and the bank newsletter, in a university setting, special librarians, through exchange of information with their colleagues in foreign country universities, would become invaluable sources of information for the university faculty and staff.

Special librarians in museums communicating with their foreign counterparts would gain greatly in having first-hand knowledge and understanding of the happenings in the world of art and the culture of a particular country. For librarians in state libraries, the opportunities offered through exchange between information professionals are endless. For example, through contacts with foreign regional librarians, they would obtain business information; information on the social, cultural, and other conditions of the country; and be able to identify which information is extremely important for international business exchanges. They could also find information on the culture and the social customs of a foreign country for travel groups. As emphasized in the January 1997 issue of Information outlook: 'We cannot underestimate what it means to be a part of a global village. It is only at our perfl that we ignore events in other parts of the world, that we look for solutions with only one point of view, or that we look at opportunities for effective information management in only one geographic location. Simply put, we are living in an Information Age that allows us to think outside of the box. Our profession is no different than anyone else's. We not only live in an internationally aware world, we are often sought out to identify threats and opportunities in the world. How aware are we of what is going on in our own field? What kinds of organizations, networks, and developments are happening outside our own backyard that we need to know about? If credibility, objectiveness, and relevancy are as important as we tell our customers or clients they, are, what are we doing to make sure we can meet those very significant expectations?"

Special librarians worldwide indeed stand to gain through contact exchanges partnerships-with their colleagues in other countries. They stand to benefit from assistance in cataloguing of specialized materials, acquisition of specialized materials, exchange of specialized publications, interlibrary loans, translations, locating rare and unique publications, specialized subject searches, keeping up-to-date on developments in a specific country and with relevant global issues-in particular on developments and issues of interest to their parent organizations, to name a few. Their knowledge and global understanding would be so much richer and their service to their communities so much more valuable. SLA is strongly encouraging worldwide partnerships between information professionals world wide. SLA Executive Director David R. Bender also calls upon the ability and the obligation of special librarians to facilitate the interdependence between businesses, governments, and other types of organizations and help make the global village a reality. In line with the thoughts expressed in this article, the author strongly advocates that "attention to international and global education is no longer a matter of passive acceptance but an imperative mandatory is sue, " as eloquently voiced by Martha Boaz in her article, "International Education: An Imperative Need." It is the author's strong belief that blending the philosophy of LIS education with a cross-cultural and world wide perspective would give LIS programmes a new vision and effectiveness previously unrealized. The greatest benefits however, derived from such a perspective would include an impact on professional development and thinking and an influence on professional style and professional concerns worldwide bringing the global element into the profession and extending it into the New Millennium.

## SECTION OF SCIENCE AND TECHNOLOGY LIBRARIES

### Ifla Science & Technology Libraries Section

The situation in scitech librarianship is characterized by sky rocketing of printed periodicals' price. That was why one of the main reasons provoking interest to electronic publishing, namely on-line access and CD-ROM, were economics and providing value-added services. The situation with on-line access and networking is shortly described by John W. Berry in "Digital libraries: New initiatives with world wide implications" (IFLA JOURNAL V.22 N 1 pp. 9-17. The disparity between US and foreign data communications environments (including networks, hardware and software) is a source of frustration to businesses and, in particular, members of the research community when they seek to effect or use international connection. Within a country, distribution-local infrastructure-is largely a matter of local policy and investment; it is the area of greatest unevenness across countries. For example, in countries such as China and Russia, the infrastructure for very high speed links is almost nonexistent.

A major finding of the 1990 Report of the Task Force on Telecommunications and Broadcasting in Eastern Europe, commissioned by the US State Department, stated: "The years of political bias against private access and dissemination of information have left all Eastern European countries, regardless of GNP, with telecommunications and broadcast infrastructure which are among the very poorest and most antiquated in the world. Massive investment will be required to bring the telecommunication and broadcast infrastructure up to developed country levels." Libraries and documentation centres are important CD-ROM marketplace. Despite for the moment the difference in price is of 10-15% (publisher's catalogue price) in favour of the printed versions the optical disc technology is less expensive than that of printed items. Well developed CD industry provides specific production costs (ca 0.03 cents per MByte) what is 2000 times less than printed version, Table.

***Cost to Store 1 MB of Data***

| Media | (in $) | Compared to CD-ROM |
|---|---|---|
| Paper | 5.00 | 2000* |
| Hard disk | 1.65 | 660* |
| Microfiche | .76 | 304* |
| Floppy disk | .42 | 168* |
| 9-track tape | .25 | 100* |
| Magneto Optical | .19 | 76* |
| WORM | .10 | 40* |
| CD-Recordable | .032 | 13* |
| E*abyte | .015 | 6* |
| DAT | .01 | 4* |
| CD-ROM replicated | .025 | 1* |

The tendency is also promising: while periodicals' cost is rising twice for ten years the CD-production costs are decreasing steadily. Due to huge capacity the CD shipping and storing cost is 1500 times less than for paper materials. In-library processing cost is 250 times higher for paper. As for service the paper is 20% cheaper due to lower investment costs. The final expenditures' comparison formulae for 1 thousand scietech grey literature volumes comprising 220000 pages versus 1 CD-ROM disk (the price of information itself is omitted) is presented in Table.

***Operation Cost in US Dollars for 1 CDcompared with Equivalent 1 Thousand Volumes of Printed Material***

| | Paper | CD |
|---|---|---|
| Pages | 220000 | - |
| Volumes | 1000 | 1 |
| Production cost | 3300 | 2 |
| Shipping cost | 1390 | 0.85 |
| In-library processing cost | 300 | 1.15 |
| Storing cost, including rent of premises, VAC, cleaning | 11*years | 0.1*years |
| Service cost, including premises maintenance, equipment | 33*years | 310*years |
| Salaries | 240*years | 10*years |
| Total cost | 4990+383*years | 4+320*years |
| | | |

So approximate comparative formulae for 1994 Russian situation will be:

For printed publications:

P = 5000 + 383 * years USD.

For information-equivalent CD:

C = 4 + 320 x* years USD.

I wish to remind once again that here costs are indicated for Moscow 1994 prices with no respect to the cost of information itself. For CD and paper these costs are difficult to compare because CD-recorded full text usually is indexed and presents more value for money. The CD technology looks viable due to the existence of a large and rapidly growing market. Electronic publishing is growing quicker than the conventional one-both as to the number of new titles and the information comprised. Besides bibliographic and reference databases the full-text and multimedia materials occupy more space in CD-ROM production. As any digitized records the CD may be easily converted in the future.

### The Project history

That is why IFLA SciTech Libraries Section project: Electronic Deposition of the Full Text Grey Literature Documents, Feasibility Study for East Europe, FSU, Asia was initiated in 1993. The proposal for a feasibility study was submitted during SCI-TECH session in Barcelona by Andrey Zemskov. SC reached consensus that there should get out a more complete and detailed proposal, with Mr. Dennis Shaw's assistance. Review committee of Mrs. Anderson, Mr. Bradbury, Mrs. Koskiala, and Mr. Shaw was nominated.

The aim of the project was to examine the problems of access to and conservation of scientific and technological grey literature in Eastern Europe, the former Soviet Union countries and Asia and to make recommendations for ensuring improved access internationally to this material. Electronic Deposition here means digital optical CD technology.

The project considers CD as additive to the traditional printed materials, microfilms and on-line access. The project was in good relevancy with Core Programmes (ALP, UDT) and

SC project on Satellite Communication and adopted by CB 26/10/93.

### *Calendar Plan of the Feasibility Study*

1. First version of the Questionnaire 15 August 1994
2. Discussion with SC members 01 September 1994
3. Duplication and dissemination 20 December 1994
4. Follow up 01 February 1995
5. Analysis, statistics, recommendations 15 June 1995
6. Report to SC and preparation for publishing 15 August 1995

Project started in May 1994. The Calendar plan and the questionnaire were discussed, corrected and approved at SC sessions in Havana, Marty Kesselman being very helpful. After that 300 copies of questionnaire were made (200 for starting dissemination and 100 for the follow up).

The feasibility study included:

*Questionnaires and Discussions with librarians, information specialists, publishers and suppliers at seminars, conferences to identify the institutions (with names of individuals) in Eastern Europe, FSU and Asia prepared to experiment with electronic deposition.*

The 300 questionnaires were mailed or handed over during seminars in Shangkai, Warsaw, Crimea, Habana, Prague etc. Of 300 disseminated forms the response till now was 136 forms (45.3%). Data processing was performed with respect to the Questionnaire topics, selecting 4 kinds of libraries (Regional, Central, Corporate and University libraries) and 5 subregions (Asia, East Europe outside former Soviet Union, former Soviet Union, Russia, Moscow). The latter regions (Russia and Moscow were selected because information from these regions only enabled to get some statistics. Other regions and countries gave 1-3 answers per country. The only absolutely the same answer "Yes" was to question concerning the necessity of the given project. So in the following I'll speak rather of whole project but differential illustrative statistical information will be for Russian libraries. Some questions discussed during personal contacts were:

Are electronic publications relevant to libraries' need?

Is user training a problem?

Is hardware and software available?

As for grey literature problem this project was much influenced by discussions with D. Farace, Th. Larr, at GL conferences in Amsterdam and Washington. The detailed discussion with Mr. D. Marquis, vice-president of Special Interest Group on CD-ROM Application and Technology (SIGCAT), Annapolis, USA on the conservation and reliability of CD and relevant topics should be mentioned.

CD is combining holdings and access to best advantage. The CD technique is more compact, facilitates search and has no considerable training difficulties due to wide spread CD players and no fear of counter. The CD-ROMs combining several titles within a disk are very advantageous. On-line methods are more vulnerable, more expensive and need well developed infrastructure. The project was discussed with UNESCO representatives, with EC mission and representatives in Moscow and with members of International Association of Research and SciTech Libraries during Crimea'94 Annual ARSTL Conference.

Study of Findings of ongoing sister projects (LC's Digital Library, ADONIS, Tilburg University projects, UNESCO projects on electronic publications). The valuable experience of Hartlib Papers Project (conversion to digital form 25, 000 pages and preparation of CD with original handwritten letters) is very encouraging.

The problems of conservation are very important. Testing suggests that a properly produced CD-ROM can last more than 100 years ensuring the integrity of the data for the life cycle. Reliability of the digital records preservation is not necessarily connected with the physical integrity of documents, although it can be solved in the better way taking into account the compactness of records and automated service (an untrained user will not touch the documents). We should speak rather of the reliability of the rewriting, because for CD it is quite sufficient and rather easy to rewrite the whole collection. Compact discs offer a small probability of errors in rewriting

(1 mistake in 2 thousand discs), that is approximately one letter in 1 million volumes. Even if in the electronic storage the rewriting of the whole collection is done annually, the rate of information losses will be considerably lower than in case of the paper version. A possibility of accommodating full-text collections in a rather small premises allows for creation of inexpensive reserve depositories. There should be initiated a research of CD-ROM conservation including high-temperature- and water resistance in cases of disasters.

Pilot project in the NPLS&T included:

*Monitoring the full-text analogs of sci-tech journals. Special databases were generated and updated.*

The electronic files collection generated during desk top publishing and which will be in-house transferred to CD. The problem revealed to be rather more difficult as it seemed during proposal preparation. The Western publishers are reluctant to develop the electronic publishing access due to very complicated and heavily discussed Copyright problem. As for Russian publishers they are not considering yet libraries as an important customer. They prefer to solve problems at upper levels by establishing of financial support on the ground of state supported programmes.

Preparing for the in-house transfer to CD of full texts of printed publications available in the Library collection. Two full text one-off CD-Recordable publications of 1994 and 1995 Crimea Conferences Proceedings were done in our library.

## Statistics Available

***Library System in Russia:*** There are several groups of libraries in Russia clustered according to user communities, collections, supervising and financing institutions. With respect to collections there are:

- school libraries, children libraries and libraries for youth; the target groups are the youngsters.
- public libraries and trade union libraries which build their collections keeping in mind common people;
- special libraries (central and corporate SciTech libraries, Academical libraries, University libraries, etc.). The

target group consists of students, scientists and specialists. We have chosen two groups of Russian libraries for comparative analysis of the Project results. Position of special libraries and documentation centres was investigated on the ground of questionnaires. We have replies of 53% regional libraries and 67% of central scitech libraries.

The technical awareness of these groups is roughly equal, see Table IV; staff awareness and enduser awareness of these groups (estimated by themselves) are given in Table.

Regional libraries. In total there are 48, 9 thousand public libraries (38, 6 thousand of them are in rural area). Total stocks comprise 901, 8 mln. volumes, the number of users is 52 mln. There are 10 major Federal level libraries.

On the local level there are 77 Russian regions supplemented with 12 national entities. We'll consider here regional libraries but not national ones. These libraries cover whole territory of Russia. They have universal collections, the total stock-138, 8 mln volumes, the number of users-2, 6 mln. The attendance of these libraries has grown 2-3 times during last three years because of drastic increase of books prices, introduction of new programmes in the secondary schools and high schools, necessity to change profession for not to be unemployed.

***Technical Awareness (items in average) of Regional and Central Scitech Libraries***

| Items/libraries | PC | Local Area Networks | CD readers | Scanners | Desk Top Publishing |
|---|---|---|---|---|---|
| Regional | 23 | 1,4 | 2,3 | 0,6 | 0,5 |
| Central scitech | 23 | 0,3 | 2,3 | 1,3 | 0,1 |

In average each library has 23 LAN connected PCs, more 2 CD readers. Several libraries have bought integrated systems of computerization (TINLIB, LIBER, VTLS, ALEPH). Ministry of Culture initiated the networking of libraries. The first step was "LIBNET" project (1993-1994) which provided mutual access via switched public telephone lines to independent catalogues of 5 major Moscow region special libraries. On the provincial level the networking starts slowly. There are several academic and commercial networks in Russia, but due to very high costs of commercial X.25 and TCP/IP networks Russian libraries are forced to use low quality and unreliable public telephone switched lines.

***Staff Awareness for CD Service, Percent of Replies***

| | Needs training | Satisfactory | Good |
|---|---|---|---|
| Regional | 55 | 25 | 20 |
| Central scitech | 50 | 17 | 33 |

***SciTech Libraries:*** Special libraries now are in more difficult position compared with public ones. Special libraries are under the same pressure as the Russian industry and science are. Amidst special libraries we'll consider here central scitech ones thus excluding corporate scitech libraries, academical and university libraries. (University science in Russia is relatively weak if compared with Western traditions. For instance, university scientists is 7 times less equipped than average Russian scientist.)

The Russian National Public Library for Science and Technology (NPLS&T) is the major library of scientific and technical libraries system. The NPLS&T has 160 PCs, 90 of them are in a LAN. The library databases include: Russian Union catalogue of ScieTech literature; OPAC; 11 specialized and 18 subject-oriented; 4 databases have English version with abstracts. More 60 databases on CD-ROM are accessed locally on 7 workstations and remotely via local CD-network connected to LAN. Central SciTech libraries are part of information systems of Federal Ministries, all of them are in Moscow. Total stock is 9, 2 mln volumes, there are 62 thousand registered visitors. Most of CSTL are centres of the subsystems that unite affiliated scitech corporate libraries (ca 7 000) of institutions and enterprises. All CSTL and about 40% of the lower level libraries have IBM-and DEC-type computers which are changed now by PCs.

***Enduser Awareness for CD Service, Percent of Replies***

| | Needs training | Satisfactory | Good |
|---|---|---|---|
| Regional | 78 | 8 | 14 |
| Central scitech | 69 | 23 | 8 |

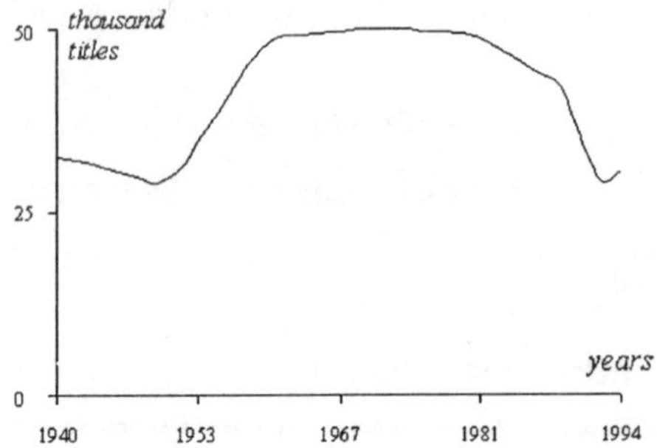


*Publications in Russia, books and brochures, thousand titles*

The issuing of books and booklets in Russia is shown on Fig 2. Having reached the level of 50 000 titles a year in the late 1950s-early 1960s, the country kept it stable till the second half of the 1980s. And then-the dramatic fall to the publishing level of 1940-ties. This drop is a structural one: publishing of political literature reduced by 10 times, while the amount of reference publications remained at the same level. Publishing of children's literature and fiction increased thanks to the new private publishing houses. There are ca 7000 registered publishing houses in 1995 compared with ca 200 publishing houses at the mid-eighties.

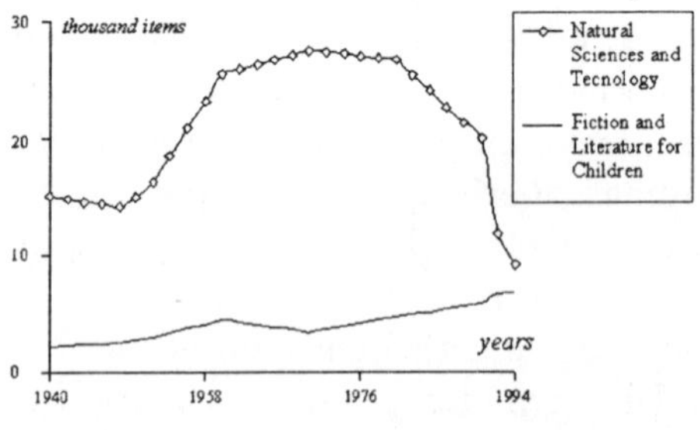


*Subject Publications in Russia, thousand titles*

Decreasing the number of authors. Several very strong teams of physicists and computer science specialists in Ukraine, group of mathematicians in Beylarus and Georgia, physicists and astronomers in Armenia, chemists and economists in Baltic republics stopped to publish in Russian. The most active part of Russian young scientists have emigrated: the losses in high tech laboratories (electronics, physics, biology) are 17%-25%. Estimations indicate that 40%-45% scientific results in nuclear physics, high energy physics, plasma physics, computer science are published in English directly. Besides numerical losses there appeared economical and psychological obstacles to publish. Russian industry has not free market competition yet so there is no motivation to improve quality or to reduce prices.

The reasons of reduction of scitech publications are:

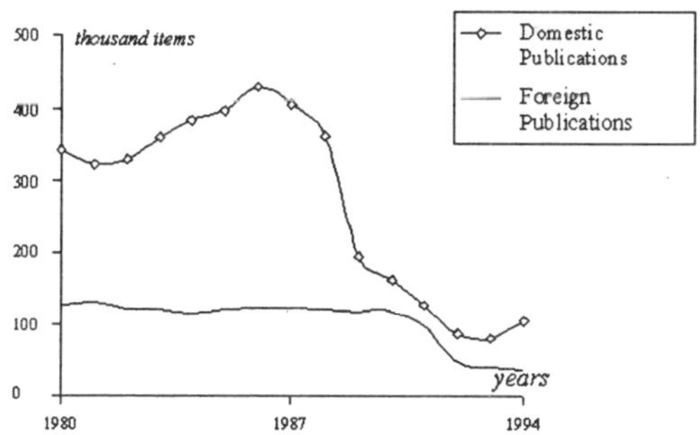


*Acquisitions of NPLS&T, thousand items*

Large libraries suffer from wide spread disobedience to Mandatory Copy Act obligations. The stipulated by this Act quantity-25 mandatory free of charge copies-is neglected. As soon as more 80% of publications are made in Moscow and S-Petersburg the regional libraries are not informed. The difference in acquisitions between the same level libraries could be astonishing, more 7 times. Estimated total 1994 publications in Russia were ca 30400 titles.

The dynamics of the NPLS&T acquisition of domestic and foreign literature. The Interlibrary Loan requests for domestic books. One could see drastic fall of the requests on ILL and DD. The informational isolation is augmented by unacceptable growth of transportation costs. In eighties the price of business trip from Siberia to Moscow equalled one-week salary of librarian; in mid-ninties the same business trip will cost as 6-month salary of the same librarian.

In the document delivery one should mention the multifold drop of the domestic and East European countries transactions.

The demand on Russian STI reduced due to pronounced orientation to the West markets. Quite opposite, the supply of scitech documents from Russia to the West has grown twofold during 1994.

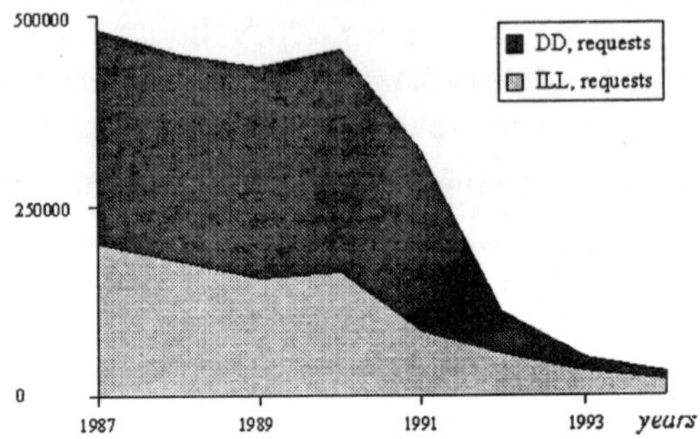


*Interlibrary Loans (ILL) and Document Delivery (DD) Activity*

CD project in Russia. The CD applications are very common now for all kinds of Russian libraries. Optical compact disks have emerged at Russian market in early 90-s. Despite CD holds less 3% of audio/video entertainment market this part of market is growing steadily, see Table VII. Russian 1994 domestic CD publishing was 500 titles, approximately 9 mln copies. Legal import was 10 mln copies and illegal import or illegal production altogether equals 10 mln disks.

***CD sales in Russia, mln disks***

| **1991** | **1992** | **1993** | **1994** |
|---|---|---|---|
| 0,3 | 2,0 | 8,0 | 30,0 |
| portion of illegal disks | | | |
| 100% | 95% | 66% | 30% |

Many CD projects began as part of Russian conversion of military industries programme. Till now capacious consumer market exists in education, entertainment and banking. CD ROM with special information production is strongly Western customer oriented. For many institutions CD publishing is not a business (profit oriented activity), but is an ambitious declaration of existence, of high-tech community membership. Choice of CD-ROM with special information is rather limited. Data reliability and updating are serious problems for many

Russian databases. Statistics. Librarians of both groups highly appreciate the importance of a full text grey literature CD-ROM development but only regional libraries are seriously planning to start deposition of electronic documents, Table VIII. The difference of intentions here is striking!

So summarizing the difference between central scitech and regional public libraries one should emphasize different scenarios of relevant publication, different strength of supervising bodies and different demand for information from target groups. Common features for these library groups are lack of money and striving to new technologies.

## ROLE OF COOPERATION

Cooperation is a social activity as old as human civilization itself. The aim of any cooperation activity is to achieve what the members of the group can not achieve individually. So library cooperation may be defined as a combined effort of two or more libraries to share their resources for providing better services to their user community.

Library cooperation is age old and can be traced to 200BC when Alexandria Library shared its resources with Pergamon Library. According to Kraus, there existed library cooperation among monastery libraries in the 13$^{th}$ century. There were exchanges of agreements among the universities of Lund, Abo and Greifswald as early as 1740. The other examples of library cooperation include a projected union catalogue of the libraries of Weimar and Jean and a proposal for a coordinated acquisition scheme for Walfenbuttel and Gottengen.

The 'Catalogue of Manuscripts in various parts of India' complied by Whitney Stokes in 1868, and in 1863 Part I of Sanskrit manuscripts in private libraries of Northwest provinces covering Varanasi was published. The first major union list entitled 'A Catalogue of Scientific and Technical Periodicals' was complied by Henry C.Bolton in 1885. With the advent of the 20$^{th}$ century, the Library of Congress started cooperative cataloguing projects and began working on the National Union Catalogue. Thereafter, in the 20$^{th}$ Century the compilations and publications of union catalogues of different types increased in number in most countries.

The first library cooperation activity in India is reported to be the Catalogue of Manuscripts complied by Whitney Stokes in 1868. Union catalogue development was one of major cooperative efforts in Indian libraries up to the 1960s. We can look at the following union catalogue development activities:

1918:-Catalogue of Scientific Serial Publications in the Principal Libraries in Calcutta complied by Stanley Kemp, Asiatic Society of Bengal.

1931:-List of Scientific Periodicals in the Bombay Presidency. Royal Institute of Science, Bombay.

1953:-Catalogue of Periodicals in CSIR organizations corrected up to December 1953 CSIR, New Delhi. Union Catalogue of Learned Periodical publications in South Asia, vol.1: Physical and Biological sciences compiled by S.R. Ranganathan and others. ILA, Delhi.

1956:-Catalogue of Medical Periodicals in Indian Libraries corrected up to December 31, 1955.4$^{th}$ ed. Director General of Health Services, Delhi.

1968:-A Union List of Learned American Serials in Indian Libraries. Indian Council for Library Development.

The 1960s also saw a large number of ILA and IASLIC national seminars devoted to the concept of library cooperation. However, with the advent of computers in library work, a change occurred. It is reported that the first use of computer in library work for the production of the Union List of Serials in 1964 using the IBM/602 machine at INSDOC. Since then library automation has been a matter of primary importance in Indian Libraries.

With the establishment of the National Informatics Centre (NIC) in 1975 and the development of NICNET in 1977, networking and communication technology in India received a major boost. This as a whole had a major influence in resource sharing among various libraries and information centres through networks. In 1984, the working group of the Planning Commission headed by Dr. N. Seshagiri recommended modernization of library services and inter linking of library systems in the seventh plan. The 1990s are said to be the golden period of library networking in India. There has been a plethora of publications and seminars on library networking during this period. Today besides INFLIBNET, there are various local library networks in India such as ADINET, BONET, BALNET, CALIBNET, DELNET, MALIBNET, MYLIBNET, and PUNENET etc.

We therefore notice that the efforts made for library cooperation in the $20^{th}$ century began with the compilation of union catalogues, as no cooperation could be effective without the knowledge of the resources of other libraries. The scope of co-operations soon took big leap. It became diversified and incorporated the various activities of the libraries such as Abstracting and Indexing, Acquisition, Bibliographic access, cataloguing, Circulations development, continuing education for staff and users, literature searching, management and accounting, microfilming, photo coping, processing, referral services, storage and union lists.

## Resources Sharing: Meaning, Need and Scope

Resources sharing is sharing of library resources such as document collection, staff members, technical facilities and mechanical aids among the participating libraries on the basic principle of cooperation, "All for one and one for all". In this respect it is possible to consolidate the document collection of participating libraries, exchange their technical capabilities and share their services. In this way it is possible to share the resources to provide on access to the vast amount of library and information sources to a larger user community at the least-cost. The objective of resource sharing is obviously to make the greatest amount of best information available to the most users at the reasonable cost.

Thus Resources sharing is a need-based concept founded on the sound principles of give and take. It is not the quantum of exchange but the real desire to do so, that is essential to become part and parcel of the important programme of resource sharing activities.

### NEED

There has been a voluminous growth of published documents in the recent part. As a result no library in able to procure, process or store all documents that its users demand. According to Kent " it is difficult to anyone single library to acquire even one percent of the total document published in the world" due to one or more of the following reasons:

(i) Growth of Knowledge in different subjects

(ii) Rapid increase of literature and growth of publication

In the second half of the $20^{th}$ century, the growth of new publication became unmanageable for traditional libraries. Its impact was felt primarily in major programmes and later by the smaller libraries.

In the field of Science and Technology alone about three million documents are published each year which includes articles, conference papers, books, technical reports and these the rate doubles every eight to ten years according to V.A. Kamath. There has been an alarming growth lately in journal articles. According to Faxton Company in USA, the number of journal titles rose from 38,079 in 1974 to 1,04,714 in 1989 an increase of 175 percent

According to Conen, Two articles are generated in the sciences alone every minute or over 10 lakh articles a year. Also fast production of literature takes in different places in different formats and in different subjects

(iii) Increasing trend of new born subjects and specialization

(iv) Limitations of funds

(v) Increase in the cost of publications

- According to Faxton company in USA, the average price per serial title paid by college and university libraries in 1979 was $50.11; by 1959 it has risen to $ 125.87. Scientific and technological libraries pay an average of $ 234 per serial title a year.
- The average price for foreign titles has risen from $41.34 per title in 1976 to $143.09 in 1989
- According to Bowker Annual 1989-90, the average prices of a monograph rose from $32..43 to $38.39 from 1986 to 1988

(vi) Increase in the number of members of user community teachers, scholars and students in universities.

(vii) The information needs of academic community being wide in scope and varied in nature

(viii) Such information needs being often repetitive and recurring

(ix) Lack of environment to make use of available computer and communication technology for efficient and production use in libraries.

Therefore some resource sharing is necessary between one library and another library to acquire more information in a specific subject with low cost as published records are increasing at on incredible rate and their prices are keeping pace, is such circumstances library cooperation will assume a pivotal role and resources sharing will become the focal point of cooperation.

## Scope

The idea of resource sharing for a long time was restricted to the area of lending of books and periodicals now it has become diversified and incorporated the various activities of the libraries such as abstracting and indexing, acquisition, bibliographic access, Cataloguing circulation, collection development continuing education for staff and user, literature searching management and accounting, microfilming photo coping, processing, referral services, storage and union lists. The resource sharing in modern times is helpful in the following four main activities.

*Acquiring books* – selection, ordering and purchase, etc.

*Recording books*-cataloguing and classification

*Making them available* –their own books by consultations and lending books not held by them by borrowing from elsewhere

*Storing books* – for present and future uses

***Shared Acquisition:*** The shared acquisition involves procurement of books, periodicals and other materials from publishers and booksellers of foreign and own country through mutual agreement among the participating libraries. By the process of shared acquisition the saving of money and time, avoiding wasteful duplications and building up a sound and large cumulative collection is possible. The savings on this count may be utilized for further utilization of documents to enrich the library collection. All the acquisition activities such as placing order, reminding the suppliers, passing bills and other activities, besides book selection can be reduced to a great extent through cooperative acquisition of documentation. This may bring down cost, care discount and save time and labour of individual libraries participating in the system. The various problems associated with subscribing foreign journals can be avoided through cooperative acquisition.

***Shared Cataloguing:*** The processing of library materials is claimed to be the highest shares of bottleneck in library work. Serious attentions being paid to document processing under the concept or resource sharing. The shared cataloguing projects of USA, UK, Australia and Canada have shown how processing work could be done very effectively, and economically, saving lot of time, effort and money. The on-line computer Library centre (OCLC) project and the library of congress shared cataloguing projects have shown how shared processing of library documents can undertaken and how the individual libraries can save their time and lab our.

***Future Scenario:*** The future scenario of resources sharing could be termed as 'Global resources sharing interconnections' Not only are these interconnection going to grow because of INTERNET and electronic publishing, but their growing trends are felt at various regional groupings two. There will be a gradual move towards greater integration of services and resources sharing.

## Resource Sharing through Network

As indicated earlier, the past few decades have witnessed knowledge and information explosion the world over and inadequate financial resources to do the best in terms of dissemination of knowledge and information. Under these circumstances, resource sharing and cooperative functioning of libraries and information centres through networking becomes vital. Efficient resource sharing can be achieved by using recent advances in Information Technology, *i.e.* networking of libraries and information centres through Local Area Networks, Metropolitan Area Networks, Wide Area Network and so on. Network of information/Resource sharing is to use the computer and telecom link for transmission of information or data from one library to another. Keeping this concept in view, various library networks have been established for cooperation and resource sharing among libraries. They have grown mostly during the last thirty years in different geographical environments in order to cater to the specific needs of users. In the United States, there has been a proliferation of them. Library networks in other countries are also growing. Several models have emerged that provide specific services. Not all networks conform to the essential functions of library networks. However, it is noted that the essential functions should include:

- promotion of resource sharing,
- creation of resource sharing tools like bibliographic databases such as union lists of serials, union catalogue of books, periodicals, bibliographic databases of articles and other types of materials such as CDs, Video recording, sound recording, theses, dissertations etc.,
- rationalization of acquisition,
- adoption of international standards for creation of records uniformly,
- delivery of documents, etc.

### India

In India, as elsewhere, economic pressures, enormous growth of publications and emergence of subject specialization have compelled the libraries and information centres to think of sharing the information resources and optimizing the use of existing resources within India as well as from abroad through various networking systems. Some of the notable networks in India are NICNET, ERNET, SIRNET, INDONET and INET. In addition, there is a major initiative from the University Grants Commission called INFLIBNET, interconnecting universities, colleges and resource institutions countrywide.

### National Level Resource Sharing

As stated earlier, INFLIBNET, a national level resource sharing of university libraries was set up in 1986 under Professor Yashpal Kapoor, the Chairman of UGC, INFLIBNET is a multiple functions/service network with focus on resource sharing and cooperation through computer communication links. It is very useful to all libraries and their readers. For this purpose, it is possible to create data banks in different subject fields, produce a number of bibliographical tools and information services. It is also possible to conserve a lot of library resource avoiding duplication at the national level.

But under the present conditions, it is not congenial to initiate a network of libraries at the national level, because all universities in India depend on the finance from central and state governments. The various universities have their own district characteristics based on factors such as geographical, linguistic and political. Each university library is following its own pattern and procedure in its routine work. For this reason, there is no uniformity and standardization. However, such a networking can be initiated in a limited environment, regional or state level.

## State Level Resource Sharing

In India, formation of a network of university libraries in all states is possible only if the concerned administrative and professional staff and supporting agency make a sincere attempt in this direction. They should plan to co-ordinate programmes of all universities in the state to form a uniform academic calendar.

They have to establish a body like Council of Higher Education to initiate a network of libraries in the state say KAULIBNET (Karnataka State University Library Network) in the interest of larger academic community. They should bring all the affiliated colleges within the fold of state level library network and extend the services to colleges.

It is not difficult to bring uniformity and adopt a standard procedure in all participating libraries within the state. After achieving the success in running the network at the state level, it is possible to link all such state level networks to the national level network. Further, it will not be difficult to link university libraries network with specialized networks in the field of library and information in India, using sophisticated modern technology and satellite facilities.

## City Level Resource Sharing

Specialized library networks have come up for individual cities like DELNET, CALIBNET, MALIBNET, PUNENET, BALNET, ADINET, BONET, MYLIBNET, etc. These networks are meant essentially for providing a centralized database of library information to be accessed by its user libraries, mostly in a particular city for the purpose of resource sharing.

In the present day of limited resources, it is imperative that an integrated view of these networks and National Information Systems and Centres on the possibility of sharing resources among them should be taken to explore avoiding duplication of efforts, materials and resources and maximizing the utilization as they form the base for successful networking. Access through any network in the globe can be obtained virtually through INTERNET which is widely used international network.

## Criticism of Resource Sharing

Resource sharing, despite its various advantages, has certain disadvantages too. The critics voice concern on the following points:

- If all libraries depend on resource sharing, no library will have books to lend;
- If cooperative acquisition doesn't operate well, serious gaps in the collection of a library will result;
- Without the sophisticated technology, resource sharing would have very limited value;
- Cost consideration may not permit resource sharing;
- The reaction of the publishing trade, if their sale gets reduced;
- Large libraries have to share a greater burden of lender rather than borrower which is not beneficial to them.

The criticism of resource sharing is no doubt sound and partially valid. But there seems to be no alternative to this. INSDOC's document supply service is an example which has been continuing for over the last four decades. INSDOC sources approximately 28,000 orders annually. We may conclude that Library cooperation is the key to the successful functioning of a library and without it, it cannot provide effective service to its users. Without cooperation, it is impossible to start sharing of resources. We notice that the sharing of resources can help:

- acquire library materials;
- share holdings;
- provide researchers with an increased number of research materials;
- avoid duplicate purchases;
- ensure collection of special material and services;
- establish efficient communication systems;
- prepare union catalogue; and
- develop an information marketing mechanism through cooperation and control of the quality of collections.

**Steps to Promote Resource Sharing through Network**

As we have seen networking of libraries is essential for sharing of library resources, the same should be promoted at local, regional, national and international level. Following steps are to be taken to promote resource sharing through networks:

1. Important libraries, information centres and institutions get their catalogues and bibliographies prepared in machine readable form to provide computer aided information services to users and promoting automation of the functions in their libraries such as cataloguing, circulation, preparation of bibliographies, union catalogue, etc.
2. To promote sharing of resources among the libraries in India by developing and disseminating information and by offering computerized services to the users.
3. To optimize information resources utilization through shared cataloguing, interlibrary loan services, catalogue production, collection development and avoiding duplication in acquisition to the extent possible.
4. Encourage cooperation among libraries, documentation centres and information centres so that pooled resources can augment weaker resources centres.
5. The promotion of non-bibliographic databases in India, especially by National Informatics Centre has enabled

institutions to perfect computer and networking technology.

6. In house functions like acquisition, cataloguing, classification, serial control, circulation, SDI, current awareness services, etc.; the network should support these library operations and the libraries should use the data in the central port for this purpose.
7. The participating libraries should follow the rules and regulations of the network and be willing to create bibliographic records according to standards laid down.
8. Anglo-American Cataloguing Rules (AACR-2) should be used as the code for cataloguing. It will help in creation of standard records.
9. Library of Congress Subject Headings (LCSH) should be used as a guide for creating subject descriptors. Other thesauri available on specialized subjects could also be used whenever needed in specialized libraries.
10. The network should provide technical assistance to participating libraries in the creation of bibliographic databases.
11. A panel of experts should be maintained for providing assistance to libraries.
12. A central host machine should be installed for creating a union catalogue, combining catalogues of all participating libraries.
13. As libraries in India use mainly Dewey Decimal Classification (DDC), Universal Decimal Classification (UDC) and Classified Catalogue Code (CCC) for classification of books, it would not be within the means and worth the effort to have one classification scheme in all participating libraries.
14. The network should promote inter-library service and sharing of foreign periodicals should be attempted. As far as possible, foreign exchange should be saved on avoidable duplication titles. A courier service should be established to support the sharing of resources.
15. All serials should also be published in electronic format and the availability of serials in electronic format, either outline or CD-ROM.

16. Most of the abstracting and indexing services have cumulated the entries forming into databases, which can be searched online.
17. Networking activities should increase in India. Government should take an interest in this field. Some of the important networks established are NICNET, I-NET, ERNET, SIRNET, INFLIBNET.

Thus we see that with this network, we can pool together all resources of all libraries, resources of all universities, colleges, research institutions, various departments and also the resources of individuals. It will be possible for us to acquire a greater number of information sources taken together in all the libraries in the country. These can inter-connect people, *i.e.* students, teachers, researchers, users, etc. It is, therefore, assumed and expected that in order to have quick access by educated or creative member of the society to whatever is happening in their own country or the world over, networks are considered as a boon.

## IMPACT OF IT IN LIBRARIES

### Information Technology

Information technology simplifies the coming together of the disciplines of electronic, computer hardware and software, communication (in particular telecommunications), artificial intelligence and human machine interface. UNESCO has defined information technology as "The Scientific, technological and engineering disciplines and the management techniques used in information handling and current interaction with men and machines and associated social, economic and cultural matters".

It acts as one of the major tools to shape our society and our institutions – particularly our libraries as one of the most important influences in education, culture and society. Information technology, through the moulding of computer technology with communications, digital imaging and full-motion video and sound, can be a powerful ally to improve education and thus improving skills for gainful employment. Cut, in order to do this, libraries and librarians will have to change. If the right changes are made by iibraries of every persuasion, there would be a good information technologies. These systems would become major information delivery systems to a wide variety of societal segments.

## Information Technology: Its impact on Information and Communication Media

The rapid and exponential growth of information has made it necessary for librarians and information scientists to employ new techniques to cope with the massive proliferation of literature in all subject fields. Research in the science and social sciences has led to high productivity in document publication. To bring this vase amount of information under bibliographic control and to render it useful and accessible to potential users is a great task. The information is valuable only if its is retrieved timely and cost effective. The scientific application of knowledge has necessitated to keep abreast of the latest information and makes necessary to keep interaction with working in advanced and frontier areas. So, in this age of information explosion/overload, keeping track of information resource and managing the same are the key to achievement and success.

Acquisition, organization, delivery and storage of information have always been the main tasks of any real library. Emerging new technologies offer new ways of handling these tasks. We can summarize the impact of ever renewing information technology on communication media and information in the following manner:

| Work | Technology (Form Old to New) | |
|---|---|---|
| 1. Communication | • Personal Travel<br>• Postal | • Teleconferencing<br>• Teletext<br>• Satellite transmission |
| 2. Inputting (Pri mary Form at) | • Oral Presentation<br>• Writing & Typing | • Word processing<br>• Optical scanning through computer |
| 3. Multiplication | • Printing | • Computer Visual Display Terminals<br>• Video discs and cassettes<br>• Computerized photo printing |
| 4. Storage | • Book shelves & Pamphlet<br>• Microform storage devices | • Computer based digital and analogue storage |
| 5. Information | • Browsing through surrogates in catalogue and through shelves | • Browsing through on-line terminals<br>• Database software |

## Information Technology Environment

Computers have made possible the availability of information and have brought many benefits in library and information systems and services. The computers' application to the information storage, retrieval and dissemination are the inevitable consequences of the information explosion/overload. The application of computers to information storage and retrieval has brought new possibilities of automatic indexing and free text searching for the words or phrases on the subject, which is likely to occur in any document, and the computer is set to read entire document for the appropriate words or phrases. The development of digital representation of information has made the computer an effective tool for data processing.

The qualitative changes in design and architecture of computers and their software have enlarged the sphere or computer applications in library and information centres. The computers are of great significance with the advancement of telecommunication and reprography technologies in the library automation. When computers interconnected by some of the modern communicable vehicles, *i.e.* through networking one can have information over vast distances in no times.

## Applications of IT

Information Technology provides an excellent opportunity for library professionals to manage themselves better. Application of communication technology and electronic data processing of information have made a great impact on libraries and information centres, and the computers and associated facilities have come to be recognized as indispensable for accurate storage, processing, retrieval and dissemination of information. All librarians should be perfectly familiar with the benefits of modern technology and perform efficiently. The main features of the recent development in Information Technology can be briefed as follows:

- Increased reliability of hardware and software
- Cheaper data storage, *e.g.* optical storage media
- Increased software knowledge leads to speedier and cheaper computer processing

- Wide use of communication (particularly telecommunication) techniques

These have led to the development of

- Local, national and international online systems
- Automated library systems
- Public Access Catalogue
- Electronic journals and electronic knowledge banks
- Computerized databases and floppies/diskettes, magnetic tapes, CD-ROMs, DVD, etc. for storage.

There has been a very considerable increase in the amount of information available in the form of full-text documents, bibliographical references, factual and numerical data and at the same time increase in the complexity of information handling and storage system.

***Computerized Databases/Library Software:*** In this modern scientific world, manual handling of information has become difficult and complicated. This old system is not accurate and speeding to channetise the information. In order to meet these problems, computerized databases like CDS/ISIS and other advanced useful library packages have already been set up in advanced countries like USA, UK, Germany, Japan and other developed countries. In developing countries, cheaper databases like CDS/ISIS and others are going to be used, in few cases these are widely used but in majority cases, they are still unfamiliar with the utilities of these library software.

In India, along with the use of CDS/ISIS, many purposeful packages like Sanjay, Libsis, Granthalaya, Basisplus, Techlibplus, Libris, Librarian-4 and other relevant packages have come into existence. These innovative software packages are helping the modern librarians in processing and distributing the information and extending the scope of sophisticated kinds of information technology.

Many hardware industries like Wipro and Penguin India Ltd. Have come forward in manufacturing library-relevant packages which give users almost instant access to a large portion of scientific and technological knowledge by means of On-line communication technology.

***Computerized Services:*** Since information literature grows at exponential rate causing problem of space for storage and speedy utilization of vast amount of information, the librarians may take advantages of the computer while searching and retrieving the required information useful to users. The computers are being increasingly used in library and information services for information processing and repackaging of information and on improving products and services of Library and Information Centres. In modern days, many librarians prefer to adopt computers because of their following advantages:

- its low-cost
- its fast and constant response
- its availability and portability
- its software
- its freedom from establishment

Recently, there has developed an awareness of the importance of computers and librarians have started using non-book materials for information transfer. Librarians can utilize computers in their various house keeping activities and information services as mentioned below:

(i) *Computerized services – Technical Section:* The technical processing desires occupies significant role in the channel of library administration. Computerization of these services would facilitate the library staff as well as information seekers while searching the relevant information.

(ii) *Computerized Services – Circulation Section:* Computerized information facilitates the librarians to deal with day-to-day operations, planning and decision making. This is an informative package useful to the library managers and other subordinate staff for carrying out their regular work and routine processing of the transactions. For example, facts such as book orders, bills and other matters must be available to them to carry out daily works efficiently. If this information is made available speedily, library staff can do routine duties perfectly and promptly.

(iii) *Computerized Services Periodical Section:* The acquisition and processing of periodicals are common functions in academic, special and public libraries. In order to maintain and process the details, a library has to maintain large volumes of various registers. The maintenance of register is tedious and every year a large set of data has to added. Accession registers occupy much space and they are expensive. Manual cataloguing also may not be at uniform standard. It is time consuming and difficult to maintain the large set of data also. Manual calculations are likely to have errors and it is difficult to check all types of errors. To a librarian the modern technology would have a great boon.

***Networking and Network based services:*** In this information age, with enormous growth of publication and emergence subject specialization and economic pressures on libraries, it has become essential for the libraries and information centres to think of sharing the information resources among libraries and optimizing the use of existing resources thought the use of computer and telecommunication technology by establishing various networking systems.Through library networking, users can scan and monitor the information they require, which a particular library doesn't hold but other library holds that particular information, without loss of time and at a minimum cost. Resource sharing networks offer:

- Document delivery and interlibrary loan services
- Shared cataloguing
- Cooperative collection development
- Coordinated acquisition
- Reference assistance
- Consultation and staff training
- Email, facsimile service, bulletin boards etc.

Access through any network in the globe can be obtained virtually through INTERNET which is widely used international network.

Automated libraries can also help sharing of information through CD-ROM networking. With the increasing tend in electronic publications particularly on CD-ROMs and networks, automated libraries are going to be converted into electronic libraries. The introduction of multi-user and multi task CD-ROM systems has made more economic for most of the organizations, especially where the same data or database are required for several users.

It is relevant to monitor that a number of Indian libraries have a status of rich document collection. Through automation and networking, these rich resources can be put to best possible are not only in their respective states but even outside whenever there would be demand for the information.

## AREAS OF LIBRARY AUTOMATION

As stated earlier, libraries should adopt the new sophisticated information technology tools to provide accurate and instant information and to cope up with the demands of new knowledge, the enormous increase in the collection of documents, their problems of storage, dissemination and retrieval of information. Today, the term 'Library Automation' is used to refer "the extensive use of mechanical, electronic or microelectronic equipments to perform the functions and activities associated with the libraries, such as acquisition, serial control, cataloguing and circulation and also to library and information services and networking". Computers are used in libraries to assist in a number of library routines necessary for efficient day-to-day functioning what we call 'house keeping activities'. They are also used for formatting and generation of indexes.

The computers are of great significance with the advancement of telecommunication and reprography technologies in the library automation – when computers interconnected by some of the modern communication vehicles, one can have information over vast distances in no time. The computers are being increasingly used in library and information services for information processing and repackaging of information and on improving products and services of library and information centres. They offer a versatile tool for organization and retrieval of information.

## House Keeping Activities

Library took necessary for efficient day-to-day functioning and falling into the area of 'house keeping' consist of procedure for acquisition, cataloguing, circulate and serial control.

***Acquisition:*** Acquisition and ordering systems in libraries cover the selection, ordering and accessioning of items into the library's collection. Computers are used:

- to send order slips and 'chasers' for unacknowledged or overdue orders to the booksellers.
- to produce lists of books on order
- to keep accounts of money spent
- to produce accession lists of recently acquired books.

The detailed input to an acquisition system covers

- new orders
- amendments to existing orders
- bookseller's reports
- acknowledgement of receipt of items in the library

Selection of new books can be done from commercially available services which disseminate information about forthcoming documents, or directly from MARC tapes or any local inputs.

Two files are maintained in a computer-based acquisition system. One is the main file containing records of all current orders. The second is a file with the names and addresses of booksellers used by the library. A code number for each bookseller links the two files, so that booksellers information is not repeated in the order file. The system prints out the orders addressing the appropriate supplier printing of orders can also be done on special pre-printed stationery that can be sent directly to the book-seller.

By checking with the date of entering the order record into the file, 'chasers' can be sent to the booksellers, if no information regarding the order has been received within a predetermined time.

When the item is received in the library, the order record with the bibliographic details becomes the basis of the catalogue record. The edited record is merely added to the catalogue file in an integrated system. Other processes that can be performed by a computerized acquisition system are:

- listing items on order, by author, department or subject;
- new accessions listing;
- notifying individuals who have recommended a particular book, about the receipt of that book;
- control of accounts;
- production of relevant statistics to help management decisions.

***Circulation Control:*** This is one library service that is most accessible to computerization. The advantages are especially seen in the amount of time saved in issue and discharge routines, and the avoidance of bottlenecks, which are the basic of any library. Circulation systems using computers have the details of the book issued and the person borrowing it is entered on files. Dates of return are on the basis of the period of loan (one week, a fortnight etc.). Daily check of the files will identify what books are due or overdue and notices can be typed and sent to the users who have borrowed them. Provision for reservation data will make it possible to pick out these books for which there is a request and a user can be asked to return that particular book.

The circulation process in a computerized system depends on giving unique identification codes to books and to users. An accession number or a call number can be used as this is a unique identification key for a book. Users can be given individual identity codes.

***Cataloguing:*** Cataloguing includes the job of describing, recording and displaying details of the holdings of the library. Computers are used to aid in the production, maintenance and updating of catalogues. The quality of the catalogue depends ultimately on the cataloguer. In other words, initial input data is still the cataloguer's work.

Bibliographic details are gathered from relevant sources or from the acquisitions system. Usually there is one main or master file for the holdings of the library, and a temporary file for cumulating the additional records, because printing the master file is done only once in while.

After initial input of the records, the computer can perform simple tests on the record structure, and errors can be located and checked. Again, if a basic record structure of a package format as that of the CDS/ISIS is used, entry of data becomes a very simple process. The computer can be asked to generate added entries, if required, which can later be sorted into the main file. Separate listings for authors, subject and key points of access can be created. A postings file and an inverted index helps the computer search and display record relevant to a specific query.

***Serials Control:*** Serial control through the use of the computer is perhaps one of the most complicated tasks of housekeeping. This is perhaps because of the literally unpredictable nature of serial publications. Some of the functions of the serials control system that can be handled by the computer are:

(i) Listing of Serials holdings: is basically producing a catalogue of serials. However with serials, there are problems relating to change in title, periodicity etc. A listing system will depend on the bibliographic record for each serial being available in machine readable form. From a master file of such serials records, individual listing can be made based on title, subject, publishers/suppliers etc. Union lists of serials holdings by librarians within a geographic region can also be produced by computer.

(ii) Accessioning of serials: must take into account receipt of issues, and periodicity of the serial, likely date or receipt in order to be able to send claims notices to suppliers for items not received, and to update the holding file. To predict the arrival of periodical parts. Each record must contain information about the publication pattern of the serial. This relates to the number of volumes per calendar year, number of parts per volume supplements, if any, the pattern of numbering parts, and the frequencies of publication. Algorithms can be written with reference to the real calendar which use information on the details given above, to predict the arrival of each issue. Prediction cards called 'chaser' notices can be sent to the suppliers when an issue is overdue. Details of the suppliers and the price per volume are necessary for the system to handle subscription, renewals and accounting functions.

## Information Search and Retrieval

Creation of bibliographic databases has become one of the essential and key activities of library automation. The search process on a computerized database has many advantages over search from a catalogue by manual methods in term of speed, and accuracy. Any library or information can create first a set of machine readable records of its holdings, based on a structured format, or using a database package like the CDS/ISIS.

Users can search the database through key terms of author, subject or title, which are formulated into a search expression using Boolean operators (logical connections AND, NOT OR). Computer will display relevant terms/records that match the terms of the user's request. Current Awareness listings, Selective Dissemination of Information (SDI) and retrospective searches are the services where the computer capabilities can be used very effectively.

Index generation is another area where computer are generally of use. Computer can be used to format the entries in a permuted index and also to generate the entries for an index. Keywords can be derived from the bibliographical description, or assigned to describe the document (subject keys) and then put into the required format. KWIC indexes for instance, can be produced from titles of documents, with keywords and content generation performed by the computer. Stop lists of put forward lists prevent words like 'a', 'the', 'of', etc. from being used as the key terms. Fully automatic indexing can also be done through statistical analysis and word frequency counts with weighting, provided the text is machine-readable form.

## Advantages of Library Automation

Library automation or computer applications in library and information functions and services has the following advantages:

(i) *Speed:* Information processing is done much faster which ensures better work flow through the library.

(ii) *Accuracy:* The degree of precision and accuracy in processing information is high. However, it is dependent on the accuracy of information led into the system.

(iii) *Cost Effectiveness:* Operating costs can be reduced if the system is well designed and well managed.

(iv) *Reduction in Library Work Loads:* Library workloads can be reduced as the computer can do vast amount of work and processing.

(v) *Improved Services to Users:* High rate and better quality in performance is possible through the use of computers.

(vi) Avoids/eliminates duplication of work.

(vii) Easier access to external databases

(viii) Providing on-line access and search of information possible.

Looking at the advantages of Library automation in library functions and services, it is highly recommended that libraries/ information centres should follow the same in India, as here more than 97% libraries are still using the traditional and orthodox systems in their library services. India should keep pace with the changing scenario and acknowledge and utilize the computers as an internal part of library house keeping and services as libraries in the USA, UK, Japan and other countries are making their full use.

## LIBRARY NETWORKS: MEANING, NEED & OBJECTIVES

***Meaning:*** The development of sophisticated technologies in computer and communication field has upset libraries world wide in storing and transmitting information. The computer and its communication circuits link to other computer or to terminals constituting an integral information machine.

This technology introduced the 'Network System'. When a group of libraries using computers decide to exchange information, a network is developed. The National Commission on Libraries and Information Science (NCLIS) in its National Programme Document (1975) defines a network as:

*"Two or more libraries and/or other organizations engaged in a common pattern of information exchange, through communications, for some functional purpose. A network usually consists of a formal arrangement whereby materials, information and services provided by a variety of libraries and other organizations are available to all potential users. Libraries may be in different jurisdictions but agree to serve one another on the same basis as each serves its own constituents. Computer and telecommunications may be among the tools used for facilitating communication among them".*

***According to Martin:*** "A network is a group of individuals or organizations that are interconnected. The linking must include a communication mechanism, and many network exist for he express purpose of facilitating certain types of communication among their members. In the library world, institutions from network primarily to achieve better sharing of resources – resources consisting of bibliographic information and of collection – and better services to patrons". It must be emphasized that the particular focus in this gathering will be on online networks, those using computers and linking members to the computer resources by means of telecommunication connections. A library network is a description of an activity which existed before the term itself was devised. When any two libraries talk to each other, we have the fundamental condition for networking, that is exchange. When one library provides a service to another, we have the rudiments of network behaviour. Inter-library loan or bibliographic exchange in any form, is the chief justification of a network. Networking is a system with a predominant How of service and a reverse flow of demand. When a librarian asks his neighbour for a book or a citation and his request is honoured networking begins. Librarians now tend to view a collection as not merely what they possess in their institution, but all materials they have access to through photocopying, inter-library loan and reciprocal borrowing privileges.

***Data:*** Bibliographic records (MARC) frequently

***Retrieval:*** Author/title/number (subject) (keyword)

*Access:* Telecommunication network/Private network/Hard wired network

*Users:* Librarians (Public)

The above classification shows that library networks have the following features:

- One type of data
- Committed user base
- High Professional needs
- Low end-user needs

Networks enable librarians, faced with clients' information needs beyond their local resources, to identify and obtain materials and services for those clients. As we move increasingly into electronic information era, we see technology and networks working together to reduce the physical movement of materials.

## Need for Networking

As a universal phenomenon, libraries the world over are facing two major problems. These are:

a. Information explosion

b. Price escalation of library documents

c. Increased cost of library services

The number of publications in various disciplines, especially in Science and Technology is alarming. It is estimated in the past that the primary source of literature in the field of Science and Technology is doubling in every 15 years whereas it now doubling in 10 years. According to UNESCO statistics of World Book Production, about three lakh books are published every year. The number of learned journals in the field of science and technology alone has now come to the tune of 60,000 adding at the rate of 1000 journals a year approximately.

Another important problem the librarians/information professionals are facing is the constant increase in the prices of library documents. Since Indian libraries have to depend mainly on foreign publications, especially in the case of science and technology journals they have to face sharp increase in the rates of subscription and downward changes in the value of rupees. This hydro-headed problems have forced the librarians and information specialists to cut down the number of journals they procured to manage the situation within the available resources. Another problem is increasing cost of library services as costs of library services have skyrocketed, libraries have realized that through cooperative arrangement there is the possibility of providing new services whose cost would be spread over many institutions. The concept of cooperation proves much effective and satisfies the user needs in a better way.

Thus, we notice in order to find a solution to the problems faced by libraries/information centres regarding information explosion and costs, library networks have been established for cooperation and resource sharing among libraries so that one individual libraries may not feel burdensome while handling vast amount of information and price escalation of library documents and services.

## Aims and Objectives of Library Networks

As we have seen earlier, the basic purpose for creating a network is to provide information services to member libraries through sharing of resources of the participating libraries of the network. This may lead to member libraries to depend more on access to documents held in the other member libraries than on depending only on their respective collection. The main aims and objectives of library network are stated as the following:

To promote resource sharing and cooperation activities among libraries by providing efficient and reliable means of resource sharing, *e.g.*

- Inter library loan for maximum use of resources
- Document Delivery Services – providing the copies of the copies of the document what is not available in their respective libraries
- Manpower training and refresher course facilities – stimulating, promoting and coordinating research and training programme for library staff and network members
- Access to national and international databases
- Communication link through publication and interpersonal communication.

To improve resource utilization and service level at the individual libraries by providing automation facilities in the following areas:

- Acquisition and fund accounting
- Cataloguing – assist member libraries in cataloguing of books, serials, non-book materials and catalogue production
- Serials control
- Circulation
- User services – implementing electronic services in the libraries for fast communication of information.

To coordinate efforts for suitable collection development and reduce unnecessary duplication wherever possible. The purpose is:

- To develop collection by mutual cooperation
- To reduce the operational cost of the collection development
- To control the rate of rising cost of the collection development

To establish referral centres to monitor and facilitate catalogue search and maintain a central on-line union catalogue of books, serials and non-book materials of all the participating libraries. To develop a specialist bibliographic database of books, serials and non-book materials for search and access. To create a database of projects, specialists and institutions for providing online information services. To coordinate with other regional, national and international networks for exchange of information and documents for the use of libraries and users.

To evolve standards and uniform guidelines in techniques, methods, procedures, hardware and software, services and so on and promote adoption in actual practice by all libraries, in order to facilitate pooling, sharing and exchanging resources and facilities towards optimization.

## FUNCTIONS OF LIBRARY NETWORKS

Library Networks have been established with the main purpose of sharing resources so that unnecessary wastage of limited finance with them can be avoided.

However, not all networks conform to the essential functions of library networks. It is noted that the essential functions should include the promotion of resource sharing, creation of resource sharing tools like union catalogues, rationalization of acquisitions and adoption of international standards for creation of records uniformly and delivery of documents. Keeping these things in view, functions of a typical library network might fall into the following three categories:

(i) Information services to users

(ii) Technical services to member libraries

(iii) Management service to the network administration

Information and technical services are goal-oriented, *i.e.* to fulfil the primary goal of the network. Functions that serve the users directly, *i.e.* information services to users are:

**Information Services**

- Inter-library loan service – it means that each member library may require to have the facility to photocopy for delivering the documents.
- Reference and Referral – each member library may require the facility of having dedicated telephone and/ or E-mail service.
- Access to databases – to prepare retrospective bibliography for the purpose of browsing to know whether or not a document is available.

**Technical Services**

Functions that serve the libraries *i.e.* the technical services are:

- Cooperative collection development programme
- Technical processing involved in acquisition
- Cataloguing and other means of resources to identify and to locate documents
- Circulation control system

**Management Services**

The management services, *i.e.* functions that support the network administration are:

- Establish an operational system that implement the functions mentioned above
- Evaluation of the networks. This is done through
- collection of statistics
- analysis of performance of the network
- user studies
- Training activities. These are done through
- staff development programmes
- user oriented programmes
- Cost analysis

It involves:

- determination of costs, fees to be collected, etc.
- allocation of budgets
- Communication of activities such as
    - holding of meetings
    - publication of newsletters, etc.

**STRUCTURE OF NETWORKING**

The earlier stated functions of a network can be implemented in different models of networks.

The structure of a network will depend upon the purpose for which libraries use it. A number of libraries should join the network that offers the facilities to make their functioning simpler, better and more cost effective. For instance, university libraries in a state may choose a model which is of totally decentralized type.

However, the affiliated colleges in a university system can be linked to the respective university library, such a model may be known as distributed type. The public library system may choose a model of hierarchical type. Special libraries in a city may choose a model, which is of totally decentralized.

These are three basic anatomical structures, namely:

- Star network
- Hierarchical network
- Distributed network

### Star Network

In a star network, one of the members maintains and operates a centralized bibliographical database. This database consists of all the bibliographical records of every member libraries. The configuration may be

The node P holds all the bibliographical resources (databases) with all other members A, B, C, D, E utilizing these resources. It is the obligation of the node P to maintain and update the databases.

### Hierarchical Network

Each member shares resources locally; each participating library at the lower level passes unsatisfied needs to the participating library which is at the higher level. The requests remaining unsatisfied are referred to the 'library of last resort' which may be obliged to check other centres to locate required materials. The configuration is:

Users of the network, members $A_1$, $A_2$, $A_3$, $A_4$ are mostly satisfied with the resources available in their respective libraries. Unsatisfied requests are passed on to the higher level resource centre B, finally the few remaining unsatisfied requests are referred to the library of last resort C which may be obliged to check other centres $B_2$ and $B_3$ to locate required materials.

### Distributed Network

In a totally decentralized model, a type of distributed model, all network members hold in theory different resources which they may share with one another.

Here all members A, B, C, D, E, have different resources which they share with one another.

A modified model of a decentralized network looks like

Here A, B, C and D are themselves a network, either to star type or a hierarchical type.

## NETWORK TECHNOLOGY: A BRIEF IDEA

The world over, library networks and consortia have developed technologies to facilitate the process of accessing databases, retrieval of information, processing of interlibrary loan requests and the delivery of documents. So we must have some idea about the network technology in general – various terms used in the context of networking, standards, protocols and the software that convert data from one format to another and the technology relevant to Information and information Service field in particular.

### Basic Network Architecture/Topology

A network's architecture is the way the data flows within the network. The basic building blocks of a network are nodes, hubs and backbones

- Node-a node is any piece of hardware on the system that can be addressed by a message from another node, that is, a computer, printer, fax, modems or CD-ROM drive

Hub-It is a device that accepts multiple connections. Nodes are connected to it. It, also known as concentrator, simplifies the wiring of the nodes to each other and routes signals between the nodes. There are many different types of hubs. Some are simple hardware devices that only accept connections called passive hubs; others are complicated electrical components that monitor and control the flow of information to various network locations called active hubs.

### Ring Architecture

It arranges the nodes on the network in a circle. When one of the computers on the network sends a signal, it passes it to the next node on the network. If it is not addressed to that node, it is retransmitted to the next node and so on around the circle until it reaches the node it is addressed to. The connections between computers are not direct, instead, each computer attaches to a hub and the ring itself resides inside the hub.

### Star Architecture

It has the nodes connected to a central, host, computer when one of the computers as the network sends a signal, the next routes it to the node it's addressed to. There are no direct connections between the nodes on the network except through the host computer.

## Bus Architecture

Bus, or linear, architecture connects all nodes to a single bus much as the components are organized within the computer. A signal addressed to another node is sent to the bus. All other nodes on the network examine the signal to see if it is addressed to one of them. Typically, wires connect each node to the network's backbone, which is a fixed length of cable with terminator at both ends to stop reflections when signals hit the end.

## Hardware Components of a Network

*Servers:* A server on a network is any computer that can shared by other computers working on the network. In many cases, the server has to be the most powerful computer on the network, because it is shared among so many users or clients. These clients (computers) depend on the server for programmes and data, or connection to other computers and devices.

## File Server

It stores data files and some application programmes. It has large amounts of secondary storage in the form of hard disks, CD-ROM drives, tape drives and other storage dievices.

## Print Server

It stores print jobs on a hard disk until the printer is ready to handle them.

## Communication Server

It can be a fax or modem over which data from any other node can be sent. It can also be used as a gateway to the Internet.

*Network Interface Card:* It is the key component of the network workstation. It serves a number of purposes:

- It makes the physical connection or bridge between the computer and the network.
- It converts the parallel data on the computer's bus into serial data for the network.
- It boosts or amplifies the signal's strength so it can flow through the cables.

***Cables:*** When signals are sent through a hard-wired network, they are sent along a common set of wires or cables, the network's circulation system. Three types of cables are used to connect the devices:-

(a) *Twisted Pair:* They are the least expensive way to connect computers because the wire is cheap and easy to install. However, they are relatively slow and have a tendency to pack up noise that can cause high error rates.

(b) *Coaxial:* It is the most common type of networking cable. It consists of an inner wire surrounded by a layer of insulating material that is, in turn, surrounded by a braided wire. They are more reliable and durable.

(c) *Fiber-optic:* It connects of the glass or plastic filament, protector by thick plastic padding and an external plastic sheets. It uses a pulse of laser light instead of an electronic frequency to transmit a signal. Fibre optic cables are fast and reliable, as well as small and light. They have an extremely wide bandwidth, so a large number of signals can be sent simultaneously.

***Baseband Cable:*** A cable that transmits only one signal is called a baseband cable.

***Broadband Cable:*** This can handle simultaneous transmission of different signals by sending them at different frequencies. Broadband cables are more expensive and require additional frequency modulating equipment.

***Network Devices:*** When signals are sent through a network, they must be sent in the right direction, and they must also sometimes be amplified so they travel farther or converted so they can be transferred to a different network. These are the roles of a series of hardware devices called repeaters, bridges, routers and gateways.

(a) *Repeaters (or Physical relays):* They connect segments of a network, and since signals get weaker and less distinct with distance, these small devices refresh and enhance them before sending them along. They are usually used to extend the network in effect joining two networks together by passing a cable signal between them.

(b) *Bridges (or Data Link Relays):* They connect networks, which use different physical links. For example, a network running on twisted pair wires is connected to one using coaxial cable with a bridge.

(c) *Routers:* They control where messages are sent on networks. The router keeps the addresses of other nodes in a table. If the address of a message sent through the router is on the network, the message is forwarded. If the address is not on the network, the router towards the message to another network by sending it to a gateway.

(d) *Gateways:* Gateways are used to connect different types of networks. Since two networks may not share a common protocol, these devices translate each network's protocol so the other network can understand the data.

## TYPES OF NETWORKS

### Client Server Based Networks

In this system, clients are usually computers on the network that are operated by human beings, making changes to the data files they receive and when these changes are complete, sending the data back to the file serve for storage.

This arrangement has the virtue of processing efficiently, especially on large networks with dozens or even hundreds of machines. With the full processing power of a very powerful computer allocated solely to sending and sorting files, individual clients are not kept waiting for data and they can process different files with different software independently of each other.

The only disadvantage with this kind of network is that if file server goes down, the whole network comes to a halt.

### Peer-to-Peer Network

Each computer has the same potential to access and process data. These types of networks are called peer-to-peer network. A peer-to-peer network has the virtue of simplicity in both design and maintenance. It is usually less expensive to set as well. However, it is also slower and less secure than the client/

server network. It is suitable for smaller organizations with a limited number of computers on the network.

### Complex Networks

A network can be connected to other networks and networks can consist of different types of machines from different vendors each with its own unique way of handling electronic information, not directly understood by other machines on the network. Special software and hardware can be attached to the network to handle this complicated set up. These devices are called bridges, routes and gateways, perform in different ways the task of "translating" the electronic information supplied byt one machine into a format that can be understood by another.

### LAN, MAN, WAN

These networks are classified according to their geographical coverage

***LAN – Local Area Network:*** A network is called Local Area Network if the computers comprising it are located within the same building or within a distance range less than one kilometre from each other.

***MAN – Metropolitan Area Network:*** It inter-connects computers within a metropolitan city. Cellular phone networks are a good example of such networks.

***WAN – Wide Area Network:*** A network is called Wide Area Network if the computers comprising it are distributed over a large geographical region may be all over the country, all over the world or any distance range more than 30 kilometre. Parts of the network may be connected by the cables and other parts by microwave or satellite transmission. Typical wide area networks are those operated by the telephone companies. The Internet is probably the widest of all networks in that it links not only LANs but also other WANS.

### Network Protocols and Standards

If computers are to talk to each other, they need an agreed set of rules called protocols by which they can communicate. The protocols are techniques to govern the flow of data from one computer to another. For different types of computer to be able to communicate effectively, standards need to have been set for the periodicals.

***Network Standards:*** These standards may result from international agreement or do facts, from a particular manufacturer becoming dominant in the networking field. The three most important bodies involved in setting standards in the field of computer networking are CCITT, ISO and IEEE.

CCITT (Comite Consultatif International Telegraphique et Telephonique) International Consultative Committee for Telegraphy and Telephony, are responsible for the V, X and I standards. The V standards are for data communication, over in Public Switched Telephone Network (PZSTN), *e.g.* the modem standards $V_{21}$, $V_{22}$ of 300/300, 1200/1200, 2900/2900, 1200/75 and 9600/9600 bets per second. The X standards are for dedicated data communication services *e.g.* X.25 for packet switching services and X.400 for messaging. The I standards are for Integrated Services Digital Networks (ISDN)) *e.g.* I.400 series specifies the interface between the user equipments and the network.

ISO, the International Standard Organization, have developed a 7 layer model known as Open Systems Interconnection (OSI) model to describe the way in which computer networks operate. This model ranges through from the physical connections at level 1 through the transport protocols at level 4 to end-user applications at level 7. The purpose of this model is to help develop 'open' standards.

IEEE, the Institute of Electrical and Electronics Engineers, an American body, have developed and recommended standards for the physical connection of computers. In the networking field, since 1985 they have developed standard 802.5 for Token Ring Networks and 802.3 for an Ethernet connection between computers. These standards have been adopted by ANSI (American National Standards Institute) and ISO.

***Protocols Controlling Data Transfer Over the Network:*** In the early 1960s when researchers tried to connect computers with each other, they thought of various techniques to govern the flow of data from one computer to another. Some of them are:

(i) *Netware Core Protocol (NCP):* Developed by Novell Netware, it manages the flow of data between Netware Clients and File Server for maximum efficiency. It is earliest of the protocol among different Network protocol to govern the flow of data from one computer to another. It is a combination of Bits with different portions representing functions to be performed.

(ii) *Transmission Control Protocol/Internet Protocol (TCP/IP):* TCP/IP works on the principle of packet switching which involves breaking the data into small chunks and sending these chunks along the network. TCP devides the data into small chunks with each chunk not exceeding 546 bytes and pass them to IP, the next protocol in the transmission process. Each pocket is attached with information about source and destination; this resulted into many packets flowing through the same network line with each data pockets reaching its correct destination.

(iii) *Internet Work Packet Exchange (IPX):* It handles data verification and addressing responsibilities for flow of data between different networks, *e.g.* between Netware Networks and other networks. It adds a header to the information received from TCP Protocol containing the address of the destination, then it passes the data to Network Interface Card for transmission.

(iv) *Sequenced Packet Exchange (SPX):* It verifies the accuracy of the data by using Network Operating System (NOS). It also verifies the accuracy of the remote station to which the data is to be sent by performing some initial communications with the destination workstation. If it gets a confirmation back from the remote or destination station only then, it sends out the data, otherwise it reconfirms by sending the repeated communications. If it fails to get a response from the destination, it issues a notification to the application programme about the failure of the data transmission.

***Standards & Protocols: Library and Information Science Field:*** Resource sharing technology cannot work effectively unless appropriate tools are developed. These tools include the creation of standard bibliographic databases such as union catalogue of books and periodicals, union lists of serials, bibliographic databases of articles and other types of materials, such as CDs, Video-recordings, Sound recordings, theses and dissertations.

It becomes necessary to use the methods and tools that help in quick and identification and deliver of documents. However, the adoption of different bibliographic standards creates incompatibility problems and that acts as a major barrier in the use of bibliographic and related information. The standards, protocols and the software that convert data from one format to another should be of international standard.

***Bibliographic Standards:*** Format compatibilities are necessary for computerized catalogue data and these are being standardized by the International Standards Organization. ISO 2709 has been adopted the world over and the efforts to harmonize MARC formats are on.

The Library of Congress and National Library of Canada achieved the result in harmonizing their MARC formats in 1997. It is hoped that various MARC formats will also get harmonized in due course.

Maintenance of bibliographic standards uniformly is essential for quick exchange of records, *e.g.* Delhi Library Network (DELNET) has adopted the following standards:

- AACR-II. It is widely accepted code for cataloguing. It helps in the creation of standard records.
- MARC format
- LCSH, Library of Congress Subject Headings. These are used by many networks and libraries in the world. They are a major guide for creating subject headings. Other thesauri available on specialized subjects are also used whenever needed in specialized libraries.
- DDC is commonly used.

Standards have been developed by the International Standards Organization and National Information Standards Organization of the US besides a number of national standards organization for creating standard bibliographic and information products. Some examples are as following:

National Information Standards Series: ISSN 1041-5653

z39.2-1994-Information Interchange Format

z39.901992-International Standard Serial Numbering

z39.14-1997-Guidelines for Abstracts

z39.14-1993-Guidelines for the Construction, Format and Industry

z39.44-1486-Serials Holding Statements

The other standards include:

- z39.50-1995 Information Retrieval. Application Service Definition and Protocol Specification (version 3)
- z39..53-1999 Code for the Representation of Languages for Information Interchange
- z39.57-1989 (R1995) Holding statements for Non-serials Items
- z39.58-1992 Common Command Language for Online Interactive

Information Retrieval

- z39.63-1989 Interlibrary Loan Data Elements
- z39.64-1989(R1995) East Asian Character Code for Bibliographic use
- ANSI/NISD/ ISO 2108 International Standard Book Numbering (ISBN)
- ANSI/NISO/ISO 9660 Volume and File Structure of CD-ROM for Information Exchange
- TRO2-1997 Guidelines for Indexes and Related Information Retrieval Services

***Communication Standards:*** The effective electronic resource sharing has been hampered by the inability to interconnect, effectively and economically, many diverse electronic library and information databases, which exist worldwide. These standards provide the mechanisms to reduce the existing fragmentation of information and service delivery.

z39.50 (ANSI/NISO z39.50-1995 (ISO 23950)) is an American National Standard for Information Retrieval Prepared by the National Information Standards Organization (NISO), it defines how one system can cooperate with other systems for the purpose of searching databases and receiving records. As a network protocol, the z39.50 standard provides a set of rules that govern the formats and procedures for the exchange of messages between a client and server, enabling the user to search remote databases, identify records which meet specified criteria and to retrieve some or all the identified records. It is concerned, in particular, with the search and retrieval of information in databases. It simplifies the search process and enables uniform access to a large number of diverse and heterogeneous information sources. In library networking, z39.50 has assumed greater importance and is the most important protocol available today. In sum, this protocol:

- Provides a mechanism, using clients server model for transmitting and managing queries and result sets
- Is a generalized mechanism and can be used for bibliographic, full text and other types of databases
- Enables the client to perform searches and creates result sets. The records pertaining to the results can be presented to the client or used for creating new result sets with other searches
- Conforms to one or more common syntaxes and yet it is not necessary that he same syntax is shared in all databases.

The methodology for interaction between a client and server is as follows:

1. A client sends an INITIALISE request and server responds with INITIALISE response.
2. As soon as the session is established, the search request can be made by the client.
3. The server respects with the search results
4. Only one search result is made at one time and is served.
5. Records are transmitted to the clients as soon as the client makes the PRESENT request.

There are other facilities like account control, deletion, termination of the session and enhanced features like sort, browse, ILL, etc. For libraries, z39.50 could very well provide a single interface allowing libraries to support a number of different services. Various library applications include

- Reference searching of other system
- Copy cataloguing
- Collection Development and Interlibrary loans
- Virtual libraries: Access to digital collections

In India, Indian Agricultural Research Institute, Pusa Road, New Delhi has taken the lead to install the first z39.50 server in India and make to databases available to the z39.50 clients.

## ILL Protocol

The ILL protocol is used to provide just ILL services. Several vendors use it in their software. In the ILL protocol, the services represent the activities. These services are such as ILL request, RECEIVED, RETURNED, RENEW, LOST (item requested is lost) and CANCELLED (cancellation of the request). There are optional messages such as SHIPPED, RETURNED, RECEIVED and CHECKED-IN. When the requests are in operation, the messages such as PENDING and IN-PROCESS are used. These are several other services used by the protocol and they are requested by messages such as ILL-ANSWER, FORWARD-NOTIFICATION, etc.

The National Library of Canada has developed a protocol for ILL communications in order to facilitate resource sharing in a networking environment. The protocol has been designed to encourage software developers and members of the library and the information community to adopt the protocol and incorporate it into ILL systems.

The protocol is expected to be POST (Open System Interconnection) based and is able to communicate with all types of hardware, software communication facilities used. OSI provides interconnectivity and interoperability in order to communicate with all types of hardware and allow transfer and communication of data among them. Improvement of interlibrary loan facility through electronic messaging is possible if we use Open System Interconnection (OSI) Reference Model and improve the telecommunication infrastructure.

## ESSENTIALS AND REQUIREMENTS

Since Library Networking is meant to promote and facilitate sharing of resources available within a group of participating libraries, several factors are to be considered for planning such on a network. The following are very important:

(i) Member libraries must justify need for a network. The development of a viable network demands planning not only among the network members but also between the members and users themselves.

(ii) Member libraries must agree upon a network policy is to be implemented. The policy must clearly state:

  (a) *Objectives of the Network*-e.g the main objective may be to share the resources among the member libraries. It may be achieved in several ways, for example,

  - Users of the member libraries may be allowed only to refer the documents in any of the other participating libraries.
  - Limited number of periodicals/book may directly by issued to users of all the member libraries.
  - Providing photocopies of the articles/ monographs
  - Cooperative collection development programmes

  (b) *Network Structure:* Member libraries should adopt that structure of a network, which will fulfil the purpose for which libraries use it. The lack of arrangement in developing a network structure undermines both the approach of functions and planning.

(iii) Member libraries must identify the funding agencies and mobilize the resources in advance. The financial resources must freely flow while implementing the system. If necessary, network fee may be collected from each of the member libraries. The examples of library networks in the western countries suggest that all networks based on a fee structure can be maintained without grant and are viable in the long run.

(iv) For resource sharing among member libraries, it is necessary to create bibliographic tools like union catalogues and union lists based on the resources available in the participating libraries.

Depending on the objectives or type of network model, databases of library collections should be developed. If the network is of star type, a centralized database consisting of all the records in all member libraries is necessary. If the network is of any other type, database for each of the library collections has to be developed separately.

(v) For the purpose of creating databases, it is essential to agree upon a standard. All libraries should follow a standard MARC format, AACR-II, a standard thesaurus like Library of Congress Subject Headings (LCSH) etc. uniformly.

(vi) Although efforts should be made to have one classification scheme in all participating libraries but use of different numbers should not become a hurdle as search requests are mostly by authors, titles, editors and subject descriptions.

(vii) Member libraries must agree upon indexing system to be followed. In a centralized database system (a star network), it is preferable to adopt a single systems of indexing, *i.e.* POPSI, chain indexing or any other system. However, in a decentralized or in a hierarchical system, each library may have a freedom to adopt an indexing system of their choice. In such cases, the software must be developed to switch from one database to another database and then one indexing file to another indexing file while searching.

(viii) For the success of network in a long run, each of the member libraries must have a policy to automate every function of the library – acquisition, cataloguing, classification, serials control, circulation, SDI, current awareness services etc. – in the shortest possible time.

This helps the library to have computer culture which is required to design, develop, maintain and to operate several databases, to reduce the cost of library operations as well as network operations.

(ix) The major problem in each of the member libraries when attempts are made to prepare the machine-readable records for the existing catalogue. Prior to creating such records, one has to identify frequently used and infrequently used documents. Then prepare the machine-readable catalogue appropriately for the frequently used documents or alternatively use the existing machine-readable databases by down-loading from CD-ROMs or from other databases and reformatting them, one can select the appropriate records for their respective database.

(x) The network should be able to recommend to participating libraries the type of hardware and software they need for their in-house functions and for networking purposes. Hardware should be selected considering the number of entries the participating libraries can generate within the next 3-5 years. The hardware at the Central Host speed with which participating libraries generate records and the network pools them into the Central Hose.

The network software may or may not support the in-house operations of the libraries in the beginning but eventually the network software should not only be able to create union catalogues or full text databases, etc. but also get integrated with the in-house operations.

(xi) If there is no adequate trained manpower in each of the member libraries, attempts should be made to train or/ and recruit library personnel.

(xii) In addition to the databases, hardware, software and trained manpower, it is preferable to have certain communication facilities such as Fax, Telex, Telephone, etc. as a part of the network system in each of the member libraries for the effective working of the network. E-mail and INTERNET facilities should be available with the libraries and they should be able to access international databases, preferably individually or through the network host to begin with.

(xiii) Inter-libraries loan services should grow and may be interlinked with the search of the union catalogues. Delivery of documents should be fast, either electronically through fax or through courier or Mail. Rationalization of acquisitions needs to be undertaken.

(xiv) The member libraries should be willing partners, ready to buy hardware, etc. and should be willing to send professional staff for training. They should be willing to pool bibliographic records to the Central Host of the network besides adhering to other network obligations.

(xv) A performance criterion should be developed and agreed upon to evaluate the working of the network.

## HARDWARE AND SOFTWARE REQUIREMENTS

### Hardware Requirements

Each of the member libraries must have at least some of the following hardware. However, the main library (Central Host) may require most of the hardware mentioned below, but with additional disk space. Hardware specifications are given below:

*I. Server:*

- Pentium @233 MHz with 64 MB RAM
- 1.2 GB HDD
- 32 x CDROM Drive
- 1.44" Floppy Drive
- Colour Monitor (SVGA)
- Windows-NT Operating System
- MS-SQL Server 6.5

*II. Client:*

- Pentium @233 MHz with 32 MB RAM
- 1.2 GB HDD
- 1.44" Floppy Drive
- Colour Monitor (SVGA)
- Windows-98 Operating System

*III. Other Hardware*

— Fax (with dedicated phone line)
— Modem (with dedicated phone line)
— Telex
— CD-ROM drive
— At least two determine printers
— One letter quality printer (preferably laser printer)
— Cartridge type drive

**Software Requirements**

Each of the participating libraries must have the following:

— Software for effective network operation as well as the library automation
— DOS (latest version) and/or
— UNIX (latest version, to begin with, it may be optional)
— LAN (Novel/Ethernet, to begin with, it may be optional)
— Software for E-mail (at least PROCOMM)
— Word processors
— DBMS packages
— IR packages CDS/ISIS
— Library automation: Libsys/Granthalaya/any other similar packages
— Programming languages: C/C$^{++}$

**Software Evaluation**

Software evaluation is quite often a difficult task. We have to consider the following procedure, criteria and features to evaluate software packages.

***Procedures for Evaluation:*** The following procedures may be considered to evaluate software packages:

— Select a software after carefully examining the existing literature
— Examine carefully its literature and documentation
— Compare it with various other packages, keeping in view the following points

- Is it easy to understand?
- Is a separate training required?

- Is it menu driven?
- Can it handle records of variable sizes?
- Is it easy to edit a record?
- Is it difficult to update the files (inserting or deleting records?)?
- How much memory and hard disk space are required?
  - On-site evaluation
  - Post installation service (if the software is corrupted for various reasons, will the vendor replace it?

***Criteria for Evaluation:*** Some of the criteria for evaluation of software are::

- Ease of operation
- Quality of documentation
- Hardware limitations
- Speed of operation
- Security in multi-user environment
- De-bugging facility and proper error messages while executing
- Support from vendor

***Features of Software:*** Some of the important features of software are:

- User friendly
- Provision to on-line interaction, especially while editing inputting, retrieving and in data management.
- Provision to obtain outputs in various formats
- Compatibility and portability.

***Factors to be considered:*** Finally, one has to consider several factors while acquiring a computer. These are:

- Memory and Storage Capabilities
  - memory size
  - auxiliary storage devices like tape, disk, cassette, etc.
- Availability of input output devices
  - availability of terminal
  - speed and capabilities of input and output devices such as the ability to process lower case letters and special symbols.

- Facilities to extend the memory and input-output devices
- Maintenance facilities provided by the manufacturer
- Compatibility with
  - other machines especially with locally available machines
  - with main frame computers, which may be available in the parent organization
- Availability, capabilities and portability of software
  - availability of computer for popular languages
  - capabilities of operating system
  - availability of special purpose software are

Therefore, we should take into account various specifications regarding establishment of a Library Network. The objectives, functions, requirements for hardware and software and structure of the network should be pre-defined before the establishment of a library network.

## LIBRARY NETWORKS: INDIAN SCENARIO

### Networking in Indian Context

Libraries are storehouses of information and knowledge. In this modern world, access to information holds the key to development.

The rapid and exponential growth of information has made it necessary for librarians and information scientists to employ new techniques to cope with the massive proliferation of literature in all subjects fields Research in the science and social sciences has led to high productivity in document publications. To bring this vast amount of information under bibliographic control and to render it useful and accessible to potential users is a task of great magnitude which the information people face. So through the application of communication techniques and electronic data processing, library and information centres have now begun to realize the need of computers and associated facilities as indispensable for steady and accurate storage, processing, retrieval and dissemination of information and above all sharing resources among libraries.

For libraries to use their resources more efficiently and effectively for the users is a great task. This task can be solved to a great extent by resource sharing and cooperative functioning among libraries. And for this, networking of libraries, applying latest modern techniques is a must.

In India, networking of libraries is even more necessary than in the developed nations. The important factors that may be considered for networking of resources (Libraries holding resources) in India are:

1. It is not possible for all the organizations and agencies to design a system to cater to its resource needs because their main aim is to provide resources rather than designing the system for providing resources. So they have to purchase an appropriate latest system to cater to their needs. Generally, it is very difficult or rather impossible to find a system which could entirely satisfy its needs. In India, manually such technologies are purchased from abroad and afterwards people face a number of maintenance problems. So while opting for networking, annual hardware maintenance, some initial training is required.
2. The cumulative collection of scientific serials held by many important libraries in India is quite poor when compared to USA, UK and other developed countries while in India, some libraries have a very good collection, the majority of libraries suffer from very inadequate collection. There is a great need to consider the entire resources of the country as a single entity that can be available to the entire user community of the country. Networking the libraries is the best way to make resource sharing very effective in order to ensure equitable availability of required information.
3. Literature being generated as a result of research activities being carried out is doubling every five years. Over 10 million journal articles are published every year besides news items, editorials and articles appearing in popular print media. It is not possible for all the libraries and information centres to acquire all the

bibliographic material at one place due to storage problem as well as paucity of funds. Even to maintain a reasonable level of acquisition of journals, books and reports, calls for heavy budgets in libraries. Therefore, networking with other institutions, libraries, information centres, etc. is easy and economical way to get what a particular centre does not have in its capacity.

4. Budget to the libraries/information centres/institutions and restriction on staffing has also forced institutes to opt for networking in the country and this is on the increasing trend. As for example, it is not possible to give a laser printer to each individual in many of the organizations, so best way to provide printing facilities to each of them is put the printer in the network and let all the computers users share it by way of networking operating system.

   Similar methods can be adopted to share other hardware resources like Modem, CD-ROM drive, etc.

5. India is a vast country with caste, cultural and linguistic diversities. Planning for their development is done at the centre only. Planning for such a big country by sitting in the capital requires an extremely fast flow of information from all parts of the country to the centre. This can be done effectively by networking all the information centres in the states with the centre. Poor infrastructure is a hindrance in this flow of information. With the introduction of better telecom facilities like optical fibers, satellite communication, powerful computer, this is likely to increase but still many parts of the country do not have these facilities.

Because of the above mentioned reasons, resource sharing and cooperative functioning through networking have become inescapable for libraries and information centres in this country.

## NATIONAL EFFORTS AND STATUS OF NETWORKS

### National Efforts

There have been many attempts in the country in the last two decades in computer application to library and information activities. During last so many years, libraries and information centres have become more earnest to computerize their operations and services. While NISSAT (National Information System for Science & Technology) has been promoting an integrated approach in library automation in the country, the efforts have been by and large, at the institutional level. Some of the major organizations engaged in computerized information handling are:

- BARC-Bhabha Atomic Research Centre, Mumbai
- DESIDOC-Defence Scientific Information and Documentation Centre,Delhi
- DRTC-Documentation Research and Training Centre, Bangalore
- IISc-Indian Institute of Science, Bangalore
- IIT-Indian Institute of Technology (Delhi, Chennai, Kanpur)
- INSDOC-Indian National Scientific Documentation Centre, New Delhi
- NIC-National Informatics Centre, New Delhi
- NISSAT-National Information System for Science and Technology, New Delhi
- PRL-Physical Research Laboratory, Ahmedabad
- TIFR-Tata Institute of Fundamental Research, Mumbai

Besides the above, University Grants Commission (UGC), Department of Electronics, Department of Telecommunication, Planning Commission and other various Departments of Government of India have also been engaged in establishing various networks. There are possibilities of mounting bibliographical databases on these networks for providing online access to access.

The growth of Indian Library Networks may be traced to the efforts made during the last forty years. The chronology is given below:

## Planning Commission Efforts

The Planning Commission, Government of India, has been taking considerable interest in library resource sharing and library networks. Its efforts in these areas have increased since the Seventh Five Year Plan covering 1985-90. The Commission appointed a working group on modernization of Library Services and Informatics in November, 1983. In July 1984, the working group submitted its report. It recommended among others, interlinking of library systems through library networks. This report was to be considered for the Seventh Plan.

The Commission appointed another Working Group which submitted its report in May, 1989. It again recommended among others interlinking of library systems in the country.

The Planning Commission appointed in Feb, 1995, a Core Task Group to prepare an approach paper for enhancing inputs of Science and Technology for library resource sharing.

The Commission again constituted a working group on Libraries and Informatics under the Department of Culture, Ministry of Human Resource Development, Govt. of India, which report was to be considered for the Ninth Plan for the period 1997-2002. The report of the Working Group of the Commission includes many important recommendations for the networking and modernization of libraries in the country.

All these initiatives by NISSAT, UGC, Planning Commission and other departments of Govt. of India have led to increased efforts to the establishment of library networks and library automation in the country.

## Networks in India

Current computer Networks in India can be decided into three categories:

I. *Networks connecting Educational and Research Institutions all over the country*

   a. *ERNET – Education and Research Network:* It was launched by the Department of Education (DOE), Govt. of India in late 1986 with financial assistance from UNDP (United Nationals Development Programme) to provide academic and research institutions with electronic mail facilities. It is currently used by DSIR Labs, research centres and academic institutions.

b. *SIRNET – Scientific and Industrial Research Network:* It was established by INSDOC in late 1989 to interconnect all the CSIR aboratories and other R&D institutions in India. Its main objective is to harness the vast S&T information resources available with national laboratories and inculcate the habit of resource sharing among themselves. Its ultimate aim is to link the entire scientific community of the nation with the national library system and the international links to achieve efficient scientific communication.

c. *OPNET – Open Education Network:* Open University Network – Many institutions are venturing into the field of education and are offering professional and technological courses by using communication technologies. They are using television, computer communication, email and network to reach the students. Indira Gandhi National Open University (IGNOU), which is an apex body for open and distance education, is engaged in the task of developing a network of open universities in India called OPNET. This is a network of physical, intellectual and academic resource organized under the aegis of the Distance Education Council (DEC), an independent arm of IGNOU and distance education in India. All the open universities are partners of OPNET. The resources that are pooled together include academic programmes, norms and sharing programmes, delivery mechanisms and interactive software for student services. The OPNET will be an umbrella network with the subnet of every partner university for delivery of their own courses.

II. *Networks connecting the libraries in the country*

(a) INFLIBNET–established by UGC in 1988, operations began in 1991. It is a network of university and college libraries. It has also provided financial assistance to a large number of university libraries in India.

(b) CALIBNET – established by NISSAT in 1986. NISSAT decided to establish a network of scientific libraries in Calcutta. At a meeting in 1986 in Calcutta, DSIR initiated action for preparation of a feasibility study for networking about 40 libraries in Calcutta. CALIBNET was the first library network visualized. At present, it has now become the centre for CD-ROM databases which are acquired from outside sources. Libraries can access these CDs. The basic purpose of the library network is to share the resources available in participating libraries. However, no resource sharing is done as there are no union catalogues prepared. This activity, is however, in progress.

(c) DELNET: established in 1988 by India International Centre with the initial financial support of NISSAT and later officially registered as a society in June 1992. Its main objective is to promote sharing of resources among the libraries located in Delhi and outside Delhi. It is the first operational library network in India.

(d) MALIBNET – The need for interconnecting libraries and information centres in Chennai was visualized by INSDOC in 1991. INSDOC undertook a feasibility study which was completed in March 1992. MALIBNET was registered as a society in Chennai in Feb. 1993.

(e) PUNENET in Pune in 1992
ADINET in Ahmedabad in 1993
BONET in Mumbai in 1994
MYLIBNET in Mysore in 1994
BALNET in Bangalore in 1995

All these networks are supported by NISSAT. They have not, as yet, created their value added databases such as union catalogues, though work is in progress. They are, at present, mostly offering Email and CD-ROM facilities

III. Others

(a) *NICNET:* It was established by National Informatics Centre (NIC) in 1977 and started in the late 87's. It was launched basically for getting and providing information from/to district levels to facilitate planning process. It links for regional nodes at Delhi, Pune, Bhubneswar and Hyderabad and has established 32 nodes at state and union territory levels and 439 nodes at district headquarters. By 1991, NICNET has achieved success in the creation of databases and networking. It also provides E-mail and other facilities to users using its already existing infrastructure.

(b) *INDONET:* India's first data communication and computer network was started in March 1986 by CMC Ltd. It was launched as a solution to the growing need for providing timely well processed data to various institutions. In the First phase, they have mainly networked Mumbai, Calcutta and Chennai. Later, Delhi and Hyderabad were also linked as additional stations. INDONET presently has an international gateway which provides access to world wide pocket switched networks like USA's Global Networks Systems (GNS) and Internet.

## Present Scenario of Library Networking in India

The present status of library networking in India is that most of the libraries covered by some network are creating databases of their holdings and in automating the library activities. Generally, the periodical holdings are attempted first in building up the databases as it takes less time than for the other types of library documents. This is followed by the databases of holdings of books, reports, dissertations, standards, etc. The Library Network Centres, *i.e.*, the coordinating agencies of the networks also are concentrating on acquiring them to provide the user with access to the total records. They provide such access either by email or online through the telephone network. In addition, these centres also try to provide a common software for database development and automation of library activities and services. Table below gives the details of status of some important library networks in the country.

However, this scenario networks doesn't provide a growth of ideal library networks in India.

From the above table, it can be seen that except DELNET and INFLIBNET, most of the other library networks have yet to develop databases of library holdings in a significant way. Even these two networks have to go a long way, to cover in their databases, the entire holdings of all the participating libraries. Unless this is achieved, the networks would not be able to achieve significant resource sharing as well as rationalization in library acquisitions. Most of the networks are, however, making efforts towards this end by conducting training programmes for the staff of the participating libraries in data capturing, database development and automation of library activities and services.

## Networking of Public Libraries

The public libraries in the west have developed into a true community information and reference systems with such computerized data access and facilities for providing a variety of information to the general public from housing and social security to legal and medical aid and temperature and travel schedule.

In India, development of public libraries has not been a priority and their growth as a result has been uneven. Public libraries which could serve as the backbones of literacy mission, suffer for want of adequate funds, trained staff, modern equipment, good and adequate collections, proper reading rooms and stacking and user facilities. In order to provide to the public, access to the latest information and educate them, public libraries have to be technologically advanced so that they have access to INTERNET and international databases and networks.

According to UNESCO public library Manifesto 1994 (Revised)

"The public library acts as a living force for education, culture and information and as an essential agent for the fostering of peace and spiritual welfare through the minds of men and women" The Manifesto recommends that: "The public library network must be designed in relation to national, regional, research and special libraries as well as libraries in schools, colleges and universities".

So there is a need to establish a public library network which is in conformity with the other networks in the country. Due to lack of up-d-date, actual number of public libraries could not be ascertained, however, nearly about 60,000 exist in the country. They can't be called libraries in the real sense as most of them are simply reading rooms. Most of them are without computers and the librarians working in the distances in general, are not conversant with the application of computers in libraries. Training of library staff in the computer applications for library operations and services becomes one of the basic requirements of automation and networking.

In the rural areas, as rural settlement are generally scattered and their libraries are neither up-to-date nor well staffed. Since the level of users is not of a high standing and also various problems in information infrastructure, it is not possible in the first phase to connect rural libraries with the public libraries network for networking purposes. However, with the wide use of telecommunication technology, it is possible for institution located in remote area to join the network.

Therefore, we notice that if the public libraries are to really reach the public and achieve the status of national network system, the adaptation of new sophisticated techniques and technologies is a highly important pre-requisite. We must change with the times and learn from the latest trends in the west.

For this, we have to develop the infrastructure of public libraries and give attention to the manpower development, training given in the use of computers, AACR-II, use of MARC format Library Congress subject headings, handling of software, etc. and use of electronic mail and INTERNET.

## MAJOR LIBRARY NETWORKS AND THEIR SERVICES (INDIA)

The chapter includes major library networks, *viz.* DELNET, CALIBNET, INFLIBNET and MALIBNET, operating in the country. All these networks provide various services, and their activities extend from automation of library activities to specialized services intended for their members and interested users.

**DELNET**

Delhi is growing as a major centre of information resources in India. These resources cater both to the specialized and the general users.

They are located in activities, information and documentation centres, institutional libraries, research libraries, government libraries, public libraries, department libraries besides the libraries of the universities, colleges and schools. During the recent years, increase in information has led to increase in the demands of the users. It has been noticed that in this area of information explosion, libraries in India are generally ill-equipped to handle and retrieve information effectively, the financial resources and the space requirement for housing library collection are limited in almost all of the libraries.

No a single library can afford to house every necessary document even in the area of its interest. Resource sharing, thus assumes great importance at this juncture the option left with the forward looking librarians has been to promote the sharing of resources by automation and networking. With this objective, in January 1988, the India International Centre initiated efforts for the establishment of Delhi Library Network (Now Developing Library Network).

DELNET is the first operational library network in India. It was started as a project of the India International Centre in January 1988 with the initial, financial and technical assistance by National Information System for Science and Technology (NISSAT), Department of Scientific and Industrial Research, Govt. of India. It was registered as a society in June 1992 under the Societies Registration Act of 1860 and is currently being promoted by the National Informatics Centre (NIC), Planning Commission, Govt. of India and India International Centre, New Delhi.

## Objectives

The following are DELNET's main objectives:

- to promote sharing of resources among the libraries by developing a network of libraries, by collecting, storing and disseminating information and by offering computerized services to the users.
- to offer guidance to the member libraries on cataloguing database services, circulation, acquisition, serials control, online services, selection of hardware and software, etc.
- to coordinate efforts for suitable collection development and reduce unnecessary duplication wherever possible.
- to establish a referral centre, to monitor and/or facilitate catalogue search and maintain a central online union catalogue of books, serials, and non-book materials of all the participating libraries.
- to facilitate and promote delivery of documents manually and mechanically.
- to develop specialist bibliographic database of books, serials and non-book materials.
- to develop a database of projects, specialists and institutions.
- to possess and maintain electronic and mechanical equipment for fast communication of information and delivery of electronic mail.
- to coordinate with other regional, national and international networks for exchange of information and documents.
- To undertake facilitate and provide for the publication of newsletters/journals devoted to networking and sharing of resources.

## Membership

At present, DELNET has Two Hundred and Forty Three libraries as its members, including both institutional and associate-institutional members: in India 235 and outside India 8.

Fees Details: Following are the fees details for its members

*Admission Fee* : Rs.5,000

*Institutional membership*: Rs.7500/-per year (For libraries with 10,000 or more book collection)

*Associate institutional membership* : Rs.10,000/-per year (For libraries with less than 10,000 books)

*Overseas Institutions*: Admission fee: US $100/-

Annual Membership fee: US $500/-

The membership is progressively increasing and includes universities, diplomatic missions, college, government department, institutions and public libraries. Some institutions from far off places like Shimla, Bhopal, Punjab, Andhra Pradesh, Lucknow and Pondicherry in India have also joined DELNET as members. DELNET's membership has increased from 103 in Feb'99 to 243 to date (August, 2001).

## DELNET Activities/Services

***Promotion of Database Creation:*** For effective networking, standard bibliographic data should be available in machine readable form with the libraries. So, efforts were made from the very beginning to promote the standardization of databases in the DELNET libraries. Experts were sent to the libraries to solves day-to-day problems. A panel of experts was seeing maintained for this purpose. Regular meetings of the librarians and computer specialists were organized to discuss mutual problems and the areas of cooperation.

Nevertheless, there have been some libraries in Delhi that took keen interest in database creation on their own. But the practice of regular meetings for database creation and resource sharing continue. DELNET provides technical assistance to member libraries in the following areas:

- creation and maintenance of bibliographic databases
- serials controls
- user services
- hardware and software requirements
- union catalogue preparation
- current awareness and SDI services
- authority data compilation
- subject profiles construction

- abstracting services
- inter-library loan and user services
- document transfer/copying facilities
- access to local, national and international databases

***Resource Sharing:*** DELNET saved foreign exchange worth Rs. 10 million by rationalizing subscriptions to foreign periodicals during 1991, 1992 and 1993 through resource sharing.

This was mainly achieved in the fields of physical science, medical science and agricultural sciences. It is hoped that in the years to come, DELNET would be able to save more foreign exchange for India through sharing of periodical resources.

In 1991, a courier service was started on contract basis will a private agency for inter library lending among the participating libraries but it was not very effective. Later, DELNET has introduced its own courier service with the financial help of NIC. The service is well used.

***Standardization:*** A standardization committee of DELNET has been meeting from time to time. The standardization committee takes into account the following areas:

- Communication format for interchanging bibliographic data
- Input output format
- Bibliographic description: Mandatory and optional data elements
- Classification scheme and subject headings
- Thesaurus
- Authority files
- Language scripts into roman script
- Forms of heading
- Identification numbers, codes and abbreviations
- Data input for abstracting and indexing
- Search/command language

It was noticed that colon classification, universal Decimal classification and Dewey Decimal classification were mostly used in Indian libraries and therefore, it would be almost impossible to impose a standard classification scheme on all libraries. It was decided to use Dewey Class Number.

As searching by class numbers was done by very few librarians, it was decided that the participating libraries could search by the classification numbers or they could pass on such requests to DELNET central office for necessary action.

With regard to the standardization of subject headings and to usage DELNET recommends the use of LCSM.

Specialized libraries may use additional thesauri that are available in each major discipline such as social sciences, humanities and science and technology.

***Online Databases:*** DELNET has around twenty databases available online for its users. These are:

- Union Catalogue of Books: UCF
- Union Catalogue of Books: MARC Format
- Union List of Current Periodicals
- Union Catalogue of Periodicals
- Database of Periodic Articles
- Indian Specialists Database
- CD-ROM database
- Union list of Video recordings
- Union List of Sound Recordings
- Union List of Newspapers
- Union List of Serials of Management Libraries
- Union Catalogue of Hindi Books
- Multilingual Books: Sample database
- Urdu Manuscripts Database
- Database of Theses and Dissertations
- DEVINSA Database
- Serials: Petroleum and Natural Gas
- Books in-Print Database
- Jain Database
- Directory of Libraries

Table gives the DELNET databases and their records:

| DELNET DATABASES | NUMBER OF RECORDS | | | | |
|---|---|---|---|---|---|
| | March'96 | Dec'97 | March'98 | Feb'99 | Nov'2000 |
| 1. Union Catalogue of Books (Record holdings) | 1,50,227 | 2,07,185 | 39,68,54 | 4,72,754 | 7,01,324 |
| 2. Union Catalogue of books (MARC) (Record holdings) | - | - | 16,000 | 16,965 | 20,000 |
| 3. Union List of Serials | - | 16,000 | 16,000 | 16,146 | 16,497 |
| 4. Union Catalogue of Serials | - | 3,105 | 6,935 | 10,203 | 10,599 |
| 5. Database of Periodical Articles | - | 48,605 | 60,000 | 1,15,103 | 1,91,432 |
| 6. Specialists Database | - | 1,200 | 2,000 | 2,000 | 2,000 |
| 7. Multilingual Books (Sample Database) | - | - | - | - | - |
| 8. CD-ROM Database | 0 | 0 | 138 | 138 | 1,064 |
| 9. Union List of Video Recording | - | - | - | 1,217 | 1,983 |
| 10. Union List of Sound Recording | - | - | - | 500 | 500 |
| 11. Urdu Manuscripts Database | - | - | - | 210 | 210 |
| 12. Union List of Newspapers | - | - | - | 70 | 70 |
| 13. Database of Theses & Dissertations | - | - | - | 251 | 16,587 |
| 14. DEVINSA Database | - | - | - | 20,000 | 20,000 |
| 15. Union List of Serials, Petroleum & Natural Gas | - | - | - | 871 | 900 |
| 16. Union List of Serials : management Libraries | - | - | - | 800 | 800 |
| 17. Union Catalogue of Hindi Books | - | - | - | 3,000 | 3,000 |
| 18. National Bibliographic Database Pilot Project | - | - | - | 30,000 | |

## ILL Online

DELNET members can place their inter-library loan requests through our ILL online facility, which is available on the union catalogue of books database. The member requests appear on the main server, which are monitored by DELNET staff at regular intervals and the books are acquired and supplied to the requesting library through the courier. Photocopying charges for journal articles etc. and courier charges for sending books to member libraries outside Delhi are extra.

## DEL-LISTSERV

DELNET has created a Listserv service called DEL-LISTSERV to provide the current awareness service to users and allow the member libraries to receive the latest daily information from the INTERNET automatically in the form of electronic mail. The following listservs have been created and are available online through DELNET:

- Net-happenings – This Listserv appraises the users about the latest new sites along with their web addresses on the INTERNET and has proved to be a major source of information for the users on the INTERNET.

- Med-clips – This medical clippings listing discusses the various topics of medical interest like AIDI, cancer, etc. and is informative in nature.
- IFLA – This Listserv allows the users to get the latest information from the International Federation of Library Associations and Institutions, which includes the issues of concern to library and information professionals.
- LIBJOBS – Through this Listserv, the library professionals are able to find out daily, the jobs/vacancies available throughout the world.

**Book: New Arrivals**

This is a new service through internet giving a list of recent publications in all subjects. The service covers education, management and physical sciences. Other subjects can be introduced on demand.

**Book Reviews from INTERNET**

This is an INTERNET service of reviews of latest published books covering different subjects. The service covers in the field of Arts and Music, INTERNET and military history. From time to time, other subjects will come into this fold.

**Current Contents**

This service gives the current contents of the latest issues of journals. It is particularly useful for rationalization of periodicals and resources sharing in member libraries.

**Index to Hindu**

DELNET has started offering Index to Hindu online to its members. Indexed news items are available on the system covering different periods of the Chennai edition. More updates and archival data is being added into the system regularly.

**Retro-Conversion**

DELNET offers retro conversion facilities to the libraries through specialized agencies and also facilitates the use of modern tools such as CO-ROM's and online facilities for retro-conversion.

### Referral Services

DELNET maintains a referral centre that provides reference facilities to participating libraries. The referral centre also looks after the access to the central databases and monitors access to international databases.

### Document Transfer/Copy Facilities

DELNET provides the facility for transferring or copying of the documents to its users.

### Training Programmes

DELNET conducts training programmes in the use of DELNET services, software, E-mail, AACR II and LC subject headings, Internet, etc. from time to time. Information about future training programmes is available on request.

### Lectures and Workshops

DELNET organizes lectures by networking specialists working in different parts of the world. The lectures are open to members, specialists and users in general. DELNET also organizes national workshops, seminars and meets on library networking from time to time. DELNET had organized National Annual convention on Library and Information Networking (NACLIN) in 1998 & 1999.

### Newsletter

DELNET publishes a newsletter in order to spread the message and increase the awareness about library networking in India. Through this Newsletter, DELNET communicates to its members the progress, it is making in various fields. The Newsletter is also a forum for communication on the advances, achievements and needs of the libraries and their services.

### INTERNET

***Electronic Mail:*** DELNET provides RENNIC Email facility to its member libraries, which is introduced by National Informatics Centre. This gives them access to both national and international E-mail users and also to INTERNET users. DELNET Email reaches the libraries, institutions and individuals in India as well as abroad having E-mail connection.

Email is being used not only for communication between institutions but also for inter-library-loan requests.

Subscription rates for E-mails are as follows:

***Full INTERNET (TCP/IP) Connectivity:*** DELNET is providing full INTERNET SLIP/PPP dial up access at a concessional rate of Rs. 8,500/-per annum for Rs. 500 hours of connect time through NIC to the member libraries. Also the shell account facility for INTERNET access is available for Rs.4,000 per annum for 500 hrs of connect time. A number of DELNET member libraries are already availing these facilities. These rates are subject to change by NIC.

***Web Page:*** DELNET has a web page on INTERNET. This enables all INTERNET users the world over to know about DELNET and its activities. The web page also includes a list of Member-libraries along with their E-mail addresses. The Web page is being updated from time to time.

## Products

***DELSIS:*** A major breakthrough has been achieved by DELNET with the launch of DELSIS, a powerful library networking software. DELSIS (DELNET System for Information Services) is an integrated modular system, which supports DELNET online databases.

It has been developed by DELNET on a Relational Database management System called BASIC plus, a product of Information Dimension Inc. of USA, which has been provided to DELNET courtesy National Informatics Centre, New Delhi. It handles not only the Online Public Access Catalogue (OPAC) but also has the administrative tools for building up the union catalogues on BASISplus. It provides powerful and extensive facilities for online enquiries for books, serials, biographical details about the specialists and supports the cataloguing of books in Indian languages.

Features of DELSIS:

— DELSIS is a user friendly menu driven package

— Its versatile options allow the users to retrieve the information quickly.

— It contains the modules for Online Public Access Catalogue as well as the modules for the creation of databases *e.g.* addition, deletion, inserting of records etc.

— The Online Public Access Catalogue (OPAC) components of DELSIS can meet the needs of the users, irrespective of whether the user has little computer experience or is familiar with using computers to perform various library tasks.

***DEL-WINDOWS:*** DELNET has released the DEL-WINDOWS version 1.0 after the successful creation and implementation of DELSIS Unix version. It is an efficient tool for creating and retrieving bibliographic databases and catalogues.

DEL-WINDOWS can convert the simple PC into a powerful management information system. Some of the *salient features* are:

— It is simple and easy to use. The novice library professionals and end users can interact with the software without any prior training.

— It is user-friendly with adequate windows-menus for data inputting and search capabilities.

— It provides the option for creating the bibliographic records either using ECF or the MARC format.

***DELSEARCH:*** DELNET has opened a new chapter in the information retrieval procedure by devising a new database access mechanism through DELSEARCH. It is an off-line remote database access system through E-mail. It is the first of its kind and is the most economical and user-friendly remote database access system. It helps institutions, information specialists, research scholars, librarians and users interested in bibliographies and tutorial information on South Asia. It allows them to search the DELNET union catalogues through E-mail and is a great tool for research scholars. The software is developed on UNIX platform and allows the users to send their search requests through E-mail. As soon as the query is received by the system in the form of an E-mail, the respective databases are searched for the query word and the results are returned to the addressee immediately. The searching of the database does not require any human intervention and the searches are done by the system automatically.

**The Future of DELNET**

The future of DELNET is very promising. Its membership with India and outside India is going to take a quantum jump. The DELNET databases are growing in number and size and as a variety of information on South Asia is becoming available through DELNET, it is expected that all institutions outside India specializing in South Asian studies to take DELNET membership.

DELNET databases are going to be accessible through INTERNET which will made accessibility very fast. INTERNET users in India are increasing and it will increase DELNET presence in different parts of India. DELNET has already created software, *viz.* DELDOS and DEL-WINDOWS for creating MARC records.

These software will so on be developed to perform library operations as well. There developments are likely to give more revenue to DELNET and provide justification for more and more libraries to join DELNET. As a resource, it is hoped the DELNET will grow faster as a service based resource sharing model in India.

**CALIBNET**

It was the first library network visualized and started by NISSAT. At a meeting in 1986 in Calcutta, DSIR initiated action for preparation of a feasibility study for networking about 40 libraries in Calcutta. CALIBNET now is a society under West Bengal Societies Registration Act 1961 and responsible for Calcutta Library Network, a project sponsored and supported by NISSAT. NISSAT also contributed to the development of MAITRAYEE software package based on INGRESS 5.2 for CALIBNET. This package was developed through CMC Ltd. And given to CALIBNET. So far, no data has been created in machine readable from using MAITRAYEE. At present, CALIBNET has become a centre for CD-ROM databases.

## Objectives

CALIBNET has made significant studies towards fulfiling its dual objectives:

- Launching its library network programmes, facilitating remote online access to the holding data of Calcutta libraries and other specialized databases as well – a significant step towards bibliographic resource sharing amongst Calcutta libraries; and
- Providing electronic access to globally available information, imbibing its information centre approach.

Both are essential for advanced learning and scholarship. In the process, CALIBNET aims at covering a wide panorama of information end-user interests, with diffusion of new electronic information technology as the primary concern.

## Present Status

*Software Developed and Library Network Launched*:

Intense in-house research and development efforts have now achieved the Library Network capability by three significant studies:

- A multi-user storage and retrieval software 'SANJUKTA' to support CALIBNET's centralized Database (CDB) and to provide online access to its from remote locations.
- A conversion software package 'PARAPAR' to support interchange of bibliographic data between USMARC, UNIMARC and CCF files and also from non-standard formats to standard ones.
- Evaluation of a centralized Database (CDB) of holdings data of Calcutta libraries, and specialized databases as well.

These apart, CALIBNET'S pioneering study and research led to its publication of the "Guidelines for Implementation of UNIMARC in Indian Libraries". This will be an invaluable aid for the national database development programme under consideration, that favours adoption of UNIMARC format.

With the support of SANJUKTA, the centralized database hosted on CALIBNET server and located at the Network Service Centre, can be accessed and searched online by any one from a remote location, provided one is equipped with a computer, a telephone, a modem and a password from CALIBNET.

The efficacy of SANJUKTA has been tested by successful remote logging of the CALIBNET server at Jadavpur, hosting the CDB from a workshop venue at Great Eastern Hotel, Calcutta. Online access to the locational information of bibliographic resources via the CDB and sharing up such resources amongst the libraries of this metropolis is now a reality.

The capability of PARAPAR was established through exercises and tests on sample records furnished by a major library in New Delhi and conducted in-house at Calcutta at their instance and eventually demonstrated at a workshop-cum-meeting in New Delhi.

## THE CENTRALISED DATABASE

Since library network capability has been established, the most crucial and indispensable activity is to develop the basic resource – the Centralized Database (CDB), that constitute the very backbone of any library network – by inputting the holding data of Calcutta libraries. The centralized database, launched only recently, currently held around 30,000 record covering:-

- — conference documents held by Calcutta and contiguous libraries.
- — social science management and economics, behavioural sciences, quantitative methods, computer science, etc. including predominantly journals held by management libraries in South Asia libraries of Indian Statistical Institute and the Indian Institute of management, Calcutta and
- — Index to contents of serials published by Asiatic Society in previous two centuries.

### Library Network

The Centralized Database (CDB) is the bedrock of CALIBNET and its development essentially calls for a cooperative movement, whereby each library par rakes in the movement by contributing its own holdings data to be incorporated in the CDB and thereby enrich it. The CDB needs to be now augmented by inputting holdings data of as many libraries as possible and getting the data continuously updated. Optimum coverage of libraries, which alone will progressively transform the CDB into a truly resourceful online searchable central pool of Calcutta's bibliographic holding data, is now on with the cooperation of libraries.

## THE PARTICIPATING LIBRARIES

The responses from institutional libraries are very encouraging. The libraries of following institutions have extended cooperation by way of furnishing their respective machine-readable database and current journal subscription lists:

1. Calcutta University
2. Jadavpur University
3. Indian Statistical Institute
4. Indian Institute of Management
5. Central Research Institute for Jute and Allied Fibres
6. Anthropological Survey of India
7. Botanical Survey of India
8. Geological Survey of India
9. Zoological Survey of India
10. Bengal Engineering College (a deemed university)
11. National Atlas and Thematic Mapping Organization
12. Bose Institute
13. University College of Medicine (Calcutta University)

These are being now inputted into the CDB. In coming years, holding data of many more libraries are expected to go into the CDB.

## LIBRARY NETWORKS ABROAD

International programmes like UNISIST of UNESCO, Universal Availability of Publications (UAP) and Universal Access to Information (UAI) of IFLA and a few others have helped in promotion and coordination of information services through out the world. Global Information Systems, characterized by decentralized input, centralized processing and decentralized distribution such as INIS, AGRIS & DEVSIS have been evolved towards universal bibliographic control and dissemination of literature. International information networks/ centres such as Lockheed/Dialogue, SDI/Orbit & ESA/IRS hold various databases in several disciplines and offer on-line services to users through out the world.

**Library Networks in USA**

The library networks in USA are in a most advanced level of development. Networking is based on three major areas of technology-creation of bibliographic information in machine-readable format for storage & retrieval, hardware and telecommunication mechanism for transmission of information. The major point of success of library network depends upon availability of machine-readable catalogues in the constituent units. A great progress has been made by USA in this regard. Three foremost bibliographic utilities and networks in USA are:

- *On-line Computer Library Centre, Dublin, Ohio (OCLC)*
  - — Established in 1967, it was formerly known as a Ohio College Library Centre
  - — It includes all type of libraries-academic, government, public and special. It has nearly 27,000 libraries as its members.
  - — It has developed its own telecommunication networks besides various products and services. It has 30 million bibliographic records with 520 million holdings locations in its union catalogue. The database increased at the rate of 400,000 records every month.
- *Research Libraries and Information Network (RLIN), Stanford, California*
  - — Established in 1978 it supports the cooperative programmes of research libraries group comprising libraries and other research institutions.
- *Western library Network (WLN), Olympia, Washington*
  - — Established in 1972 it provides on-line computerized services to promote resource sharing and automated library functions.

Besides these, there are various other library networks, some of which are listed below:

- *SOLINET*-Southeastern Library Network
- *Metropolitan libraries Network of Central Oklahoma* is a multiple library network.
- *OLC*-Oakland library Consortium, Pittsburg, Pennsylvania.
- *PLAN*-Panhandle Library Access Network Inc.
- *AMIGOS*, Dallas
- *BCR*-Bibliographic Centre for research, Aurora
- *CAPLON*, Washington
- *ILLNET*, Springfield
- *INCOLSA*-Indianapolis library Cooperative Services Authority, Indianapolis
- *MINITEX Library Information Network*, Minneapolis
- *MLC-Michigan Library Information Network*, Lansing
- *MLNC-Missouri Library Consortium*, St. Louis
- *NEBASE-Nebraska Library commission*, Lincoln, NE.
- *MELINET*, Newton, MA
- *PALINET*, Philadelphia
- *PRLC*, Pittsburg,PA
- *VALINET-veteran Affairs Library Network*
- *FEDLINK Network Operations (FNO)*, Library of Congress
- *LIMS-Library Management Information System*

**Networks in UK**

- *BLCMP (Birmingham Libraries Cooperative Mechanization Project), Birmingham:* It contains 13 million bibliographic records of books, serials, music, maps, Audio-visuals, etc. in its database. There are more than 60 libraries comprising public libraries, college libraries, university libraries and special libraries using its catalogue.
- *LASER (London and South Eastern Library Region):* It is an independent company under the University of London. It promotes library cooperation among 80

libraries in London and South East England and has more than three million records in its database.

- *The British Library:* Though not a network, it has nearly 21 databases including BNB(British National Bibliography) holding 15 million bibliographic records
  - *Blaiseline (*British Library Automated Information Service)-The automated information service of the British Library services offers search services to its users.
  - *British Library* holds one of the largest patents database in its Patents Information Network. About forty million patents are held and the database is growing at the rate of one million patents per year.
  - *Business Information Network*
  - *BIDS* (Bath Information and Data Services) offers several services in the field of public health, medicine and also provides access to British Library databases

**Networks in Canada**

*The National Library of Canada* promotes decentralized networking through the use of protocols conforming to the Open System Interconnection (OSI) reference model.

- It has nearly 10 million bibliographic records in its online database.
- It adds 800,000 to 1,200,000 records per year to its database and holds 1 million authority records.
- Besides its 275 concurrent users, it has 600 external institutions across Canada that use its union catalogue. It provides an in-depth ILL service to non-Canadian who need Canadian publications

- *CISTI – Canadian Institute for Scientific and Technical Information*
  - It holds books and conference proceedings, over 50,000 serials and millions of technical reports from around the world.
  - Maintains union catalogue of 50,000 serial titles with over 20,000 current titles.

— It offers a number of services such as CAN/OLE (Canadian Online Enquiry Service),Document delivery, CAN/SND (Canadian Scientific Numeric database service) online at a very cheap rate to users outside Canada on several scientific subjects.

- *UTLAS International Canada-formerly University of Toronto Library Automation System*
  — Established in 1971, it was the first library network utility in North America to go private by becoming a subsidiary of International Thomson Library Services (ITLS)
  — It is a computer based service organization for Libraries and information industries
- *Ottawa Public library*
  — It has an online database of more than 1 million volumes
  — It offers highly advanced service to the general public.

**Australian Libraries Gateway**

The Australian Libraries Gateway (ALG) is a free Web-based directory service which has improved access to information about more than 5,400 Australian libraries, their collections and services since March 1998. It aims to be a directory of current information about every library in Australia, a tool for worldwide users, for both library professionals and the general public.

The Gateway has been developed on behalf of the Australian library community by the National Library of Australia and received initial funding as part of Australia's Cultural Network (ACN). While the Australian Libraries Gateway site is hosted by the National Library of Australia and staff there, are responsible for maintenance, individual libraries are responsible for maintaining the currency of the information about their own library on the Gateway (via online forms and passwords, fax, telephone, email and/or post). Many resources, such as library catalogues, online exhibitions and image databases, are maintained remotely by libraries around Australia-the Gateway simply links to these resources. There are various other library networks which are working around the world:

- Library Network of Southwest Germany
- Nordic Libraries: Information Servers
- Strasbourg University Library Network
- LIBWEB

## LIBWEB: LIBRARY SERVERS VIA WWW (LIBRARIES ON THE WEB)

Here documents are maintained on server http://sunsite.berkeley.edu, Berkeley Digital Library Sun SITE (Software, Information & Technology Exchange). The Berkeley Digital Library Sun SITE builds digital collections and services while providing information and support to digital library developers worldwide. This is sponsored by The Library, U.C. Berkeley and Sun Microsystems, Inc.: The Library, 385 Doe #6000, University of California, Berkeley USA 94720-0001.Any library having a new or correct URL can add to the list by filling on-line form and submit. The bookstores, publishers, or other companies without a specific library connection are not listed.

Libweb currently lists over 6100 pages from libraries in over 100 countries. Following are the no. of libraries as the LibWeb members in the different countries:

United States (4555)

Academic Libraries (2077)

Public Libraries (2141)

National Libraries and Library Organizations(26)

State Libraries (51)

Regional Consortia (85)

Special and School Libraries (175)

Europe-

Scandinavia (113). It covers Denmark, Finland, Iceland, Norway, Sweden.

British Isles (199): England, Ireland, Northern Ireland, Scotland, Wales.

Western Europe (217): Belgium, France, Italy, The Netherlands, Portugal, Spain.

Germany and Central Europe (192): Austria, The Czech Republic, Germany, Hungary , Slovakia , Switzerland.

Southeast Europe and the Balkans (29): Bulgaria, Croatia, Cyprus, Greece, The Republic of Macedonia, Romania, Slovenia.

Baltic States (34): Estonia, Latvia, Lithuania, Poland.

Russia, Ukraine, and Eastern Europe (21): Belarus, Moldova , Russia, Ukraine.

Africa and the Middle East (57)

Asia (186)

It covers the following countries:

Bangladesh(2), Brunei(1), China (16), Hong Kong(11), India(18), Indonesia (3), Japan (55), Kazakhstan (3), Korea(1), Macau (1), Malaysia (13), Pakistan (3), Philippines (6), Singapore (5), South Korea(18), Sri Lanka (6), Taiwan (7), Thailand (16), Uzbekistan (1) Australia, New Zealand, and the Pacific (103) Canada (252) Alberta(32), British Columbia(45), Manitoba(6), New Brunswick(4), Newfoundland (31), Northwest Territories (1), Nova Scotia (15), Ontario (66), Prince Edward Island (1), Québec(38), Saskatchewan(12),Yukon(1) Mexico, the Caribbean, Central America, and South America (83)

From the above figure it can be guessed how much developed are the library networks in USA, Canada and European countries as compared to the developing nations around the world.

## POSSIBILITIES OF NETWORK BASED INFORMATION SERVICES IN INDIA

Today with the emergence of global network infrastructure, wherein local networks (LANs), national and regional networks and international networks are rapidly getting interconnected, a host of networked information services have evolved over the years. Library and Information networks are designed to support basically library and information services.

Library networks offer these services:

- Union Catalogue
- Current awareness & SDI services
- Authority data

- Library automation-Acquisition and fund accounting, serials control, book and journals maintenance, user services, creation and maintenance of bibliographic databases, etc.
- Inter Library user services
- Document Transfer/copy
- Access to national/ international databases

The details of the above services have already been discussed in the context of Library Networks and their Services. The development of INTERNET has drastically changed the way communication among different libraries, professionals and users is taking place these days.

Communication services offered by computer-to-computer networks like INTERNET include electronic mail, file transfer and remote log-in. E-mail is a store-and-forward messaging facility available on all the networks. It is probably the most widespread of the three network services because it is often the only way to exchange information among the networks. Users on the networks can also invoke file transfer commands (ftp file transfer protocol on INTERNET) to copy computer files. Remote log-in is the most sophisticated service provided on the networks through programmes like TELNET on INTERNET which allows a user at one site to work on a computer at another site.

Network information service applications are developed using these above communication services.

An important requirement for wider use of the services is the inter-connectivity, at least for E-mail, among the various networks in the country, including library specific networks like DELNET, CALIBNET, INFLIBNET, etc.

Possibilities of offering different network based information services are many; a few have been described below:

***Monitoring Information Resources and Services on INTERNET :*** There is urgent need for setting up a network information monitoring facility, consisting of a core group of two to three staff members and a suitable computer connected to ERNET (Education and Research Network which connects the major academic institutions in the country) or similar other networks connecting major library and information centres in the country.

Main responsibility of this group should be to systematically scan and monitor information resources and services on INTERNET and provide relevant information to Indian users. Two interesting applications / services that can be offered from this facility are:

i. Creation and maintenance of a directory of S&T information resources on INTERNET. This can form the basis of both on-demand and in-anticipation referral service. It is also possible to put this directory on ERNET, accessible by all users on ERNET and other networks in the country, by E-mail

ii. Creation and maintenance of an Infoserver consisting of bibliographic data downloaded from open-domain bibliographic information sources available on INTERNET, *e.g.* pre-prints of Astronomy and Astrophysics, content pages of top Biological Science journals. Data accumulated in such fashion can be freely made available to our researchers.

***Creating an Electronic Discussion Forum for Library and Information Science*** : An electronic discussion forum is an E-mail based conferencing medium for a group of people, geographically far apart, to discuss issues related to their profession or discipline. A forum for library and information science can be established to discuss, for example, issues related to library practices and use of new information technologies in libraries and information centres.

Such a forum can also act as an electronic news medium for sharing information pertaining to new initiatives, plans, projects, information sources and services, international development, etc.

While a few real-time electronic discussion forums (also called Bulletin Board, Computer conference, interest group, discussion group, discussion list, etc.) exist today, majority of them use e-mail to set up an informal discussion by interconnecting people of specific interest over a network.

Members of such forums can exchange messages with others irrespective of the network they are on and their geographic location.

The software used for setting up an electronic discussion forum is known as a mail server. Mail servers are electronic mail delivery systems, which when they receive a message can resend it to a group of users/subscribers whose e-mail addresses are maintained as a mailing list. Each subscriber sees all the mail forwarded by the server and if he/she wants to add his/her comments on the issue, sends in a message to the server.

Many discussion forums also archive the messages and support batch search and retrieval from the archive. Several hundred such electronic discussion forums exist globally today. They are bringing radical changes in the conduct of research and scholarly communication. One example of a discussion forum for librarians and information specialists is the Public Access Computer Systems (PACS-L) forum, moderated from the University of Houston, USA. PACS-L participants discuss many topics ranging from specific hardware and software considerations to issues involving online catalogues, CD-ROMs, networking and locally mounted databases.

While such a forum will improve communication among the professionals in our country, it will also encourage librarians to develop more sophisticated network skills and to explore more fully the potentials of electronic communication.

***Creating E-mail based Bibliographical Database Servers*** **:** While online, interactive searching of bibliographic databases is a desirable feature, e-mail based access is an interesting and less expensive solution considering the computing and network technologies currently used by our libraries and information centres. It is not difficult to create an e-mail based front-end to a bibliographic database, which will receive user queries, formulated in a specific syntax, by e-mail, carry out the search and the results to the user, by e-mail.

***Monitoring, Filtering and Re-distribution of Discussion Forum Postings*****:** As already mentioned earlier, several hundred discussion forums exist today on INTERNET on a wide variety of topics. The messages posted on these forums are an important source of information, raw knowledge and often untried new ideas. There is a need to identify important forums, in the context of our research priorities, scan these regularly, extract significant postings, and re-distribute these among our researchers. Such messages could also be archived into a database. Such a service will help our scientist to become part of the international network of scientists in their field of specialization and get to know the latest developments and research results, well before these appear in published form. This will have positive influence on ongoing research and stimulate new directions in research. Furthermore, such a service will relieve an individual researcher from the burden of getting to know what discussion lists exist, procedure for their subscription, usage, etc. Even if this were to be possible, this will result in 'network flooding' due to multiple subscribers to the same list and subscription of multiple lists by one person. The cumulative time saved by use of a single facility of this type will be enormous. Thus we see that networks are radically changing the way information is disseminated. Several useful network information services can be provided to researchers in the country using just e-mail facility. More sophisticated network information services could be evolved as the time progresses. This would also give the Library/Information professionals the required time and experience to plan for better coordinated efforts.

# Bibliography


Alfred Aho, John Hopcroft, and Jeffrey Ullman: *Data Structures and Algorithms*, Addison-Wesley, 1983.

Bazirjian, Rosann: *The Acquisitions Librarian,* New York: Haworth, 1995.

Cargill, Jennifer: *Technical Services Today and Tomorrow,* Michael Gorman. Englewood, Colo.: Libraries Unlimited, 1990.

Dennis S. Arnon. Scrimshaw: *Electronic Publishing: Origination, Dissemination and Design*, 1993.

Magrill, Rose Mary, and John Corbin: *Acquisitions Management and Collection Development in Libraries,* Chicago: ALA, 1989.

Mark S. Ackerman and Roy T. Fielding: *Proceedings of the Second Annual Conference on the Theory and Practice of Digital Libraries*, 1995.

Paul S. Adler and Terry Winograd: *Usability : turning technologies into tools*, Oxford University Press, 1992.

Ricardo Baeza-Yates and Berthier Ribeiro-Neto: *Modern Information Retrieval*, Addison-Wesley-Longman, 1999.

Strauch, Katina, and Bruce Strauch: *The Acquisitions Librarian,* New York: Haworth, 1990.

Schmidt, Karen A.: *Understanding the Business of Library Acquisitions,* Ann Arbor: Books on Demand, 1990.

# Index

□□□